Currency Lass

Currency Lass

The moving story of a young woman
in the convict town of Sydney and the South Seas

Margaret Reeson

AN ALBATROSS BOOK

© Margaret Reeson 1985

Published in Australia and New Zealand by
Albatross Books Pty Ltd
PO Box 320, Sutherland
NSW 2232, Australia
in the United States of America by
Albatross Books
PO Box 131, Claremont
CA 91711, USA
and in the United Kingdom by
Lion Publishing
Icknield Way, Tring
Herts HP23 4LE, England

First edition 1985
Second edition 1988

National Library of Australia
Cataloguing-in-Publication data

    Reeson, Margaret
      Currency lass

      Simultaneously published: Tring, Herts:
      Lion Publishing
      Bibliography
      ISBN 0 86760 018 7 (Albatross)
      ISBN 0 7459 1046 7 (Lion)

    1. Lawry, Mary, 1799-1825 — Fiction. I. Title A823'.3

Cover illustration: Arthur Boothroyd
Typeset by Rochester Communications, Sydney
Printed by Singapore National Printers, Singapore

Contents

Hassall family showing *Duff* and missionary connections

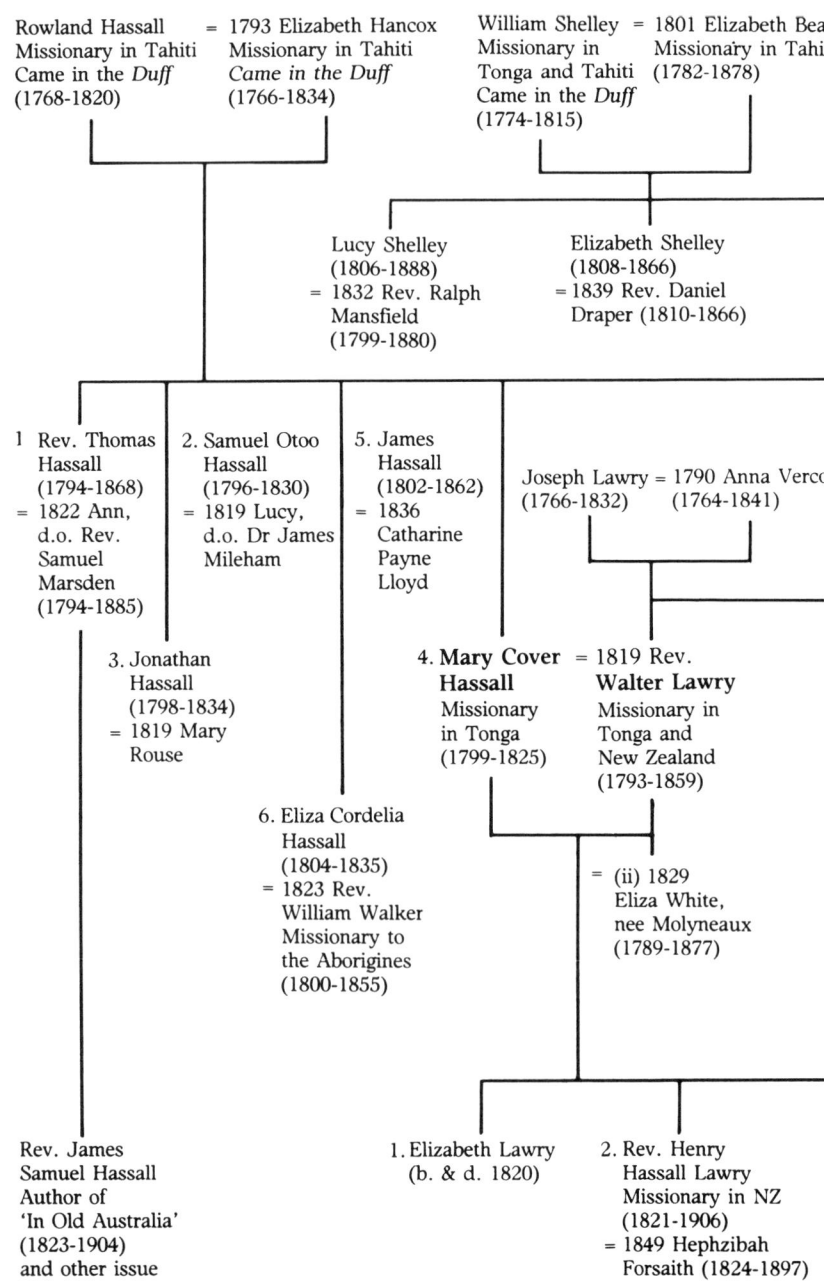

Rowland Hassall = 1793 Elizabeth Hancox
Missionary in Tahiti   Missionary in Tahiti
Came in the *Duff*   *Came in the Duff*
(1768-1820)   (1766-1834)

William Shelley = 1801 Elizabeth Bean
Missionary in   Missionary in Tahiti
Tonga and Tahiti   (1782-1878)
Came in the *Duff*
(1774-1815)

Lucy Shelley
(1806-1888)
= 1832 Rev. Ralph
Mansfield
(1799-1880)

Elizabeth Shelley
(1808-1866)
= 1839 Rev. Daniel
Draper (1810-1866)

1 Rev. Thomas
Hassall
(1794-1868)
= 1822 Ann,
d.o. Rev.
Samuel
Marsden
(1794-1885)

2. Samuel Otoo
Hassall
(1796-1830)
= 1819 Lucy,
d.o. Dr James
Mileham

5. James
Hassall
(1802-1862)
= 1836
Catharine
Payne
Lloyd

Joseph Lawry = 1790 Anna Vercoe
(1766-1832)   (1764-1841)

3. Jonathan
Hassall
(1798-1834)
= 1819 Mary
Rouse

4. **Mary Cover
Hassall**
Missionary
in Tonga
(1799-1825)

= 1819 Rev.
Walter Lawry
Missionary in
Tonga and
New Zealand
(1793-1859)

6. Eliza Cordelia
Hassall
(1804-1835)
= 1823 Rev.
William Walker
Missionary to
the Aborigines
(1800-1855)

= (ii) 1829
Eliza White,
nee Molyneaux
(1789-1877)

Rev. James
Samuel Hassall
Author of
'In Old Australia'
(1823-1904)
and other issue

1. Elizabeth Lawry
(b. & d. 1820)

2. Rev. Henry
Hassall Lawry
Missionary in NZ
(1821-1906)
= 1849 Hephzibah
Forsaith (1824-1897)

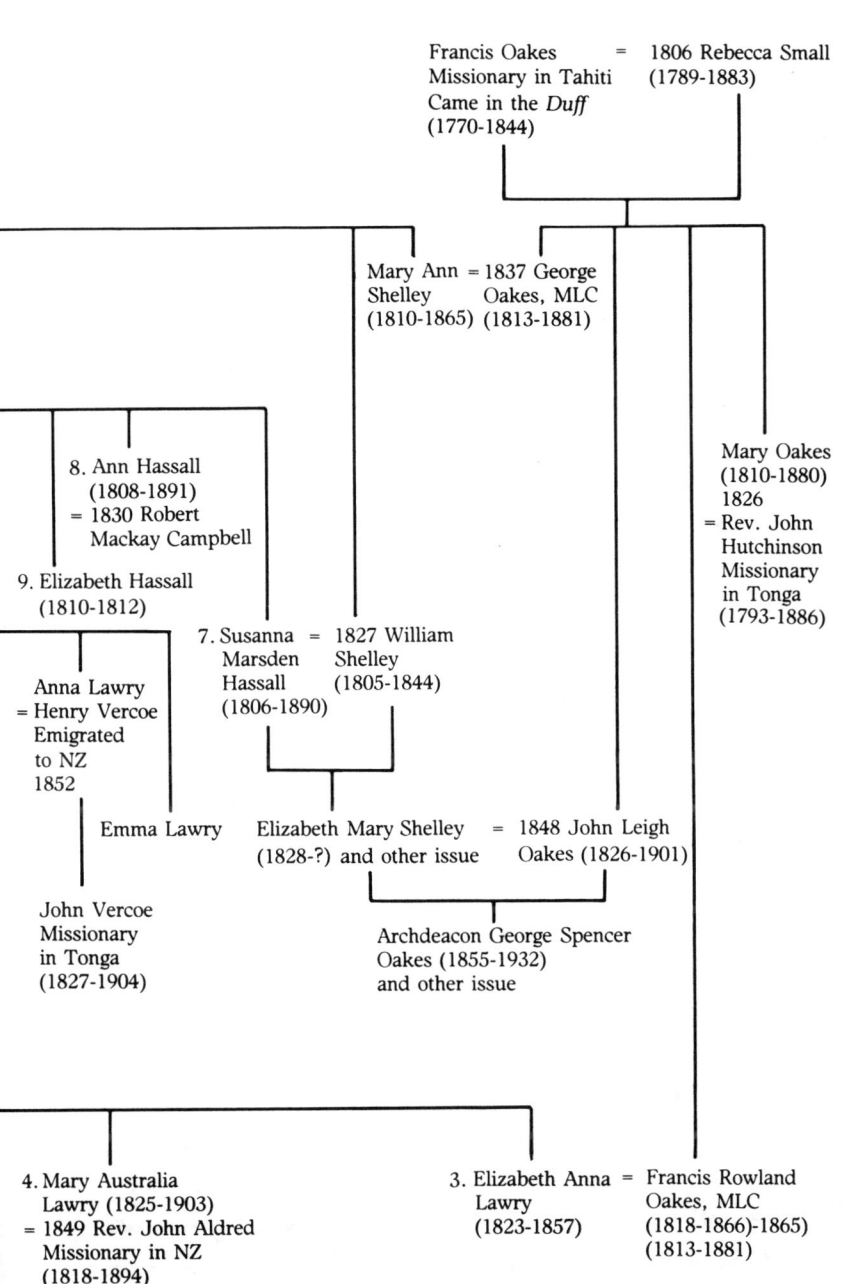

Francis Oakes   =   1806 Rebecca Small
Missionary in Tahiti   (1789-1883)
Came in the *Duff*
(1770-1844)

Mary Ann = 1837 George
Shelley   Oakes, MLC
(1810-1865) (1813-1881)

Mary Oakes
(1810-1880)
1826
= Rev. John
Hutchinson
Missionary
in Tonga
(1793-1886)

8. Ann Hassall
(1808-1891)
= 1830 Robert
Mackay Campbell

9. Elizabeth Hassall
(1810-1812)

Anna Lawry
= Henry Vercoe
Emigrated
to NZ
1852

7. Susanna = 1827 William
Marsden   Shelley
Hassall   (1805-1844)
(1806-1890)

Emma Lawry   Elizabeth Mary Shelley   = 1848 John Leigh
(1828-?) and other issue   Oakes (1826-1901)

John Vercoe
Missionary
in Tonga
(1827-1904)

Archdeacon George Spencer
Oakes (1855-1932)
and other issue

4. Mary Australia
Lawry (1825-1903)
= 1849 Rev. John Aldred
Missionary in NZ
(1818-1894)

3. Elizabeth Anna = Francis Rowland
Lawry   Oakes, MLC
(1823-1857)   (1818-1866)-1865)
(1813-1881)

Sample of Mary Lawry's handwriting

is pleasing to God, we lay our cause before him
and wait with patience the result. Pray for me
my dear more fervent than ever, I often think of
a phrase which you made use of in your first my
my time of life was the most critical. I assure
you that I find it so, and feel the deepest un-
worthyness of the station I am soon to fill but
hope the Lord will give me grace to do his will
in all things, and fit me exactly for an helpmeet
in all things to my dear love, not being an hindrance
to his usefulness in the smallest matter, but a
Spur to it. and soother to his moments of solitude
and may we bear each others burdens and take up
our cross daily following Christ in all things.
I realy do love him more than any other I know or did
know or wish to be acquainted with, I am unworthy
of such a pious good man as he is, but my Brother
will not think it too great a repetition but for the
reason of pleasing myself and the thoughts of gratifying
you more shall connect at the sentiments in a better
manner.   My prospect is that of soon being Married.
My motives for the step are all centered in my Love;
I have for him what I never had for a mother,
unalterable affection. And his love for me is every
thing but unbounded! the name of my love is Lawry
(I have before mentioned him in a particular manner)
a native of Cornwall,— he has been in the colony
14 Months, & came as a Wesleyan Missionary — his
piety is genuine, person genteel, talents excellent, his

Author's Note

Writing to her brother shortly before her wedding day, nineteen-year-old Mary Hassall spoke of her feelings. She was in love and looked forward to her marriage with the Rev. Walter Lawry, but she had no way of knowing what their life together might mean. She wrote:

> '...I tremble on the brink as I am just about to take a step which will either be my happiness or greatest grief and misery thro' life.... I feel the deepest unworthiness of the station I am soon to fill but hope the Lord will give me grace to do his will in all things and fit me exactly for an helpmate in all things to my dear love, not being an hindrance to his usefulness in the smallest matter, but a spur to it, and soother of his moments of solitude and may we bear each other's burdens and take up our cross daily following Christ in all things. I really do love him more than any other I know or did know or wish to be acquainted with...'
>
> *Parramatta, July 24, 1819*

Mary Hassall, later Mrs Mary Lawry, was a girl of early Australia – a 'currency lass', born in the colony in 1799. This account of her life is a piecing together of the patchwork of diaries, letters, newspaper articles and reports of her day. Mary wrote at least nineteen letters to her brother, Thomas, between 1816 and 1825 and Thomas kept them all. The original letters, now yellowed but still bearing the imprint of Mary's handwriting – sometimes sprawling and emotional, sometimes tidy and considered, with original attempts at spelling – can be read in the Mitchell Library, Sydney. One letter carries the shadow of a long, straight twist of hair which she sent to Thomas and which must have lain undisturbed for generations.

As well as Mary's own letters, her husband Walter kept a detailed diary during his ministry in New South Wales and Tonga, 1818-1825, and wrote long letters to his parents – as well as many letters to the Wesleyan-Methodist Missionary Committee in London. In later years he published two accounts of visits to Tonga in 1847 and 1850. In these he reflected on the past, adding contemporary descriptions of various places and people he saw.

The letters of Mary Lawry's father, Roland Hassall, as well as her four brothers, are represented in the Mitchell Library, Sydney, in collections of family letters and correspondence to London Missionary Society personnel in London and Tahiti. Letters and papers of such contemporaries as Samuel Leigh, John Williams, William Carvosso, Ralph Mansfield, Samuel Marsden, Lachlan Macquarie and others have also been used.

When in this book Mary says, 'In my letter to Thomas today I wrote...', 'Walter wrote in his diary...' or some equivalent phrase, the dates and the quotations from the original letters are authentic, including Mary's own spelling. (Punctuation has been added for ease of reading.) When Mary comments, 'Father says...' or 'Walter told me...', their quoted remarks are based on their own writings. Dates given at the beginning of sections in the book link directly with dates on which Mary wrote her letters or with other (dated) primary sources.

For any reader who is interested in detailed references, a fully referenced version of this manuscript is available at St Mark's Library, Canberra, and the Women's Archives, Australian National University, Canberra.

Margaret Reeson
Canberra, ACT

Acknowledgements

One of the special pleasures of working on this biography has been the opportunity to meet and learn from many people who have an interest in early Australia and the Pacific. Some of the most enriching contacts were with several senior people who encouraged and advised me.

The Rev. Dr Alan Tippett of Canberra opened to me the treasure trove of the Tippett Collection of Missiology and Australian and Pacific church history, lodged at St Mark's Library, Canberra, and answered endless questions from his vast knowledge of the field. His guidance has been invaluable. The Rev. Arthur and Mrs Jean Brawn of Sydney provided me with a number of clues to primary sources and told me where to look for more.

The Rev. Dr A. Harold Wood of Melbourne first introduced me to Mary Lawry through the chapter on the Lawry family in his book *Overseas Missions of the Australian Methodist Church, Vol. 1, Tonga and Samoa.*

The staff of St Mark's Library, Canberra have offered friendship and help over many months and the Rev. Eric Clancy of the Uniting Church Archives has provided information. Staff at the Mitchell Library, Sydney and the National Library, Canberra, have been helpful.

Appreciation goes also to Mrs Lucy Marshall of Auckland, historian and great-great-granddaughter of Mary and Walter Lawry, who corrected family information and provided some family folklore. Dr Niel Gunson has provided the family tree at the front of the book.

Friends in the Uniting Church congregation of Central Belconnen in Canberra bore patiently with my preoccupation with Mary Lawry and did me the kindness of listening and encouraging. Special thanks to Beattie and Alan Hatfield, who gave me the key to their front door and access to their word-processing facilities.

My family has been longsuffering over many months. The loving support of my husband Ron has been much appreciated during the project, as has the way he has provided firsthand experience of what it means to be married to a minister! My daughters Ruth and Jenni have given household help and excellent critical comment on the manuscript in progress, and have been marvellous listeners. (My son David still thinks cricket is more interesting.) They have graciously kept on loving me, even when wife and mother has been confused about whether she was living in the nineteenth or twentieth century.

Margaret Reeson

Prologue

St Austell, Cornwall: Christmas Day, 1825

Today they brought my son to see me. I think it was to say goodbye. He came to me with snowflakes still clinging to his little jacket, his eyes bright and puzzled and his hands so cold. I held his hands to warm them as he told me about his ride through the snow perched on the horse in front of his father. How can I bear to be separated from my son and his little sisters? How can I part from my husband, my other self? I'm not really afraid of dying, I don't think, but it is so desperately hard to let them go.

Some of the women of the family have been sitting with me. They thought that I was asleep. 'Poor little thing,' they said. 'So sad. She is so young – and Mary must have had such a hard life, too. Imagine growing up in a penal colony! What a poisonous atmosphere that must have been. And then all those naked savages... The poor girl has been deprived of so much, has made so many sacrifices. It seems such a waste.'

No. *No.* They don't understand. They would never understand even if I had the strength to tell them. Here in their cold, ancient land they don't understand the warmth and brightness, the fascination of the new, the challenge of taking steps of faith into a strange society, or the great love I have known.

It is too late to explain to them now. But as I lie here, waiting, I can remember...

Tahiti memories

Parramatta, New South Wales: December 12, 1816
I really didn't want to go to the schoolhouse this evening.
If I were not such an unconvincing liar, I could have complained of a headache or of some vague feeling of faintness,
but it would not have worked. Mother is no fool and knows
that I have rarely been ill in my life. I certainly don't look
unhealthy today, not on my seventeenth birthday. As for
Father, the ploy of mild illness wouldn't count at all. To
him, faithfulness, loyalty and reliability are all-important
and, unless we are at death's door, our entire family –
Father, Mother, four boys and four girls – will always be
there in the schoolroom on Wednesday nights, whether we
like it or not.

Of course, I couldn't have told the truth. How could I
have said, 'Well, there is a young man who will be there
who always seems to be *looking* at me . . .'

Father would have demanded to know who it was in case
it was someone quite unsuitable, like a ticket-of-leave
man. Mother would have twittered a bit and said, 'You are
seventeen now, Mary, and you must expect men to notice
you.' My big brothers would all have thought it was a huge
joke and my little sisters would have accused me of vanity
and giggled a lot. They would probably all say that I was
imagining it. I don't think I am. Reluctantly, I went with
my family to the schoolhouse tonight and am more sure
than ever that he likes me.

The schoolhouse is not far down the road from our house
here in Parramatta and, as we walked there this evening
through the dusk of early summer, other little groups
joined us: neighbours, close family friends, a few soldiers
from the regiment, a handful of men with their ticket-of-
leave from the convict barracks. The wooden shutters on
the windows had been swung shut and low, hanging lamps
had been lit inside, filling the room with a soft glow and
creating a second congregation of shadows moving around
the walls as we entered.

Father marched in, leading the family of which he is so
proud. We trailed in behind him and slid along the hard,
backless forms which reminded me of my school days:
Mother, who shares everything with Father, including his
strong faith, my oldest brother Thomas who was there because he wanted to be, Samuel and Jonathan who were a
little more half-hearted about it, tall James who at fifteen
would have preferred to stay home, and my younger sisters Eliza, Susannah and Anne who thought it was good
fun to go out in the evening even if it were only to the
Methodist meeting.

The classroom filled up slowly, not really crowded but
what else could you expect at a midweek Methodist meeting in a village like Parramatta? It is different on Sunday
mornings at St John's Church when the Rev. Samuel
Marsden is preaching and the building is nearly full. That
is the place where respectable and wealthy members of the
community come to show how virtuous they are, decked
out in military uniforms and smart clothes from London
and Paris. Ladies in their sprigged silk and frilly parasols
sit in their rented pews well away from the lines of convicts, marched to their places under the guard of rows of
soldiers. At least on Wednesday evenings at the Methodist
services no-one is there because he might be flogged if he
is not.

This evening, when the service began, I tried to bow my
head so low that my face was quite hidden by my bonnet.
But that is a very uncomfortable way to sit, so at last I ven-

tured to look up. The preacher stood before us, his Bible in his hand, reading the scripture to us. I wasn't listening to the words at all, I'm afraid; I was waiting for him to finish and begin his sermon. It was not, to my shame, because I was eager to hear his message. I watched him critically from under the brim of my bonnet, a tall, heavily-built young man in the sombre clothes of a preacher, dark hair neatly combed and a long face flushed with the effects of too much of our sunshine. The Rev. Samuel Leigh is no doubt a very good young man and very well respected in our community.

But he was doing it again. As he preached, his eyes seemed to drift to the corner where I was sitting and he kept looking at me, looking at me with such persistence that I dropped my gaze to my lap. Am I being singled out because I need, more than anyone else, to hear the message he is preaching? I'm not even *listening* to his sermon! Or is he looking at me – in services, at home when he often comes to visit my parents, when we meet in the street – because he *likes* me?

Tonight, after the little service was long over and I was in bed, I tried to decide what was happening. Is it because today is my birthday and soon I will have to think seriously about marriage? Seventeen years ago I was born here in Parramatta and I have never lived anywhere else. Mother says that the family had only been here in New South Wales for a year before I was born – my three older brothers were all born before they came. Some newcomers to this colony seem to think that it must be rather awful living here in a penal colony, but I can't imagine anything else. Of course, I'm glad that *I'm* not a convict – I know too many convict girls to have any delusions about the often homeless and unprotected life they have to live – but it doesn't seem so very strange to see convict work gangs on the roads and farms. And what do people do for servants in the house if they don't have convict women? Our family, the Hassalls, came to New South Wales free, so we mostly mix with free people: people like the large land-

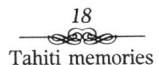
owners, the merchants, the military officers and the Anglican clergy. Everyone knows my father, Mr Rowland Hassall. I am friends with girls whose fathers have high standing in the community like my special friends Anne and Elizabeth Marsden, and wealthy parents like our neighbours the Macarthurs, or girls from British gentry like the Blaxland and Campbell families. We visit each other, ride, make embroideries and lace, garden, learn new songs together, picnic by the river and shop together for the latest fashions from England.

So I like just being myself, Miss Mary Hassall, and I am in no hurry to be a married woman. It is not so long since I was a student in that same classroom, as well as working with our governess, Mrs Rutter. I recall happy times of singing in the mornings, mostly hymns, with dust specks dancing in the brightness of the narrow windows. Many times have I worked over my slate at those same desks, trying to perfect an elegant, looping style but spoiling it when faced with real paper. Somehow the magpie quill always needed mending and the treacherous inkpowder often produced a horrible defacing blot in the middle of my work. When I sit in that classroom now, I can still hear the musical chant of voices reciting their ABC and repeating over and over the litany of spelling words, or intoning the mathematical tables, our voices growing drowsy in the heat of summer. I recall cold winter mornings, huddling over the little fireplace, and lessons about fabled places like London...

Yet it is not only a fear of growing up that makes me anxious about what might be in the mind of Mr Leigh. Because I am the daughter of a fine, God-fearing man and former missionary, I think I am afraid that I will have to be the wife of a missionary. There are not so many free young ladies in the colony. Some of those wouldn't even consider marriage to anyone but an officer of the regiment or the son of a wealthy merchant. Missionaries need wives too.

Only recently I overheard Mr Leigh telling my mother that he found it very hard being a single man in this colony with its low morals and many disgraceful habits, and had written to his Missionary Committee in London suggesting that they should not send out any more single men. Only last year a missionary from Tahiti came to Sydney looking for a wife after his first wife died. He was as old as Father and went back with a fifteen-year-old!

So I'm feeling a bit scared. It is not that I don't respect Mr Leigh and the work he is doing, but I think I would really hate to be the wife of a missionary. It seems to be such an uncertain life.

Parramatta, New South Wales: January, 1817

The old journal was found again today. I had not been looking for it and indeed had not even thought about it for a long time, but unexpectedly there it was.

It is January, high summer, and Father's orchard is laden with ripe fruit. Mother is a thrifty housewife who can't bear to waste anything and, having baked quantities of peach pies, apricot cakes, stewed fruit and fruit puddings of all kinds, made mulberry preserves and peach cider by the gallon, yet still having baskets filled with peaches, she announced: 'Pickled peaches. We'll pickle the rest. Mary, please go and find my recipe notebook – it is in the old sea-chest with some of my other household papers.'

So I went to the chest, which I rarely open, and as I looked through the papers for the recipe I came across the journal. At first I thought it was a book of household notes – of recipes for making soaps and candles, hints for the use of herbs and such like – because it was written in my mother's careful handwriting. The book was old – not old enough to be antique and therefore precious, nor new enough to be in use today; just moderately shabby and used-looking. I turned the pages and mythical names caught my eye – Matavai, Tahiti, Pomare – names which have been part of my growing-up, yet seemed so exotic written in the hand that usually pens letters to family in England or invitations to dine.

As I handled the book, I remembered the first time I had seen it. When I was a little girl I was helping Mother pack some things in her sea-chest and, seeing the book, had noticed some blank pages at the end. We were always short of paper so fragments of paper for writing and drawing were in demand. So I asked, 'May I have this old paper for drawing pictures? May I? Do you need this old book any more?'

Mother had been quite shocked. 'Certainly not! That is my *journal*,' investing the word with great importance, though I didn't understand it. 'That is what I wrote long ago when Father and I travelled from England to Tahiti to be missionaries, when Thomas was only two and Samuel was a new baby... No, you weren't born yet.'

I was only a child and, although I had heard them talk of living in Tahiti years before, it was beyond my imagination. To me, even the fifteen-mile drive to Sydney was a long way and the journey to Father's new grazing land grant twenty-five miles away at the Cowpastures almost the ends of the earth. I couldn't even imagine how far it might be to Tahiti – or to England for that matter. So I had left the question, knowing that at some time past my parents had travelled from their original home to another far-away place and had been missionaries there. What that really meant I had no idea.

Today, however, my search for the recipe was diverted by my rediscovery of Mother's journal. I am much older now and the old book fascinated me. Would Mother allow me to read it? I wondered.

'Mary! Whatever are you doing, girl? Can you not find it or are you day-dreaming again?'

Tucking the journal under my arm, my hand fell with great good fortune on the recipe notebook and I carried both books to the kitchen. So it was that, surrounded by the furry sweetness of peachskins and textured fruit stones and the aroma of cinnamon and vinegar, Mother talked to me as an adult of her experiences:

'We had never intended to come to New South Wales,'

she began. 'In fact, we scarcely knew where Port Jackson was — only that it was a penal colony and a place to be feared, somewhere on the far side of the world. We were going to be missionaries in Tahiti — or so we thought.

'When Father was a young weaver of Indian silk in Coventry, England, he heard for the first time about the London Missionary Society. It was quite new. Preachers came to Coventry and spoke in the churches about a great new vision for missionary work in the Pacific.

'Father was very open to any suggestion that he serve God in some way; he had recently almost died of cholera and come close to being mistakenly nailed into his coffin! He tells the story of how he had revived, sat up in his coffin and vowed to serve God in some way in thanks for his rescue.

'Of course, it was all very novel and unusual in those days,' Mother explained. 'Almost none of the churches, except the Roman Catholics I suppose, had had any kind of missionary societies. Then quite quickly, within about ten years, many churches decided to begin missions in other countries: the Baptists, the Anglicans, the Methodists, the British and Foreign Bible Society and others. Father and I heard about the London Missionary Society and of their plan to send their very first shipload of missionaries to Tahiti in the Pacific. We had heard stories about Tahiti after Captain Cook and Captain Bligh had been there. It sounded very interesting and exciting. The Mission didn't seem to mind that Father and I were not very well educated. They said they needed workmen — practical people to teach practical things to the heathen before they would be ready to understand the gospel.'

My parents thought about it for some time, then applied to join the group. When they learned that they had been accepted and would sail on the *Duff* in August, 1796, they were elated but also rather frightened. It was a very daring step to take.

Early on a beautiful morning (August 10, 1796) the *Duff* weighed anchor in the Thames River. Mother recalled the crowds of friends and relatives, hands waving in farewell, the new missionary flag fluttering overhead and the crowd, those on board and those on shore, singing together, 'Jesus, at your command we launch into the deep. . . '

'I could scarcely sing the words for tears,' Mother said. 'My family was getting smaller and smaller in the distance and I felt that I would never see them again in this life. And I never have.'

The *Duff* waited till it was possible to begin the voyage in convoy with fifty-seven transports and Portugese traders, to avoid enemy French ships, then sailed on alone. At first the new missionaries were strangers to each other. Mother soon learned that there were four other married ladies on board and that my brothers were the only children. As the days went by, they gradually began to know each other, to recognise each personality and each gift, each irritating habit and each helpful contribution. They knew that they could be at sea for many months – though they didn't guess how many months – and organised themselves into a disciplined group with tasks and responsibilities. They agreed to the distribution of food stuff by one member: 'They allotted one pound of tea a month to each man and one and a quarter pounds to each woman! Perhaps they thought we needed our tea more.' They appointed a librarian to supervise the books; the surgeon began classes to teach simple medical skills. All began work on a simple Tahitian vocabulary from material collected by earlier Pacific mariners and agreed to meet together twice a week for Bible study, as well as daily for prayers. Mother reflected that they were very wise to insist that the party should all be able to read, at least a little. Their captain was Captain James Wilson, a man who had only been a Christian for a few years after a very wild and adventurous seafaring past.

Sailing south, the weather became hotter and wetter but, after they left their one port of call at Rio de Janeiro in South America, the open sea stretched before them, increasingly cold and wild. Their aim was to sail south and then west around the bottom of South America, but as they approached Cape Horn the seas became more mountainous and the stormy winds beat them back. They struggled for days – cold, frightened and beaten upon by deadly seas – until Captain Wilson said: 'We must turn back. If we try to sail west we will fail. We must sail east and then south of Africa.'

In the telling it sounded simple, like turning the head of one's horse in the opposite direction. But Mother wasn't satisfied with her description. She held a peach aloft and poked a little hole near the top with her sharp peeling knife.

'There is England.' A swift slash of the knife indicated a rough Africa and on the opposite side America. 'We were here, nearly around the bottom of South America, more than half way to Tahiti, and we turned back. . . We turned back and travelled the other way, *all* the way across the South Atlantic, south of Africa, across the Indian Ocean, south of Australia, south of New Zealand, right across the Pacific. Just us, our one little ship, and we didn't see land or any other ship, not even in the distance, for over three-and-a-half months. Your father has always felt rather cheated that we sailed nearly all the way around the globe and all we saw was water and a few whales!'

Slowly rotating the scarred peach, Mother stared with eyes that looked right through our kitchen table piled with fruit, the servant girls and my sisters and I busily slicing. We couldn't see what she was seeing, but she began to speak again: of the elderly Mrs Eyre who suffered constantly from exhausting sea-sickness, of young Mrs Sarah Henry faced with her first pregnancy, of her own two little boys crawling and toddling around the ship in danger of falling overboard if she didn't watch constantly, of missionaries and crew ill, of cattle and other livestock dying, and of being deeply thankful that the food and fresh water lasted till journey's end. She spoke of the terrible storm before Christmas, of watching whales play near the *Duff*, of Christmas Day with her own efforts to make something

special from the simple ingredients available. She told us of hours spent in disciplined discussion of theology and the beautiful services of Holy Communion on deck in the sunshine, of men teaching each other their trades (even to Surgeon Gillham with his medical skeleton) – though Mother thought that some of the trades would be more useful than others to the naked heathen.

'A hatter – and a gentleman's gentleman!' she said with a twinkle in her eye. They decided that they would attempt to work in three groups: the main group with all the women to work in Tahiti, a group of ten single men to begin work in the so-called Friendly Islands, Tonga, and two men to go to the Marquesas. When at last they sighted land, they had been at sea for almost seven months and were well-prepared to begin their work.

'But I confess I was in two minds by then,' Mother said. 'On the one hand I was longing to get off the tossing ship and to feel solid earth under my feet again, to be free of the constraints of living in the same limited company with no privacy in such crowded quarters. Yet I was afraid. Would the natives welcome us or despise us? Would we be safe? I used to have nightmares about wild men hurting my little boys! We had no way of knowing.'

On a lovely tropical Sunday morning, March 5, 1797, the _Duff_ anchored off Tahiti. Mother was alarmed to see canoes coming towards them.

'We counted seventy-four of them, each loaded with about twenty people!' The natives surged on board, but in a most friendly way, full of cheerfulness and good nature, even helping the sailors to put the great guns in position without the slightest anxiety. They were unarmed. In the first mingling of greetings, the Tahitians were puzzled by the missionaries' refusal to buy their fruit and chickens (because, of course, it was the sabbath) and even more by their unwillingness to approach their women. The Rev. James Cover had the honour of preaching the first sermon in Tahiti on 1 John 4:8, 'God is love'. They sang several hymns.

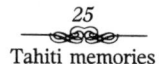
'We chose things like "Praise God from whom all blessings flow" and "Blow ye the trumpets, blow" because of their good tunes,' Mother said. The Tahitians watched this strange ceremony with courtesy, but did not understand at all what they were seeing.

The next day, the *Duff* anchored off the Matavai area and some of the party went ashore. They were offered the use of a large woven and thatched building which had once been intended for Captain Bligh. The local people brought many generous gifts of fruit, coconuts, pigs and other food and welcomed the new arrivals most warmly.

'They were really very kind,' Mother said, 'but they were so curious about us. The day that we women and our little boys came ashore, we were surrounded by people the whole time. They stared at us and we stared back at them. I'm not sure which group was more surprised! When we had gone into the building, they kept calling to see the children, but they were so gentle and full of laughter that neither the little boys nor I was afraid. Even their young King Otoo and his wife Tetua, riding around as they always did on the shoulders of their servants, wanted to see and touch Thomas and Samuel. The people kept bringing us so much food that we had no way to use it all.'

It seems that among other gifts the missionaries gave to Otoo and his wife was a gift of bright clothing. The young queen was delighted with the fancy cap and the other garments, even though the seams had to be ripped open to help them fit her. But Otoo was not so impressed and said that he would have much preferred a gift of an axe or a musket. The British group did not realise it, but that was a prophetic comment which they would have cause to remember a year later.

After the first group had settled at Matavai on Tahiti, Captain Wilson took the *Duff* with a party of ten to Tongatabu. Our special friend, Mr Shelley, was in the Tongan party and was put in charge of medicines, while Mr Crook and Mr Harris went to the Marquesas. Mother was rather evasive about what happened, but evidently Mr Crook

stayed there and Mr Harris did not – I think she felt I was too young to hear the story!

For the group in Tahiti, life settled into a pattern. The first warmth and friendliness remained, but the new-comers found that hidden problems were being exposed. The Tahitians were quite happy to have Europeans among them, but they had no interest in the gospel. Rather they saw the English party as a source of muskets for tribal warfare and other material benefits and had no interest in preaching or prayers. The missionaries had not expected an immediate response, but they had not been prepared for ridicule and laughter.

'If this story about God and Jesus and the sabbath day were true, why didn't Captain Cook and Captain Bligh and the others say anything about it?' they taunted. The missionaries were hurt to hear blasphemy and jokes about their Lord.

The Tahitians were certainly very generous with their gifts, but they expected matching gifts from the mission-aries. If the missionaries didn't offer gifts, the people felt quite free to take things, so that the group found it neces-sary to lock things up and set guards. Meal times became a misery. Crowds of happy Tahitians would arrive to help prepare the food for the meal, with great good will, but when the food was ready they and their relatives immedi-ately sat down with the missionaries and devoured most of it! Mother recalled the inconvenience of trying to prepare a meal in small quantities and eating furtively in little groups, locked in their partitioned rooms.

As they learned more of the local language, they learned things that shocked them. They were appalled to see the babies of chiefly families killed at birth, open immorality, human sacrifice, sorcery, and a group of young men in the king's household whose position Mother could not bring herself to explain. My parents had intended to honour the chief by giving small Samuel his name, but discovered that by so doing they offended Tahitian culture, and so the first birthday of Samuel Otoo Hassall was an embarrassment.

Father was set to work in the blacksmith's shop and always had a crowd of Tahitian people watching in wonder at the forge, the flying sparks and the hissing of water on metal. Once King Pomare visited and was so delighted with the bellows and forge that he grabbed Father and rubbed noses with him.

A year passed and, as well as caring for her family, Mother had gone through pregnancy and the birth of my third brother, Jonathan. Mrs Henry had her first baby, Sarah, a few months after their arrival, the first missionary baby. The Tahitians had shown no signs of interest in the gospel, but constantly asked for firearms and tools. The missionaries had agreed that it would be very unwise to allow muskets into the hands of such a warlike people, but continued to trade in other items.

The fragile coexistence was broken by the visit of the trading ship *Nautilus*, plying in furs from America to China and now in urgent need of repairs. The ship's crew planned to trade muskets for food and water in Tahiti, but the missionaries tried to supply them secretly from their own limited stock of food in order to avoid a trade in muskets. Pomare found out what was happening and was furious, refusing to allow the missionaries to buy more food. The *Nautilus* left, but a week later it returned, now even more unseaworthy because of damage in a gale and without the supplies they had so recently collected. Again the missionaries attempted to avoid trade in firearms, but the Tahitians were bitterly resentful of the white men's interference. Things became very ugly, quite suddenly, with many of the crew of the *Nautilus* deserting their ship and Pomare and his men preparing to attack the missionaries.

'I was terrified,' Mother recalled. 'A group of our men had gone to the king to ask for the deserters to be sent back to the ship, but they were beaten up by a rabble and barely escaped with their lives. They came back to say that the king had armed men ready to attack us that night. What could we do? Some stories were circulating that we younger women were in danger from the Tahitian men, while others said that they would kill us all. The *Nautilus* was right there in view, a rare chance to escape, and the captain urged us to come away with him. A number of our group packed up in haste and went on board, but others – Mr Nott, the Eyres and a few others – decided to stay on. (Mrs Eyre was quite old and said she would rather risk death on dry land than face the misery of another sea voyage.)

'Your father didn't know what to do. He said to me, "Surely this can't be the end of our mission. I can't believe that these people who have been so friendly and kind would kill us. And even if things are not good here at Matavai, there are other islands nearby – we could begin again. Would *you* be willing to stay on?"'

I listened with awe. What a question to be asked! 'Oh Mother, what did you say?'

'I said, yes, I would stay,' Mother replied. 'It wasn't easy, but I thought I could face it. In the end, they didn't let us stay. They said we *must* leave. Some said so because they thought that the Tahitians would force Father to make weapons on the forge. One man hurt your father very much by saying that he couldn't imagine how your father could possibly have thought it right to bring a wife and young children to such a place as Tahiti in the first place and, of course, he should take us to safety.

'So, not really sure we were doing the right thing, we gathered our belongings, our three little boys, Thomas, Samuel and the new baby Jonathan, some food that remained and a few pigs, and rowed out in the darkness to the *Nautilus*. At first light we sailed – not free to stay and face what might be a massacre, yet frightened about a voyage on the battered ship.'

It must have been a dreadful voyage. Because of the desertion of so many crew members, the missionaries had to act as sailors. That included manning the pumps constantly as the ship leaked badly. They were desperately short of provisions, struggling with torn sails and being tossed through storms. They almost ran aground on Pyramid Rock near Lord Howe Island.

'We thought of happy days on board the *Duff* and the hopes we had had for our mission in Tahiti. Everything seemed to be lost. We weren't even going home to England, but to the nearest place inhabited by white men – the miserable penal colony of Port Jackson. Why had God allowed this awful thing to happen to us?' The desolation of that time was still reflected on Mother's face as she spoke.

The *Nautilus* limped into Port Jackson on May 14, 1798. Among its bedraggled, exhausted, discouraged and almost penniless passengers were my parents, Rowland and Elizabeth Hassall, and my brothers Thomas, Samuel and the new baby Jonathan. They had arrived in a penal colony remote from the rest of the world, where even the officers were being rationed with provisions as the whole colony was hungry. It must have been a dark and hopeless hour.

'If it hadn't been for the kindness of some of the people of Sydney, particularly the Anglican clergy, the Rev. Richard Johnson and the Rev. Samuel Marsden and their good wives, I don't think we would have survived,' Mother said thoughtfully. 'Mr Marsden let our family stay on one of his small farms just north of Parramatta and use the fruit and vegetables there. He found Father a job as a storekeeper at the Commissariat Department at Parramatta and Toongabbie, when the previous storekeeper was found to have been a thief. When your father was given a grant of land, Mr Marsden gave him seeds, with planting and breeding stock, to begin his own little farm. The Marsden family have been among our closest friends ever since.'

And so here we were, pickling peaches in our own sunlit kitchen, the Hassall family of Parramatta, New South Wales. Not where we would have been – the family of a weaver in Coventry, England; nor where we might have been – the family of missionaries in the Pacific. I think I'm glad we are here.

And yet, I don't think my parents have ever really detached themselves from their experience in Tahiti. For one thing, there is a very special bond between my parents and the other missionaries who were with them on the *Duff* and in the islands. People here still sometimes refer to them all as 'the missionaries', even though it is years since some of them were in Tahiti. In some ways, I think my parents are closer to people like Mr Oakes, Mr Shelley and Mr Crook, the Eyres and the Henrys than to their real brothers and sisters in England. The people of Tahiti are still very important to them and they have kept in touch by letters and trading.

Of course, the people who stayed on in Tahiti had not been murdered after all. Later, new parties of missionaries joined them, despite the *Duff* being captured by pirates on its second voyage and never arriving! So all through the years that Father had been living in New South Wales other missionaries had been going on with the work. Very recently, letters have come from Tahiti to say that at last people are turning to God and King Pomare has become a Christian. Father and Mother were so excited to hear that the years of work were beginning to bear fruit, yet also a little sad not to be there to see it. Our family has always been linked with the missionary work – Father has sent trade goods to Tahiti, we have given our gifts of money and, when new missionaries come through New South Wales, they often stay at our house.

Their flight from Tahiti has left a scar, however. It is not just a memory scar, but a scar of guilt as they ask themselves: should we have stayed there? Should they have stayed with Mr Nott and the Eyres and be there still? Or should they have gone back there again – as did Mr Shelley, the Henrys and the Crooks? (The Henrys came with my parents on the Nautilus, Mr Shelley escaped from Tonga to Sydney in 1800 after three of their party had been killed, and Mr Crook was rescued from the Marquesas by a passing American brig, the *Betsy*. He had been the sole missionary in that island group for over a year. All of them, with others, later returned to the islands.) Father was asked to go back more than once, but the more established in New South Wales he became, the harder it became to move. Maybe it is hard for a rich man to be a missionary.

Of course, Father and Mother did not go back. Since his coming to this country, Father has changed from being an anxious refugee to a confident man who has earned the trust of others. He began with two small grants of land on the Western Road near Prospect and another 100 acres on Pennant Hills Road. With hard work and care, and the help of convict labour, he has built up excellent farms there — as well as newer farms on the Hawkesbury River and my favourite property, 'Macquarie Grove', in the beautiful Cowpastures country south of here. He used to trade in all sorts of goods and, even when I was only a little girl, we already had a carriage. Men of property entrusted their land and affairs to him when they were away from the colony as they saw in him that very rare thing in a convict settlement, an honest man. He was proud to be among the few registered in the regular Muster of the population as 'Came Free'.

As the years went by, he worked very hard for many good causes and committees in the colony. There were church activities like the Bible Society and the little Ebenezer chapel out at Portland Head, and community activities like his interest in education. He could not be a schoolteacher himself as his friend, James Cover, had been — his spelling is even worse than mine — but he helped to start schools for settlers' children at Kissing Point and Toongabbie, was appointed school supervisor, and was energetic in ordering school books and supplies from England. He even paid school-fees for some of the poorest children from his own pocket.

Our family is very happily settled here now and has grown. Perhaps it is the healthy climate or the good food, but all Mother's children have survived infant diseases, which is quite rare. Thomas is my oldest brother, perhaps my favourite of a dearly loved family. Samuel Otoo, the baby named unwisely for a Tahitian chief, is now a young man who manages Father's 'Macquarie Grove' property.

Then there is Jonathan, born at Matavai on Tahiti and now apprenticed to Mr Smith in Sydney as a carpenter and joiner. I was next, born on the 12th December, 1799, here in Parramatta, and named for Mother's dear friend, Mary Cover. Every two years after that, Mother had another baby: James, still a scholar under Mr Gilchrist and Mr Bradley, Eliza Cordelia, Susannah (with Marsden as her second name for our dear friends), Anne and finally our beautiful baby sister who was accidentally drowned in a shallow pool in our garden when she was only a toddler.

So most of us Hassalls were born here in Australia and are 'currency lads and lasses', rather than 'sterling lads' born in England. (British-born people tend to be condescending about our currency, Spanish dollars with holes cut from the centre for use as extra coins – only sterling is *real* money, they say.) I think I'm quite glad to be a currency lass. Governor Macquarie once complimented Father on his family and said that he had written to England to say how much he admired the young people born here. He told Father that he had written that we were 'very robust and comely and well made... promising to be a fine race of people.'

So should my parents have gone back to Tahiti? I don't know... I confess that I am glad that they did not. I would hate to be a missionary's daughter – we hear scandalous things about some missionaries' children. Nor would I fancy being a missionary's wife like Mother. No, I like it here and life just as it is.

Early upheavals

Parramatta, New South Wales: February 1817

This evening I sat quietly in a corner of our crowded best parlour and wondered whether I had just made a terrible mistake. The room was full of people who had come to our home for the regular Methodist meeting. We meet at the schoolroom for the midweek services and in the homes of the Christian friends in Parramatta for the prayer meeting and Class Meetings. The room was full, but I was really only aware of one person — despite the fact that I had not even glanced at him yet, but seemed to be concentrating on folding and smoothing a handkerchief on my lap. My face felt hot and flushed. I hoped that people would think that it was because of the heat of the evening.

There he stood, such a good respected young man with his Bible open in his hand and such an *earnest* expression on his face. Have I made a terrible mistake? Ought I to have said, 'Thank you very much; I would be honoured to be your wife'? Will I have another chance to marry a fine Christian man like Samuel Leigh, living here in a colony where so many are convicts? Governor Macquarie once said of New South Wales that half the population had been convicted of crimes and the other half ought to have been! Samuel Leigh is a very *good* man and, I'm sure, would be a very virtuous husband.

So why am I feeling only embarrassment in his presence and awkwardness in meeting him since I refused his hand?

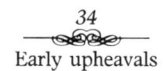
Why do I have no sense of regret or loss? In fact, I have only a very great relief at having chosen not to marry him.

Thomas and I talked about it.

'Am I stupid? He is such a well-respected and hard-working person – a minister of the gospel. Shouldn't I want to marry him because he is so suitable?'

Thomas laughed at me. 'I can't really blame Samuel Leigh for wanting to marry you, Mary. Even I think that you are an extremely lovely girl – and I'm only your brother! But no, I don't think you are being stupid. I believe that God has someone chosen for you who you will be able to love with all your heart, not just because he is a fitting kind of person. Don't be anxious; you probably have not even met the man yet.'

Samuel Leigh has been part of our community for a year-and-a-half now. He is the only Wesleyan Methodist minister in the colony, coming at the request of the little group of Methodist lay people here – including our schoolteacher friends, the Hoskings and the Bowdens, and Mr Eagar. Ever since he arrived, he has struggled with serious problems. When he first landed in Sydney, the Governor was very reluctant to let him travel around as a minister because his Committee in London had failed to send him with credentials. It was only with great hesitation that he was even allowed to stay and work.

Fortunately, all the Anglican clergy are of evangelical inclination and are in sympathy with the Methodist movement. Even so, people still watch his work critically for fear that he will threaten the establishment by making converts or that he will breed division. Mr Leigh has been so careful and cautious in his methods, however, that most of his critics have been disarmed. The poor man began his work at a disadvantage because of a misunderstanding over someone's handwriting in the letter to the Methodist Committee in London. They wrote requesting him to bring 'furniture for a house', but it was read as 'furniture for a horse'. He arrived with an excellent secondhand military saddle, bridle and so on, but nothing to make a comfortable home for himself! He began work in the Rocks area of Sydney where the most hardened criminals live, and then began to travel on long tours of the colony, preaching to scattered groups of settlers along a route of about 160 miles.

The first time I met him was one time when I was staying with our family at 'Macquarie Grove', our farm on the Nepean River. It was late afternoon when this young Englishman rode out of the bush into our house yard. His face was badly burnt by the sun and he was bitten by mosquitoes, scratched by undergrowth, and exhausted and aching from riding day after day. Of course, Mother and Father greeted him in their usual hospitable way, offering him hot water for a bath, a good meal and a clean bed. He was so grateful as he had been sleeping and eating in the very roughest of conditions and was quite worn out. After dinner, he offered to lead us in a service of worship. We were all very impressed with his warmth and sincerity. A man like Samuel Leigh can only do good in our colony. Father invited him to preach in our home in Parramatta regularly and so he has come to our home every week since then. He has become a good friend to the family and had hoped to become more than a good friend to me.

So why can't I marry him? It is not that I fear his poverty, though that rather worries Father. Quite recently, all the colonists had to present an inventory of their current property, land, houses, stock and grain at the three-yearly Muster. All that Mr Leigh had to record was his horse, Old Traveller. Governor Macquarie was quite shocked and said, 'You'll always be poor at that rate – you have been offered grants of land, but you only accept enough to build a little chapel on!'

Father came home from the Muster and described how Mr Leigh had given a brief explanation to the crowd of landowners of the instructions of the Methodist Committee in London to their missionaries: that they were sent to preach the gospel, not to become involved in trade or amass wealth. I'm sure that Mr Marsden and the other clergy must have been either annoyed or embarrassed by that statement – all of them have become quite wealthy men since they came here. Probably they see Mr Leigh as an impractical, otherworldly sort of person who scarcely deserves to prosper, but I confess that I find his simplicity rather attractive. It is probably more like the life of Jesus than that of the other gentlemen. No, it is not his poverty that has made me refuse him, though to be completely honest I think I would find it hard to be poor.

I think perhaps it is his earnestness, his seriousness, his very worthiness that makes me draw back. Is there a man who loves his Lord with joy and delight, a man who is human and yet a man of God, a man who will draw my heart to him so that I will know for sure that this is the husband God has chosen for me? I'd rather wait and see.

Parramatta, New South Wales: March, 1817

Whatever will our Sunday School do without Thomas to lead it? It is hard to believe that my beloved brother Thomas is going away, all the way to England to study, and may be away from home for years.

This morning I looked around at the great crowd of boys and girls coming into St John's Church, maybe 150 of them today, with twenty-five of us Sunday School teachers all ready to do our best to teach them. Thomas stood up in front of the flag and Sunday School banner as our superintendent, directing us all in our singing and prayers and keeping control of the whole mixed multitude in a way that made me proud that he was my brother.

When I was thirteen Thomas invited some boys and girls into our home one Sunday and began the very first Sunday School in the colony. The first children were mostly very poor, neglected children who went to no other school; they came to Thomas to learn to read. Of course, some people said that we didn't need Sunday Schools in this colony, because the children here don't need to work long hours every day as they do in England. They could go to school any day of the week. That is true, too, but not nearly all of the

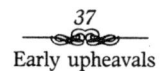
children in Parramatta go to the public school. Thomas wanted to combine the teaching of reading and writing with teaching about God.

More and more children came to Thomas' Sunday School so that, after a couple of years, they had outgrown our house and moved to St John's Church. Mr Marsden is very pleased with the school and takes a great interest in it. He even encouraged Thomas to use the mission printing press, which was stored at our house last year on its way to the mission in Tahiti, to print hymns for use in the Sunday School. As with other schools, we are always short of books for reading and spelling, but we do our best.

This morning I watched Thomas with the children. So many are the tattered, unwashed children of convicts, the sort of children most of us would avoid if we could, partly because they tend to be smelly and partly because they can be very naughty indeed. Others are young Aboriginal children from the local tribes, and some of those are the quickest and cleverest at learning of them all. Others are children of settlers and children of soldiers, all gathered here together and crowding around our Thomas. They love him, and he certainly loves them − or why would he take so much trouble with such waifs?

But Thomas is leaving us. He is going all the way to Wales to study at Lampeter College for the Anglican ministry. He'll be away for years. This comes at the end of many years of encouragement in his schooling by our father, who was so proud that his son was learning, among many other things, what Father spelled 'Lattin'. Some of his teachers included men like Mr Crook who had been Father's friend on the *Duff*. As well as the public school and the encouragement given by the Rev. Samuel Marsden, Thomas had made use of the many books Father had bought for our family, as well as the lending library his friend Mr Marsden had brought out from England from the philanthropist, Elizabeth Fry. Father and Mother keep on reminding us that we children have been very lucky to have had such a good education: 'When *we* were children . . .' they say,

and then tell us long stories about how most children of the working classes in England are forced to work in mines or factories during the week and are fortunate if they learn to read at all.

As I watched Thomas moving among the Sunday School classes, encouraging, handing out the attendance tickets, welcoming the children and supporting the teachers in their work, I realised how much the Sunday School will miss him. At our teachers' prayer meeting every first Monday of the month at our place, he has been our leader, not only guiding us in the details of how to teach but also teaching us how to love our pupils.

Parramatta, New South Wales: March 19, 1817

My eyes must be so red and swollen that I dare not look in the mirror. Even my nose is painful from so many applications of my handkerchief. Today was our Sunday School farewell to my darling brother Thomas before he sails for England. How many years will it be before he comes home again?

Today at the farewell I was watching two men who are both feeling his going very much. One is Mr Marsden, who is so proud of him. Perhaps he thinks of Thomas as his own son, certainly as his 'child in the faith', for Mr Marsden has been our minister since Thomas was a tiny boy. It is Mr Marsden's hope that one day Thomas will return to New South Wales and be the man to carry on his own Christian work when he himself is old and dies. That may easily come true.

The other man is our dear father. Father has written a moving letter for Thomas which tells a lot about himself. He has written some helpful spiritual advice and a reminder of the presence of Christ with us in all circumstances. Then he says that he hopes Thomas will be 'raised up from the midst of a sinful nation, not only to outrun me in the divine life, but to fill up all those vacancies and make up all those deficiencies which through ignorance, mistrust, fear of man and love of the world — and want of zeal

and love for Christ and souls I have been very deficient
in...'

We invited everyone to our home today and some three
hundred people walked around under the trees in our orchard in the beautiful autumn weather. There were many
old friends from Parramatta, Thomas' friends from the
farms along the Hawkesbury River where he has worked
on Father's farm, people whom he helped to rescue during
the great floods on the river, people he worked with in
Merchant Campbell's office at the wharf and in Captain
Birnie's office, Sunday School teachers and, of course, all
the children – white and Aboriginal.

Everyone loves our Thomas as, of course, they should.
He is a lovely man. Mrs Marsden was so upset when he
went to say goodbye to her in her carriage that she had to
drive off in a rather damp silence because she couldn't ut-
ter a word of farewell. All the young ladies were weeping,
including the Marsden girls. It will not only be his sisters
who will be sad to see Thomas go!

Parramatta, New South Wales: April 10, 1817
At the farewell to Thomas, people thought that I was weeping tears of sadness to see my brother go and tried to con-
sole me with kind words. If only that were the only reason
for my tears. It is not. My tears are the bitter salty tears of
shame and regret. If only I could control my horrible tongue... Why do I hurt the very people I love most with the
sharp words I say?

After the Sunday School farewell, Thomas left Parramatta and went to Sydney to board the *Kangaroo*, but his
ship did not sail immediately. All of our family went to and
fro between Sydney and Parramatta as the days of waiting
dragged on and one day I made a remark which hurt him
very much. At last, with tears, I brought myself to write a
painful letter of apology.

The trouble between us was over a girl. Perhaps I am
jealous of any girl who my Thomas might like – I am hard
to please, thinking that no girl is quite good enough for

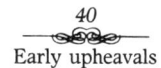
him. No-one is! But that Sarah was certainly not the girl I
would like to see Thomas marrying. So I said so, and made
my antagonism quite clear over quite a long time. Poor
Thomas was hurt by my critical attitude, but to me Sarah
Henry was an awful example of the difficulties of being
brought up as a missionary's child.

Our family and the Henrys have known each other always — or at least since our parents met for their dedication
as missionaries before they boarded the *Duff*. Mrs Henry
gave birth to Sarah only a few months after they arrived in
Tahiti, the first missionary's child to be born there. Even
then, Mr Henry had an idea that it would be nice if one day
his baby Sarah should marry the then two-year-old Thomas Hassall — perhaps he pictured them all staying there
for a lifetime and Sarah not having many choices for a
spouse.

Even as a tiny child, Sarah became part of the Tahitian
scene. Mother has told us about those days when the Tahitians, particularly the leading women, loved the white
children and surrounded them with love, warmth and extra food specially prepared. Sarah thrived on it. The Henry
family left Tahiti with ours on the *Nautilus* in 1798, but
went back in 1800 so most of Sarah's childhood was
among the Tahitians. Their language was hers; she ate
their food; she loved their friendship and their ways. She
was British by birth, but grew up almost Tahitian. The
family left Tahiti again when she was eleven years old and
came to Sydney for nearly three years. I remember her
then as a child at school and church: older than me, wild,
proud and independent and somehow different from us —
a child with other memories, other loves.

The Henrys went back to Tahiti in 1811 with Sarah and
the three younger children. Sarah said she was glad to go
back to her Tahitian friends and the strange freedom of her
life there. She was turning into a fine-looking girl of four-
teen and perhaps our Thomas was already seeing her in a
new light. Her mother died a few years later and Mr Henry
left his family in Tahiti with Sarah in charge while he came

to Sydney looking for a new wife. He went back married to young Anne Shepherd, who used to be a student at the Kissing Point School when Mr Henry had taught there. Poor Anne was only fifteen and must have been terrified to find herself stepmother to a headstrong sixteen-year-old! And Sarah had shocked everyone in her father's absence by allowing herself to be seduced by a young Tahitian chief. Most awful stories came back about Sarah's behaviour: her defiance and unrepentance, her brazen rudeness to British and Tahitian authority and, most appalling of all, the way she turned violently away from God and told the Tahitians that the missionaries had been tricking them. While all this was happening, our Thomas was pleading with Father for permission to court Sarah by letter, because he wanted to marry the girl!

They didn't know what to do with Sarah in Tahiti – she was doing more harm to the missionary cause than her father could do good, it seemed – so her father sent her to Sydney to live with former missionary families, away from the evil influence of the islands. She didn't fit in here, either. She lived with the Shelleys, down the road from us, and we could see Thomas falling more and more under her spell. She looked magnificent; perhaps we colonial girls looked pale water colours beside her vivid style. Sarah didn't seem to belong to our society. She didn't want to be a 'lady' like us. She had no patience with cooking, embroidery, painting or singing, nor did she want to teach Sunday School or join the Ladies' Committee for the Benevolent Society. She wanted to travel, to go to parties, to drink a lot, to be with men – specially to be with men.

Sometimes she said, 'Why do I have to work? Why must I be busy all day? In Tahiti, people only work when they must – they have fewer wants and they like to have time to rest, to play, to enjoy each other. Why can't I sit in the shade with a flower in my hair and a friend by my side?' Or, instead of talking at tea-parties of fashions or books, she talks of sorcerers, the supernatural or of her friends riding the surf on light boards – I wouldn't be surprised

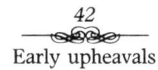
if she hasn't tried it herself. . . Late last year, Thomas asked her to marry him, but she refused him.

People say she is a bad girl. Mr Marsden says we shouldn't be too hard on her because she can't really help it, having been brought up in Tahiti. But I don't like her much. I'm relieved that she didn't want to marry Thomas. Perhaps I am threatened by her very presence here. If my parents had stayed in Tahiti, that could have been me – a misfit who in Tahiti is not allowed to be fully Tahitian, being British, but in Sydney doesn't belong to British society either, being almost Tahitian in attitudes and upbringing.

Anyway, I was miserable about the way I had spoken critically about Sarah to Thomas. He really cares about her as a person and a friend, while I see her as a threat to his happiness. So I struggled to write my letter of apology for making him feel that I would even prefer him to go away rather than see him being friends with her. The quill fought against my hand, leaving an inky trail of mistakes and sprawling words as I tried to take back the pain I had caused him. Why do I have to be so critical of people when it is none of my business who my brother likes?

I wrote in great haste, hoping that the letter would catch him before the ship sailed: '. . . your words have cut me to the heart and added much to my grief. What a cruel sister should I be if I had wished such a thing.'

I sent my letter, complete with blots. At least he knew that I was sorry to have hurt him before he sailed. My destructive tongue worries me – maybe I'm not even a proper Christian? Surely a real Christian wouldn't talk like that.

What Thomas doesn't know is that the day after he sailed, Sarah Henry ran away from the Eyre's house where she was living and eloped with the emancipist, Dr William Bland. They were married in Sydney a few days ago.

Parramatta, New South Wales: July, 1817
Some new missionaries for the South Seas arrived in the *Harriet* in May on their way to Tahiti. They are so *young*. We have been used to missionary families coming through

Sydney – for Tahiti or New Zealand missions – and some of my parents' special friends have gone back to the islands. Either I am getting older or missionaries are getting younger. John and Mary Williams in particular are barely older than I am, twenty and twenty-one, yet here they are, all ready to go to be missionaries in the Society Islands.

Mr Leigh brought them out to meet us here in Parramatta. John Williams has been preaching at some of our Methodist meetings. We drank tea together in our parlour and Mother asked young Mrs Williams about herself.

'And how did you meet Mr Williams, dear?'

Mrs Williams was very shy, but she was so proud of her husband. 'We were both Sunday School teachers at the Tabernacle, our chapel in Tottenham, London. We used to see each other in chapel and John asked me to marry him and go with him to the South Seas. Our wedding was only three weeks before we sailed.'

'You would have liked our little cabin on the *Harriet*,' John said. 'It was our first home, so we made it as cosy as possible – lamps, mirrors, bits of carpet and so on. I like to work with my hands and Mary is an excellent housewife, so we decorated it as well as we could. We look forward to a real house of our own when we arrive in Tahiti.'

Father wanted to know how Mr Williams had come to decide on this work. He was remembering, I think, himself as a young Englishman beginning his own adventure.

'I had no intentions of being a missionary in the South Seas. In fact, I was not even interested in being a Christian till I was eighteen years old. My mother worried about me a lot as I much preferred the company of my fellow-apprentices down at the local tavern on a Sunday evening to going to chapel. But one Sunday night I was waiting under a lamppost for my mates to arrive when the wife of my employer came by. (I was apprenticed to a Tottenham ironmonger.)

'She invited me to go to church with her and, partly because I was embarrassed and partly because my mates were late and I was annoyed with them, I surprised myself and went with her. That night the preacher spoke on 'What is a man profited if he shall gain the whole world and lose his own soul?' and my life was turned upside down. Then I learned about the Tahitian mission and, though the Directors thought I was a bit young, here we are.'

I rather like Mr Williams' preaching. He is certainly not a well-educated man – he seems much more a vigorous workman than an elegant gentleman – but he is full of energy and life and he speaks of his Lord as one who really knows him personally. It is good for Mr Leigh to have his company and that of the other missionaries, the Threlkelds and the Barffs. It is cheering him up to find other Christians who share some of his own visions.

Somehow, I don't think John and Mary Williams want to stay in Sydney very long. They are so anxious to go on and begin their work in Tahiti. News has been coming through with traders over the last few years that more and more Tahitian people are becoming Christians and more are crowding into the churches, so John can't wait to start work. He is a very active and busy person, interested in everything, studying everything he can find about the Pacific Islands and learning every skill that any artisan can teach him. Mary told me that he spent hours on board the *Harriet* asking the sailors questions about rigging and navigation and everything to do with ships. Here in Sydney he is constantly asking people: 'How does it work? How did you make it? If I can't get that component in the islands, what else would work?' He is a very practical man.

What does Mary Williams really think about going to the South Seas, I wonder? She is a city girl from London and even Sydney town, which seems quite impressive to me with all the handsome new buildings Governor Macquarie is having built, seems very small and unsophisticated to her. What will she think of an island in the Society group? I'm sure she is very brave and a very strong Christian – much stronger than me – but I wonder if she is a little scared. And Mother told me that Mary is expecting a baby at the end of the year. Will she be safe?

Parramatta, New South Wales: September, 1817
The wattles have been in glorious golden bloom again, the Marsdens have moved house and the missionaries have sailed. September is a lovely month, with the sunshine warmer after a very miserable wet winter and Father's orchard is breaking into waves of blossom. There is new growth on the willows over the Parramatta River at the edge of our garden and Mother is supervising a major spring-cleaning.

Amid great commotion and hurrying up and down the hill with cartloads of household goods, the Marsden family have moved into their grand two-storey mansion high up on the hill, looking north over Parramatta. For months they have been watching the building grow, and every ship from England has been watched for boxes and parcels of new things to beautify it. The Marsden girls are just a trifle superior about it all and young Charles Marsden is his usual cheerful, careless self — he always accepts any luxuries as his right without realising that he might irritate people like his friends, my brothers. But *I* think that their new house will probably be stiflingly hot in summer, facing north with no verandahs.

Now that the Marsdens have moved, they have left their old house to the young Maori men who have been living with them at what Mr Marsden rather grandly calls 'The Seminary'. Rev Samuel Marsden has been interested in the Maoris for as long as I can remember. As long ago as 1804, he had dreamed of beginning a new missionary work in New Zealand and even recruited some families in England to go as the first missionaries there. Then a number of years ago, Mr Marsden brought home some New Zealand natives whom he had rescued from whaling and sealing ships where they sometimes were being mistreated. He took them into his family and made good friends with them. In time, he became the agent for the London Missionary Society and the Church Missionary Society in New South Wales, arranging for the purchase of the missionary ship, the *Active*. He sees Sydney as a significant centre for missionary work, even though the people in England only see it as a penal settlement, miles from anywhere.

The first time Mr Marsden went to New Zealand himself in 1814, he took his party of missionaries – the Kendalls, Halls and Kings – and several work people and settled them all at Rangihoa in the Bay of Islands. I have often heard him tell the story of the very first Christian service in New Zealand on Christmas Day, 1814. The crew of the *Active*, the new missionaries, the Maori chiefs, those Maoris he had brought with him on their way home from Sydney and the local people sat near the beach, some on upturned canoes and others on the grass, while he preached from Luke 2:10: 'Behold! I bring you good tidings of great joy.' Anne and Elizabeth Marsden have been known to sigh with resignation when he launches yet again into the tale of that day, which they now know by heart!

Ever since then, the Marsdens have had a few Maoris as well as a few Aboriginal children living at their house. A couple of years ago, Mr Marsden started his Seminary for young New Zealanders, so that the sons of chiefs could come here for education. This year there are eleven young men living just down the road in George Street. They are learning some reading, writing and English language, but mainly what Mr Marsden calls the 'civilising arts', such as spinning, ropemaking, canvas work and agriculture. My brothers Samuel, Jonathan and James often spend time with them, talking about their lives in New Zealand and their strange customs.

Two young men in particular, Tui and Titore, have become special friends and often come to our house. Despite their strange clothing, with their preference for a soft, cloth-like fabric wrapped around their bodies instead of decent trousers, they are quite at home with us. They are intelligent, active boys who love to copy my brothers and enjoy their company. Perhaps when they go home to New Zealand and become chiefs themselves, they will be able to civilise their heathen people and turn them to Christianity. I know Mr Marsden hopes so.

Yesterday I visited Anne and Elizabeth Marsden at their new house. It is all very handsome, of course, and we had a lovely time looking at all their new arrangements and decorations. On one wall was hanging a big painting of the *Active*, the missionary ship which is so important to Mr Marsden. I stood and stared at it for a long time. At this very moment, John and Mary Williams, with the Threlkelds and Barffs, are on board that little ship somewhere out on the Pacific Ocean, sailing for Tahiti.

A certain young man

Parramatta, New South Wales: January 1, 1818
It is New Year's Day and I have spent the day in the heat
and dust and flies of the market here in Parramatta at the
annual Aboriginal gathering. The Governor and Mrs Macquarie had invited a great many tribespeople to a meeting
here today and, of course, quite a lot of Parramatta resi-
dents came along to look. Governor Macquarie had provided tables loaded with roast beef and potatoes, fish and
a big cask of grog.

All the natives sat in a big circle on the ground with their
chiefs sitting up on chairs. The Governor greeted all the
chiefs very courteously and gave them specially engraved
brass crescents to hang on their chests, as well as other
gifts. Then Mrs Macquarie came with the children of the
Native Institution. They showed all their people how well
they could read and spell, and displayed their workbooks.
The girls showed their needlework and all the children
looked beautifully clean and smart. The Aboriginal adults
seemed very interested and pleased, though some of the
women were crying – I don't know why.

I find I have confused feelings about the Aboriginal people. I am very fond of the children whom I know quite well
through the Sunday School and the Native Institution. One
of Father's many committees is the Aborigines School

Committee — the school was started by Mr William Shel-ley, Father's dear friend from the *Duff*. Mr and Mrs Shel-ley helped found the Native Institution during 1814. They began with six boys and six girls at the beginning of 1815. (Some of the children had white fathers.) Sad to say, poor Mr Shelley died very suddenly later that year and Mrs Shelley has been in charge since then. She works very hard at it, but she finds it very discouraging as the children keep running away. Some of them are very bright, but they don't always seem to want to learn our ways.

Mr Marsden doesn't have much sympathy for Aboriginal tribespeople. He once had a foster-son, a foundling called Tristan, living with his family for years, hoping to turn him into a civilised settler. But the lad disappointed him very deeply by getting into bad company, often getting drunk, stealing from Mr Marsden and finally running away from the family while they were in Rio on their way back to En-gland for a holiday. In the end, Tristan was brought back to Australia and he returned to a wild state in the bush. Mr Marsden couldn't understand such rejection and ungrate-fulness and has been cynical about the chances any aboriginal people may have of improvement ever since.

Then again, I have been upset and disturbed to see how sadly tribespeople are affected by strong drink. White peo-ple give it to them and then laugh when they act foolishly. And — are we safe from Aborigines when we go to the farms? Only two years ago, when Mother took all of us children out to 'Macquarie Grove' for a visit, parties of Aborigines were attacking the neighbouring farms belong-ing to the Macarthurs. Poor brother Samuel was only nineteen at the time, but he was responsible for us all, so had to go with our workmen to try to rescue the shepherds. We stayed in the farmhouse with the doors locked, won-dering whether we would see a spear coming through a window or an axe through a wall. We were very glad to get home to Parramatta where the natives are no longer fierce. Perhaps, though, the town natives are more sad than the warlike ones.

Parramatta, New South Wales: January 24, 1818

I have just been reading the description in today's *Sydney Gazette* of the King's birthday celebration in Sydney, specially the big ball Governor Macquarie held at Government House. Of course, I didn't go. Father would never hear of it, even if it were something I badly wanted to do. Mr Marsden wouldn't let his girls go, either.

'Dancing till dawn is not at all a suitable occupation for my daughters,' our father said, and that was that.

Fortunately, balls are not my favourite social occasion anyway, so I was not particularly disappointed. I'm much happier at private family dinners with friends, picnics or church gatherings. But the *Gazette* made the Governor's ball sound so pretty, with the ballroom decorated with wreaths and festoons of flowers and greenery, Chinese lanterns in the windows, the lamps all alight and the mirrors at each end of the room reflecting the colour and movement of the dancers. Next time the Blaxland girls call or the Macarthurs, they will tell us all about their new gowns, the way they dressed their hair and all the young men who paid them attention. They will giggle and flutter, whispering secrets about who is courting whom.

No, I truly didn't mind not going to the ball, but how am I to find a husband? That seems to be the main purpose of balls for some of the girls. Father doesn't like me to go out into Sydney society very much, because he thinks that some of the social occasions are too worldly or too loose in their morals. He is almost certainly right! Dear Father has a very high standard of behaviour and he most decidedly would not allow me to be mixed up in some of the wilder parties of the officers of the regiment.

More than half of the population came here as convicts, and Father would be appalled if I fell in love with a convict. There are many men who were formerly convicts and are now pardoned or have completed their sentences. People like Father are so proud of having come here as free men that they see themselves as superior to the emancipists, so I'm sure Father would disapprove of that sort of marriage.

Then, among some of the free settlers are many with whom Father has long-standing political disagreements. He has always sided with the conservative, loyalist group against those who have worked to make things difficult for successive governors. (My father has always supported the man in authority and was angry with those who deposed Governor Bligh for the sake of their rum traffic, and who criticise Governor Macquarie for some of his ideas which could threaten their power in the colony.) So he probably would not be happy to see me marry into the family of someone he has bitterly opposed. Some families are too poor, some are too irreligious, some only have daughters or children who are much younger than I am. Good, free, established Christian settlers tend to be married when they arrive in the colony.

So who does that leave? Spoilt Charles Marsden? Charles is my age and we have been friends all our lives: a carefree, lovable rogue who is like a brother, but doesn't take religion or anything else seriously. Mr Samuel Leigh? But I don't want to marry any man simply because he seems suitable. I want to *love* him.

Thomas wrote in his first letter to me after he left Australia: 'Your time of life is the most critical.' I certainly find it so. (Dear Thomas also wrote in reply to my unhappy letter of apology, and has forgiven me in a very loving way.)

Mother says that she and Father are praying for me, that the Lord will provide a good husband for me and that I need not be anxious. Perhaps, if I were a better Christian, I'd feel more sure of that, but at the moment I can see myself as a wrinkled, skinny, wealthy maiden lady of fifty, still waiting!

Parramatta, New South Wales: March, 1818

Poor Mr Leigh. He worries me. He has been working so hard that he always looks almost ill with weariness. He is constantly in the saddle, riding miles and miles and often has very small encouragement from the people he serves. Sometimes he spends hours with condemned men and comes away completely drained. He has made a number of converts, particularly among the convict population, but he always seems to be carrying around a load of care on his shoulders.

Mr Leigh is a big and heavy but not well man and his body has been forced beyond what it can manage. Also, he is very lonely. He has a few good friends among some of the Anglican clergy and has the respect of everyone, but he tends to be rather a solitary person. Since I said I could not marry him, he has been shy about spending a lot of time at our house – he comes for the preaching, but goes again quickly. There is often a sombre, gloomy air about him.

The other day he told Mother how cut off he feels from his Committee in London. Even after nearly two years he is still waiting for a letter from them. The poor man told her how he goes so hopefully to look for mail when a ship comes in – but there is never a letter for him. He is afraid it must give a bad impression of his right to be a missionary here at all. If only he had a colleague, someone to share his load, he would feel so much more content.

Parramatta, New South Wales: April, 1818

After Sunday School this morning our whole family went, as we always do, to church at St John's. It is very familiar to me as I have walked through that same church door for as long as I can remember. Mother says that Mr Marsden has been working on this building ever since they arrived in Parramatta twenty years ago, but it has been a slow process as not many people wanted to help and they kept changing it. Even today we had to skirt around the piles of bricks for the twin towers he is having built on the western end. As we moved into the church, we walked to our usual pew which Father rents in the part of the church where the free people sit.

High up in his lofty central pulpit, the Rev. Samuel Marsden looked down on us this morning, remote and holy in his vestments, bringing us the word of God with the authority of the church and the King. As the party of convicts were marched into their restricted area under the eye of a whole gallery full of soldiers, I wondered what they were thinking. Do they ever think about God, I wonder? Do they see their compulsory attendance at St John's as part of their punishment to be endured, a time to sit quietly with resignation and total boredom? Do they imagine God to be something like Mr Marsden; a stern and sometimes harsh judge on weekdays and on Sunday a giver of laws and impossible ethical demands? Do they look at the handful of free worshippers, mainly women and children, and feel even more certain that religion is something to be borne if you are under the authority of the government, but to be avoided if you are free? At least I have a prayer book in my hand so that I can follow the service. Most of the congregation just sit there, without any books, depending on the clerk to read out the hymns and call the responses and the amens in his loud, monotonous voice.

Sometimes I wonder whether I am any better off than the convicts. Church often depresses me. Not, of course, that I don't love God. I do, most truly and sincerely. Our whole family life centres around the thought that God is our mighty Creator and Lord and he wants us to be his people. I do *want* to be his and I try so hard to do what is right. But it is so hard to live up to his standards. Sometimes in church I feel that I am locked in, like the convicts in their pews, wanting to be close to God but being forced apart from him by his great perfection and my own weakness.

When I think, 'Perhaps God will be pleased with me for all my work with the Sunday School children', I am forced to remember that I'm sometimes irritable and careless about my teaching. When I think 'Maybe God will accept me for all the times I have tried to help convict girls to keep out of trouble', then I have to admit to my pride and critical spirit with girls who haven't had the opportunities that I have had. And my hopeful thought that because my *family* is such a good Christian family surely I must belong to God is soon crushed by the knowledge that not all our family has the same attitudes as our parents or Thomas.

So how can I know when — or if — I will ever be good enough for God? Perhaps I will always be locked in my pew, hearing God's word from the height of the pulpit, but never really knowing if God is willing to accept me.

Parramatta, New South Wales: May 4, 1818

Yesterday, on our way home from Sydney, brother James whipped up the horse and sent our chaise spinning down the hill away from the town, on through the bush on the road home to Parramatta. James enjoys driving, as I suppose any sixteen-year-old boy might do, and I clung to my seat as we bounced along. Perhaps James wondered why I was so silent. I hardly dared to look at my own thoughts, let alone talk about them to James.

Earlier this week, Mother asked me to take her place at a birthday celebration for Mrs Smith's little Eliza. Because Mother couldn't go, she sent me with James to Sydney. We stayed on in Sydney for a few days and, on the day after the birthday, I was invited to dinner at Mr and Mrs Eager's house. Mr Eager came as a convict, a very young Irish attorney convicted of perjury. Soon after his conviction, he became an earnest Christian and a Methodist. He has been a free man for many years now and has become a prosperous businessman. He was one of the three men, along with our friends Mr Hosking and Mr Bowden, who first wrote to ask the Wesleyan Methodists in England to send a Methodist missionary to New South Wales, and he is a special friend of Mr Leigh.

When I arrived at the Eager's place and walked into their parlour, I was startled to see a young man who was a complete stranger. Certainly I don't know every inhabitant of Sydney, but I had thought that I knew everyone who might be expected to dine at Mr and Mrs Eager's table.

Perhaps my surprise showed on my face, for Mrs Eager said, 'Hadn't you heard, Miss Hassall? The ship *Lady Castlereagh* arrived yesterday. Let me introduce to you the Rev. Walter Lawry, our new Methodist minister. This is Miss Hassall.'

The young man took my hand and smiled in such a friendly way and together we went to the table. Through the meal, he asked many questions about the colony and told us a little about himself. He is from Cornwall and has been a Methodist minister in training for two years. I think he may be about the same age as our Thomas, about twenty-five.

We asked about the voyage on the *Lady Castlereagh*.

'In some ways it was a pleasant experience,' he said, 'and only took a little over four months. But I don't think I am a very good sailor. I was seasick too often.'

'How did you fill your time on board?' Mrs Eager asked.

'Well, it was a very large ship with a big group of officers, so I spent time with them most days. I became very interested in astronomy as we moved from the northern to the southern hemisphere and learned a lot about the stars in the southern skies. Of course, I read a lot. I had brought about sixty books with me for my library here in the colony, but I have already read thirty of them: theology, history, geography, sermons, philosophy and so on. And after I had been feeling most miserably seasick, I used my time poring over my atlas, trying to work out a way I could return to England as far as possible on dry land! It is not impossible either – one could sail to India and go overland from there.'

Thirty big books in four months, I thought. Good heavens! I decided to keep very quiet or he would think me a very ignorant person.

Mr Eager is rather sensitive about the fact that he came here as a convict, but now he looks so respectable and well-to-do that Mr Lawry went on without realising that he might give offence.

'It was a convict ship and three hundred people were on board as convicts. I asked permission to preach, but it was very difficult and strange. They lined all the convicts up for a service between decks, but I found it very hard to preach freely with soldiers armed with loaded muskets and fixed bayonets standing at each elbow! And there is a certain restraint over one's freedom in the Lord when one knows that right behind one's back is a loaded cannon, hidden behind a screen, aimed into the congregation!

'Can you imagine what could happen if some enthusiastic convict who was a former Methodist should leap up to shout "Praise the Lord!" – and that it be mistaken for an uprising? The preaching and private conversations with convicts and sailors were not all lost though. Seventeen people became Christians during the voyage.'

Seventeen people, I thought. Our church here would be astonished if even one convict became a Christian each year – we simply don't expect that they might. This young man seemed to expect that people will hear the word of God and be changed.

He talked on about his family, his parents on the farm at home at 'Tregarton', at Gorran near the fishing port of Mevagissey, Cornwall, with his two younger sisters, Emma and Anna, of his poor impression of the soldiers on board the *Lady Castlereagh*, of the problems of many people confined on board ship, of the feelings of people being transported to an alien land. He talked of the beauty of the sea and described one evening when the sea looked as if a thousand boys were running over it with twinkling lanterns and candles. He spoke with a lively wit and intelligence. We at the table responded to his warmth with laughter and interest.

Bouncing along in the chaise today, I told myself not to be so silly. It is ridiculous to like someone so much on first meeting.

When Mr Leigh gets back from his country trip in a few days, he will be so pleased. He will be so thankful to have a colleague after so many years.

Parramatta, New South Wales: May 8, 1818

Mr Leigh arrived at our house this afternoon looking a new man. As Mother wasn't home, I answered the door and found a beaming Mr Leigh on the doorstep with Mr Lawry beside him.

'Allow me to introduce my new colleague, the Rev. Walter Lawry, just arrived a week ago,' Mr Leigh said.

'Miss Hassall and I have already met,' Mr Lawry responded and greeted me in a most charming way. Of course, I invited them to come in to have tea with us, but was surprised at the agitated way I found myself reacting to their presence. Not, of course, that they would have noticed anything strange, but suddenly it seemed very important for the silver to be polished, the tea delicious and the cakes light.

As we sat up in the best parlour, being very formal and polite to each other, I poured tea for the two young men.

'Do you realise, Miss Hassall,' Mr Lawry told me, 'that this is the first proper tea I have had in this country? So that makes it a very special cup of tea and one I won't forget. Thank you.'

Later at dusk, Father went with Mr Leigh and Mr Lawry down the road to the public school for the Methodist meeting. I followed them in, slipping onto a backless form among the people. Mr Leigh introduced his new friend to our people and told us how very happy he was to have a co-worker at last. He told us how they had hugged each other on meeting and were excited about all the possibilities of good work they could achieve together. Then he invited Mr Lawry to preach.

It was different somehow. Mr Leigh preaches a good sermon, but this new young man said things that struck right at my heart in a way that was quite disturbing. I must think about it.

On the way home in the moonlight, I was walking arm-in-arm with our neighbour Mrs Knight when we heard rapid footsteps. Mr Lawry slipped in between us. At first he thought that Mrs Knight was Mother, but we explained about her still being away.

'Ladies, walking along arm-in-arm with you is making me feel homesick. On board ship my home seemed impossibly far away, yet walking with you is just like walking home from chapel in Cornwall with Emma and Anna – but only after dark. When I can see everything around us clearly, so many things are different and strange. The trees and rocks, even the soil, are not like home. I suppose I will have to get used to being a stranger in a strange land.'

As we walked on, I was suddenly aware of how it must be for my brother in Wales. Is everything strange and unfamiliar to him, too? Does he feel homesick? Does he see Welsh young ladies and remember his sisters? There were unexpected tears in my eyes as I imagined how those two uprooted young men must feel, Australian Thomas in Wales and Cornish Walter Lawry in New South Wales. Our family should be kind to Mr Lawry for Thomas' sake.

Tonight, Father invited Mr Leigh and Mr Lawry to sleep at our house. (He hinted that they had been chewed up by bugs at the neighbours' where they stayed last night.) I expect we will see more of them both.

Parramatta, New South Wales: May 18, 1818
Today I have been writing a long letter to Thomas in Wales. Wales seems so very far away. Many of our friends have lived in England, or have visited there, but I have never done that. I would like so much to go to see all the things that others tell me about. Mother is proud of the great oak trees in our garden, the biggest in the colony now changing colour as the weather cools, but people say that there are whole forests of oaks in England — and trees and flowers that I have never seen. They talk about cities, great buildings and highways. They say the countryside is brilliant green in summer and that snow looks very beautiful. But I have never seen it and maybe never will.

A month ago we had letters from Thomas. Such excitement! He has been gone over a year, but the letters were written from Batavia while he was still on the journey — and a slow miserable voyage it sounded, too. By now he must surely be safely at his studies in Wales.

I have been writing to tell him about everything at home: who has had babies, who is getting married, who has died, our family health — and about Father travelling with Jonathan and James to inspect his recent land grant on the new road over the Blue Mountains to Bathurst. Of course, I told him all about the Sunday School and our special meeting last week.

It would have been so good if Thomas could have seen us on our special day. Nearly all the fifteen teachers and 117 children met at St John's Church. The children said the chapters they have been learning for Mr Marsden and were given a book or a ticket for their efforts. Mr Marsden asked them lots of questions and we were proud of the way the children answered, specially as so many of them have come off the streets with no education at all. Then we all marched in pairs in a lovely long procession behind our flag and the big banner, through the streets of Parramatta to our house in George Street. There they were all given new books and we all sang together.

Mother and the girls and I had spent all the day before baking great piles of buns, so all the children sat very politely around in our garden to eat their buns and drink punch. All the teachers came into the house and drank tea with us before our regular Sunday School teachers' meeting. Thomas would have been so pleased to see the improvement in some of the scruffy, filthy children who came to his little Sunday School at first when it was just beginning. Now some of the same children have learned to read and write, and memorise parts of the Bible. They try to be clean when they come, even if their parents don't care.

But we really miss Thomas. A lot of the teachers have left since he went and the rest of us seem to be struggling along without much leadership. Sometimes I wonder if some of the teachers even really love the Lord or care about the children. One good thing is that Anne and my special friend Elizabeth Marsden have joined us as Sunday School teachers. I try to do my best for the school by visiting children at their homes, preparing my work properly and being the Treasurer. Despite that, I am still usually tense and anxious before Sunday School begins and disappointed and irritable after it is over for the day. I have written to

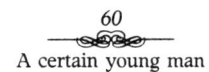
ask Thomas to pray for us, because I am afraid that if we don't improve his work will die completely, even though more than a hundred children come to us for teaching.

Parramatta, New South Wales: July, 1818

Father and Mr Lawry have spent the whole evening poring over maps. It has been a busy day with the usual round of housework, sewing and gardening for me and Mother, classes with their governess for Eliza, Susannah and Anne, and Father in and out all day with government stock work, planning with the overseer of one of his Hawkesbury farms, a meeting of the Philanthropic Society at midday, and then the Methodist meeting tonight. Since we came home, with the Methodist preacher here as usual to spend the night, he and Father have been looking at the maps.

Father has the map of the journey he and Mother made on the *Duff*, but it is rather outdated now and has big sections of vague dotted lines along the southern and north-eastern coastlines of Australia. 'Of course, those parts of the coast had not been charted at the time we were sailing to Tahiti,' Father said rather apologetically.

Mr Lawry's atlas is a modern one and much more precise. He seems to love his atlas and is always ready to explain things from it. He and Father have been happily exchanging sailing stories, while Mother has ignored them and gone on with her sewing. Eliza and James and I have sat nearby listening. Perhaps James imagines himself as a sailor one day. Probably Eliza wasn't listening very intently, but I was listening and watching a strong profile in the firelight.

They were talking about the islands. Not just Tahiti or New Zealand, but that entire scattering of tiny islands across the Pacific and the greater bulk of the islands to the north and north-east of Australia. Mr Lawry was sweeping a hand in an arc across the page with his wrist resting on New South Wales and fingers spread wide, reaching out.

'Can you imagine it? Using Sydney as a focus, a refuge, a refitting and provisioning centre — and sending missionaries right across the Pacific from here instead of working out of London on the other side of the globe. Mr Marsden has talked to Samuel Leigh and me about it and I'm sure we could extend the work to places like Tonga and Fiji, Samoa and New Caledonia, New Hebrides and New Guinea – eventually right up into Asia. If we had more funds and more missionaries...'

He *could* picture it in his mind, too. Not only could he see it himself, but Father could see his vision as well. And so could I – but his dream both excites and frightens me.

Parramatta, New South Wales: August, 1818

That man is so vain.

See him after chapel surrounded by young ladies, all twittering and giggling and gazing at him with cow-like eyes, and the vain creature enjoying every moment of it. Such popularity and flattery must surely be extremely bad for him. Those girls are just like a flock of grey and pink galahs, or rosellas decked out in their most vivid feathers, hopping around him in a flock, squawking: 'Oh, Mr Lawry... Such a splendid sermon, Mr Lawry... Oh, you are so amusing, Mr Lawry...' One of these days there will be a great fluttering of parasols and fans and the entire flock of them will fly up into a gum tree!

So why do I care? He is only a perfectly ordinary human being after all. Most certainly he is not perfect. For one thing, his emotions go up and down like a sailor in the rigging and one never knows whether to expect him to be gloomy and depressed, frivolous and full of mischief, or serious and very earnest about the fate of souls. Sometimes he comes through Parramatta on his way back from his monthly journey around the colony, full of anecdotes about the funny things that happened as he travelled. He made us all laugh with the tale of the settler's wife who greeted him at the door of her cottage with the news that he couldn't get into her parlour for a service – she had fifteen pigs penned inside!

Other times, he is full of schemes of what might be done

in the colony; he can picture Methodist chapels all over the place, even though they have no proper chapels at all yet. Recently he was also telling us about an encounter with a fine old Aboriginal man, and how sure he is that those people have good minds and could be educated. He described the fun he and the old man had with his portable shaving-kit and mirror, and the serious conversation they had shared in broken fragments of each other's language.

Other times he arrives at our house completely worn out and dejected, with an upset stomach from a steady diet of greasy pork for the ten-day trip, very short-tempered and grumpy. Maybe the settlers ignored him, as they are quite likely to do, and went on with their drinking and quarrelling and usual godless lives. Most of them are former convicts from British cities who have little interest or skill in farming, and even less in religion, so I suppose their attitude is not surprising.

Mr Lawry doesn't like to be ignored, I don't think – one gets the impression that in Cornwall people appreciated him and his preaching much more than they do in the country settlements here. He doesn't approve of our society much, I'm afraid. He seems to think we spend too much time in overeating, drinking, gossiping and making money and too little time considering our immortal souls. He may be quite right, of course.

Mr Lawry can't complain of being ignored here in Parramatta. For one young man, he receives more than his fair share of notice and flattery and I rather hope Mr Leigh is not hurt by the way people, particularly girls, flock to the Methodist services when Mr Lawry is preaching.

Why does it disturb me? Or. . . why does *he* disturb me? I feel very confused about that man. After a lifetime of listening to sermons, hundreds of sermons, I am hearing a message that seems to me to be the word I have needed to hear for a long time, a word spoken in a way that touches my heart. Am I listening to God speaking to me? Or am I dazzled by a very attractive man who preaches with fluency and style and a glowing sense of the grace of God?

Parramatta, New South Wales: September 26, 1818

With my handwriting growing smaller and smaller, I have just completed a letter to Thomas. I started writing weeks ago, with news of friends and Sunday School, then before the letter was sent we were thrilled to receive a letter from Thomas, written six months ago. Poor Thomas had had some serious difficulties during his journey to England, but we were all thankful to know that he was finally there and safe.

He wrote to Father about the high cost of paying to collect our letters when they arrive in England. To try to save him extra expense, I took the original three pages of my letter to him, turned them sideways and wrote another three pages crosswise — I hope he can read it!

There seemed to be so many things to tell Thomas. Family things, such as who has been sick. Most of our family has had illness of one kind or another over recent months, except me. I seem to be a very healthy person and I wrote: '. . . sometimes I think the reason I am not afflicted is because I am not the Lord's, for he saith "whom I love, I chasten". . . ' But then I realise that God knows best and I should be thankful to have a strong body. I told Thomas about disappointments over the Sunday School and how brother Samuel can rarely go now because he is out on the farm. I mentioned James, who has left school but doesn't seem to have anything much to do with his time — I wish he'd dig my garden when I ask him.

Then I told him about our servant Ellinor Turner, who is still waiting hopefully for her young man to pluck up courage to ask Father for her hand in marriage, and how I wouldn't give even my best friend Elizabeth Marsden the verses he had sent even though she wanted them badly — I agreed to copy them out for her instead. And I listed all the evening meetings we have these days with hardly a night free: regular Sunday School teachers' meetings, prayer meetings, house groups, the Wednesday night Methodist meetings at our house and others where Mr Leigh and Mr Lawry take turns to preach. Thomas will be

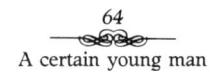
glad to know that we have so many opportunities to hear the word of God.

On the question of Sarah Henry, now Sarah Bland, I held my tongue. Thomas would be hurt to know that she had already been dramatically unfaithful to Dr Bland with a visiting ship's officer only seven months after their wedding. The officer eluded a duel with Dr Bland and even escaped without paying the court award of two thousand pounds damages. Since then, Sarah has lived with one man or another, sometimes under an assumed name, sometimes supposedly as a 'housekeeper'. Is that what people learn by growing up in Tahiti?

Even then I was not satisfied with my letter. Folding the pages carefully, with the clean sheet on the outside ready to be addressed in someone else's beautiful handwriting care of our Hancox cousins in Oxford Street, London, I calculated that I could add a little more news to the ends of the paper to be folded inside. It was there that I wrote a very small sentence for which I chose the words with particular care. I wrote of Mr Lawry: '. . .he is a Methodist preacher. . . he is a nice man and much beloved.'

With the letters I have wrapped up a big counterpane I have stitched for Mr and Mrs Hancox, our relatives in London. It is packed in with a box of Tahitian idols which are being sent from the Society Islands to London to show the mission supporters. It is strange to think of my sewing so closely linked with heathen idols for months at sea − I'm not quite sure whether I feel comfortable about it.

Father said to me once: 'Don't take those things too lightly. They are not just strange curiosities used by the heathen and now discarded. Those things have had very great power in Tahitian society. Now that many of the Tahitians have become Christians, it is as if there has been a great battle for mastery between our God and the heathen gods − the strength of these pagan objects has been defeated and now they are nothing but shabby old carvings and bits of woven cane. People in England will stare at them and probably laugh to think that the heathen could be so stupid as to worship these shabby things. But don't forget – in their day, these objects have had great power and only our God could have defeated them.'

Only recently, at our Wednesday evening meeting, we met at Mrs Shelley's house and Mr Lawry asked Mrs Shelley after the meeting about the many island curios she has displayed. Set on her mantelshelf and elsewhere around her room she has some handsome shells, carvings, delicately woven mats and some fine beaten bark *tapa* cloth, painted in designs with vegetable dyes.

'They are nearly all from the Friendly Islands. My late husband William brought them back,' Mrs Shelley explained. 'He always regretted that he didn't go back there again as a missionary. Of course, he was only a very young man when he went there first in 1797. He only stayed for two-and-a-half years, but he could never be convinced that the Friendly Islands were a hopeless cause. My husband used to say that he knew quite well that three of their original party had been murdered there – but it had partly been their own fault for getting in the way of a civil war. Although he was profoundly thankful at the time to escape with the others from Tongatabu, he was sure that it would be possible to begin a mission there all over again. In fact, he had been back there with trading ships and was trying to organise a new missionary party to Tonga when he died in 1816.'

I watched Mr Lawry run his finger over the texture of a woven fan and examine the design on a piece of *tapa* cloth. It was clear that he had a more than polite interest in Mrs Shelley's curios. He was listening with great attention to Mrs Shelley's stories of Tonga and I think we will see his faithful atlas spread out again soon.

Parramatta, New South Wales: October 28, 1818
Eliza has been teasing me again.

'Where are you going, Mary? To a prayer meeting or a party?' she asks, when she sees me before the mirror trying to smooth my hair to my satisfaction, or peering at my face to make sure my skin is free of blemishes. 'Do you really need your best bonnet, for a Methodist meeting?'

She laughs at me and, when I feel myself turning a hot red and try to pretend that I don't know what she is talking about, she giggles and says, 'He likes you, I'm sure, whether it is in your best bonnet or even with flour all over your hands in the kitchen. Everybody says so! People are saying that he should marry you, you know.'

Families can be so embarrassing. It is not only Eliza, but my little sisters, too. And Father is sometimes so *obvious* in the way he tells Mr Lawry about his farms and property and how comfortable each of his children will be one day. Even Mother does it, almost forcing me on the man's attention with remarks like, 'Mary made this cake – she is an excellent cook, don't you think?' or 'Mary is so good with the little ones in Sunday School.' (Of course, Father's statements may simply be his general pride in his possessions and his family, not that he expects his daughter to marry a particular man. Father respects Mr Lawry, but they have different views on many things. They don't even agree on which hymn tunes to sing at our meetings!)

Not everyone thinks that it would be good if Mr Lawry liked me. Some of my friends – Sunday School teachers here and young ladies around the colony – are quite infatuated with the new preacher and each one is sure he likes her. Mother has heard him say that he writes specially to one of his cousins, a Miss Vercoe of Bodmin, Cornwall, so perhaps he plans to marry her when he goes back to Cornwall. I have noticed Samuel Leigh, too. His first enthusiasm for Walter Lawry seems to be waning a bit and sometimes he looks at me with a hurt expression.

What does Walter Lawry think? Am I imagining that he is looking directly at me when he is talking to a group, that he deliberately comes to stand near me after a service, that he truly enjoys the talks we have when he stays at our house? Was he critical of me for inviting him to come to see me for a while this morning, while he was here in Parramatta for the Methodist meeting tonight? I think not.

A love declared

Windsor, New South Wales:
Friday, November 6, 1818

Today has been such a beautiful, complicated, delightful day. I was invited to go into the country to Windsor for the laying of the foundation stone of what Mr Lawry and Mr Leigh tell me is the first *regular* Methodist chapel in the southern hemisphere. (They don't really count the place where they meet in Princes Street in the Rocks, Sydney, because it wasn't a chapel in the first place and the seating makes it feel more like a tavern. Nor the tiny chapel the settler John Lees has built out on his land at Castlereagh, because that is mainly a family affair.)

The two Methodist missionaries rode to Parramatta from Sydney this morning, then Father allowed me to go with them in our gig. Brother James came, too. It would have been funny if they hadn't been taking it so seriously. First, there was the question of who would drive the gig and then the matter of where we should sit. After a polite conflict of wills we set off, the reins firmly in the hands of Walter Lawry, me tucked in between the two men and James sitting up behind us with a wicked glint in his eye.

It was a lovely bright day as the gig rolled along the Windsor road to the north-west, passing through hilly country with much of it heavily wooded, and the Blue Mountains a soft line of mauves and blues on the horizon. Walter Lawry talked about the green hills of his beloved

Cornwall. Samuel Leigh countered with stories of his home in Staffordshire in the Midlands and his student years at Gosport on the southern coast of England. Even though both men are Methodists from England, their paths have never crossed before and they are very different in background and personality; even their English accents are quite different.

As we drove along, Mr Leigh told us about the seminary he attended in Gosport. It had been established by the famous Dr David Bogue and was specially for the training of missionaries and ministers for the Independent ministry. Many of Mr Leigh's fellow students had become pioneer missionaries in faraway places like Ceylon and Mauritius, South India and China with the London Missionary Society. Maybe they would think New South Wales was also a place for pioneers! Mr Leigh told us how Dr Bogue did not agree with the idea of first sending out artisans and tradesmen to civilise the native people.

'He used to ask: "Why send out uneducated mechanics who can make a wheelbarrow or plant turnips, rather than good preachers who can explain the truth of the gospel?" and would point out that Christ called his disciples *away* from their fishing nets to become fishers of men,' Mr Leigh told us.

Mr Lawry's education was in a small Methodist seminary in Plymouth, Cornwall, where he became fascinated with his studies of Latin and Greek, began his love for geography and the scriptures and, as part of his studies, regularly travelled to Methodist circuits in Cornwall to preach. He told us of walking the twenty miles from his home back to his seminary after a short holiday, and of the beauties of the Cornish coastline.

'Unlike Mr Leigh,' he explained, 'my fellow students were not expecting to travel to distant lands as missionaries and I had thought that I would be appointed to one of our Cornish circuits. But the Committee in London of our Methodist Missionary Society asked me to come to talk to them about coming to New South Wales — and here I am!'

We drove on through farm holdings and on past Vinegar Hill. 'Did you know that the Rouse family has land here? Mary Rouse is my brother Jonathan's sweetheart,' I said. Mary is one of our Sunday School teachers and a nice girl. Of course, the two men come here regularly on their preaching trips to Windsor and Richmond, but I rarely travel on this road.

I chattered on. 'One of my earliest memories, when I was a little child of about four years old, is of the Irish convict uprising and the battle that happened on that hillside. Not that I was out here, of course. But I remember being woken up from sleep and being bustled out into the dark and up to the Barracks with Mother and all the other women and children. At the time it felt really exciting, with the bright flares of torches and people shouting. Father went with our friend Mr Crook, out into the night with their fowling pieces to defend us. I'm sure that they were both very thankful when the convict plans went wrong and they didn't attack Parramatta after all, so Father and Mr Crook were not forced to try to shoot anyone.'

Mention of Mr Crook, who returned to the Pacific as a missionary to Tahiti just two years ago, set the two men discussing what should be done there. They noted Mr Marsden's suggestion that the London Missionary Society be responsible for the Society Islands and that the Methodists look after the Friendly Islands, the many problems of the Church Missionary Society in New Zealand and what should be done about ministry to the local Aboriginal population. Both Leigh and Lawry are men of ideas and vision, and we whirled along the road to Windsor, stirring a cloud of dust behind us while they talked of faraway islands.

As we drove on towards Windsor, somehow I had the impression that Walter Lawry was showing off his driving skills and he and Samuel Leigh vied with each other to be entertaining. It was very flattering, but not easy to be between two men who were equally excited about their special day, equally enjoying the pleasant drive, but with an

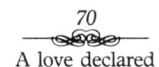
unspoken feeling of conflict between them. Behind us, I could sense James grinning.

By late afternoon, we were driving down the street of Windsor above the winding Hawkesbury River, between the scattering of cottages to the grassy block of land which the Methodists had been offered by their friend Mr Marsden. A crowd of about one hundred people had gathered for the occasion. As I climbed out of the gig I was greeted by another friend, Lucy Mileham. Together, we went to stand with the crowd as the service began.

Mr Lawry began by singing a hymn in his usual enthusiastic way – he loves to sing. (Mr Marsden quite envies the Methodist freedom to sing joyful hymns – or any kind of hymns – in their services, because the Church of England are not permitted to do so.) Then Mr Lawry read from the Bible and prayed. Mr Leigh preached from Ezra 3:11 – 'And all the people shouted with a great shout, when they praised the Lord, because the foundation of the Lord was laid.' Taking his turn at leading, Mr Lawry sang again and then preached a second sermon from Exodus 25:8 – 'And let them make me a sanctuary, that I may dwell among them.'

The crowd of settlers stood around and shuffled a bit in the grass while the foundation stone was laid. Perhaps some of them felt that two sermons were rather unnecessary, but I liked looking at my two friends and thinking of the good they are doing in the colony – and thinking a few private thoughts of my own.

This evening we stayed at Mileham's. Lucy was delighted to have my company. She is a lovely girl. Her father, Dr Mileham, is rather old and not very highly regarded as a doctor because he is old-fashioned and has poor vision, but he is a kind and generous man. Her mother died a few months ago and Lucy misses her. (We always called her 'Mrs Mileham' because it would have been unkind to Lucy to do anything else.) Tomorrow, we'll have another twenty-mile-long drive back to Parramatta. I won't mind if it takes a long time.

Parramatta, New South Wales: Sunday morning, November 29, 1818

The most difficult part of writing the letter was deciding how to begin it. In the end, after a great deal of indecisive waving of the pen, I began 'Respected Sir, I thank you. . .'

Somehow, it has seemed very important to let him know how very much that meeting meant to me. For months I have been struggling with my own private thoughts about myself and my position in God's eyes. Despite all my efforts to be a better person, a more Christian person, I have continued to have a great feeling of failure and anxiety. As I have listened regularly to Mr Leigh and Mr Lawry preach, I have begun to see more of the grace and forgiveness of God and have begun to hope that that really includes me.

Since our lovely day at Windsor, I have not seen Mr Lawry as he has been ill in Sydney. (Mr Leigh had to take his preaching appointments, not with very good grace.) He was well enough to come to Parramatta on Thursday and preached at the schoolroom on 'Who is on the Lord's side?' But it was the preaching on Friday night that reached me.

In our best parlour, surrounded by our friends and family, I heard Walter Lawry preach from Genesis chapter 32, the story of Jacob wrestling with the mysterious angel who proved to be God himself. He spoke of Jacob who had earlier won a blessing under false pretences, who had cheated his brother Esau and run away, and who was now afraid to meet Esau again. Mr Lawry described Jacob's shame and need of forgiveness, and how he was hoping to win that forgiveness from his brother by offering him gifts.

As he spoke, I could feel the agony and struggle of Jacob that night as he strove with the one whom he didn't even yet recognise as God, and how he clung to him in his helplessness and weakness. I felt the wonderful sense of relief and release Jacob must have felt when the angel recognised him by a new name, Israel, and gave him a blessing, just there alone in the dark before dawn, not because he had earned it or paid for it or deserved it, but because God loved him. I sensed for myself the wonder of God's forgiveness and grace which I can *never* earn or deserve, but which I truly believe he has offered me. By faith I thankfully accept it.

I wasn't the only one affected by that service. There was a wonderful sense of the presence of God right there in that room blessing us all, and Walter Lawry himself was like one alight with the love of God.

So I have been writing to him. It feels a bit peculiar to be writing him a letter while he is still in our house, but I feel too shy to say out loud what I want to say. I have written: 'Had you never come to this country, perhaps I should never have received the love of God, which I humbly trust I do now enjoy through your instrumentality. His holy name be praised. I really believe God owned and blessed me when you preached from Genesis 32:29 — "And he blessed him there." *This was the sermon*. No-one knows the joy and grief I went through that night, how I did weep when no eye saw me, but a compassionate Saviour whose smile makes me happy. . .' — and on and on for pages. In a way, it would be much easier if Mr Lawry were white-haired and very stout, rather than a young man whom I care about. But my sense of assurance that I really am God's person is so real that I don't suppose it matters.

Parramatta, New South Wales: December 1, 1818

The letter was handed to me privately on the evening before he planned to leave us and go back to Sydney. Ever since reading it I have been confused. The days are long now and I took the letter with me as I walked in the evening cool under the fruit trees of Father's orchard. My hands were trembling so much that I could scarcely open it. But I opened the letter and he had written that he loved me. Above my head the burdened branches of a peach tree moved, crowded with unripe fruit: small, hard and green. Will it be possible for my love to grow and ripen? Or will it be dashed to the ground in the winds of family disapproval, to lie there unfulfilled? I don't know.

I held his dear letter, hardly able to see the words for the tears in my eyes. But I knew what he had written. He loved me. For months I have thought about him, hoped to see him, been jealous of his attraction for other girls, dreamed about every time he has spoken to me, prayed about him. I love him.

But now, suddenly, I am afraid. What will Father and Mother think? They respect him as a minister and encourage him in his efforts to bring the gospel to the convicts and settlers of this colony. They admire much of his preaching and welcome him in their home as a guest. But will they welcome the idea of him courting their daughter? I fear they may not: a young, poor, Methodist preacher from Cornwall, with his family property far away; no security, a life of travel with few comforts and, worst of all, they do not agree with his theology.

Father and Mr Lawry have long, vigorous talks about the Calvinist and Wesleyan differences: about predestination and free-will, about whether we can lose our salvation. Father becomes very heated about it, indeed. Even on the *Duff*, when most of the missionaries were Calvinists like Father, he was one of the majority who forced the two lone Wesleyans to agree to the Calvinist doctrine. Father might just possibly allow his daughter to be courted by a man who was poor, but never by a man with unsound theology!

So I took Walter's letter to my room and wrote a note to give him before he left for Sydney this morning. It was hard to force cool, discouraging words from my pen when I wanted to write 'I love you' in huge letters on the page. But I wrote that I felt it would be wrong for us to have even a regular correspondence unless I had the approval of my parents and this I feared they would not give. My little sister Anne delivered the letter and I saw him ride away from our house with a puzzled and pained look on his face. I saw him go, then ran to the orchard to cry, hidden among the branches of little green peaches.

*   *   *

Parramatta, New South Wales: Sunday, January 3, 1819

Sitting in St John's Church this morning, I may have appeared very pious and demure, but my thoughts were flying in all directions. In fact, I can't recall a word Mr Marsden said, but perhaps that is not so bad. He always uses the same sermons over and over, so I must have heard it before and will hear it again.

As I sat solemnly in church, I was conscious of the summer heat, of the folds of my thin muslin gown clinging damply to my legs, of the red-faced suffering of the men in their high folded cravats and buttoned jackets, of the drowsy faces of convicts and the gleam of perspiration on the brow of the Rev. Samuel Marsden. My eyes were watching a single drop of sweat twinkling from his earlobes like an ornament, waiting for it to fall, but my mind was thinking about the Rev. Walter Lawry. I was hoping so much that he would come to Parramatta today for the preaching tonight.

All through December it has been like that, ever since he rode off to Sydney. We have had no contact, no letters, but he has been constantly in my thoughts. When Samuel and then Jonathan rode to Sydney on visits, they came back with the news that Mr Lawry was ill, very ill with dysentery. Though he was taking doses of mercury for his ailment, it seemed to be making him worse.

Our family has been away from Parramatta during most of December at 'Macquarie Grove' for the harvest. Every day I worked hard beside Mother, my sisters and the servants, helping with the baking, stewing and carrying of immense meals to the harvesters, but in my mind I was living another life. When I was free to leave the kitchen, I wandered alone through the bush and along the banks of the river.

Scuffling through the litter of curling fragments of bark and dead leaves, wandering in and out of the spiky summer grasses and tender ferns, I carried on long, imaginary conversations in my mind. I imagined what I would say to

Walter (I can even say his first name in my mind) and what he might say to me: Does he really want to marry me, or have I misunderstood him? Will my parents allow him to court me? And, oh dear, what would it be like to be the wife of a minister? I would drift back to the house with a sprig of pale creamy summer wattle or fluffy gum blossom in my cap, and pay no attention to the giggles of Susannah and Anne.

But at last, this afternoon we heard the clatter of hooves outside and a knock on the door. He had come. Mother was her usual welcoming self and was so pleased to see him. She brought him in, looking much thinner and rather pale, and bustled around trying to make him comfortable.

'Such a very hot day, Mr Lawry. You must be exhausted after a long ride in the heat – Mary, some of our fresh lemon cordial for Mr Lawry. You poor dear sir, you have been so sick, too. Are you sure you are well enough to preach tonight?'

'Yes, Mrs Hassall, I'm sure. I'm only thankful to be able to do it. It is weeks since I was well enough and it has been miserable to be unable to work.' He looked at me with a question in his eyes as I handed him the cool glass of juice and offered the basket loaded with apricots and nectarines, peaches and grapes.

Mother asked him, 'Did you have a pleasant Christmas, sir?'

'No, it was awful,' he responded. 'It was even worse, I think, than last Christmas when I had only sailed a few weeks earlier and was horribly seasick in the Bay of Biscay. This time I was ill and couldn't preach because the mercury treatment made my mouth too painful to talk. I couldn't even attend a Christmas service. My good kind servant, Thomas Wright, and I were at home together and I couldn't even eat the food he did his best to prepare.

'Thomas isn't the best cook, of course – he was a convict on board the *Lady Castlereagh* and became a Christian under my preaching during our voyage from England. When we arrived here, I asked for him to be assigned to me as

a servant and he is a most faithful friend. But even so, he is not the one I would have chosen for my sole companion for Christmas!'

Walter Lawry looked directly at me and said, 'Never have I been more homesick and lonely in my life. I felt that I ought to be meditating on the birth of Christ, but all I could think of was my loneliness – and my dear parents and sisters so far away in Cornwall sitting at the familiar table with roast goose and plum pudding, the leaping fire on the hearth where I have sat and been part of a family. . .

'The one cheerful thing was laying the foundation stone of a chapel in Macquarie Street, Sydney, with Mr Leigh on New Year's Day. Our Methodist Chapel will be right opposite the fine new buildings of the Rum Hospital and almost next to the building planned for a Court House.'

After the Methodist preaching tonight, he came back to our house and, as the heat of the day cooled, he and I sat quietly in the moonlight on our verandah. For some time we sat in silence, glad to be together and not knowing where to begin. None of my imagined conversations seemed right.

Then he said, 'Do you realise how disturbing you are, Mary? Do you know that your lovely face has been coming between me and my work for months, so that I have found it hard to concentrate? Do you realise that I am going to find it very difficult to choose excerpts from my diary to send to the Committee in London, as I am obliged to do, because your name is on almost every page?'

Surely he must have heard the thudding of my heart in the quiet evening air. He went on, telling me how he had spent hours during his illness in trying to analyse his feelings: how he had made a long list of all the things that he had always felt were essential in a wife – a good disposition, a girl who was a Christian ('that is vital to me'), sensible, educated, healthy, a good housewife and someone with a loving heart.

'I think I am a passionate person and would find it hard to be happy with someone who was cold as frost – and, of course, if my ideal wife were beautiful and rich and near my age, that would be perfect!'

He had been teasing me a little, but now he was very serious. 'That is what I have always been looking for in the girl I want to marry and I believe that God has led me to you. My lovely Mary, I do love you. Mary...?'

Foolish man. He thinks he will have to wait for me to learn to love him. Doesn't he know that girls can have strong feelings, too?

We talked and talked, until there were loud warning coughs through the window from my parents in the parlour who were preparing to go to bed. He has written a letter to my father, asking permission to write to me, but is afraid that perhaps my parents won't approve of him and his strong Methodist doctrines. He is anxious about the future. Not only does he need the permission of my parents but, under Methodist law, is not permitted to marry for another two years as he is a young minister on probation.

He told me about the long list of reasons for and against marriage which he wrote while he was sick and admitted to hoping that it would seem more scriptural and fitting for a missionary to be married than celibate. Walter told me that he had even written about me to his parents – but in code! He said that he wrote my name in Greek script *Kurei Marias 'Essall,* so that he had the pleasure of naming me without spreading my name around Cornwall before he was ready.

And now I am lying in my bed, looking through the window out onto the moonlit garden and dreaming about every word we said.

Parramatta, New South Wales: April, 1819

So many people have been travelling lately that I feel quite envious. It is a big occasion for me to travel as far as Sydney to see Walter, let alone across the sea. At least Father has given us permission to write to each other, though he doesn't want us to rush into anything.

In March, Mr Leigh sailed for New Zealand on a holiday.

He hasn't been well at all, poor man, and he and Walter have not been seeing eye to eye on some things in their work, so he was glad when Mr Marsden offered him the trip on the *Active* to try to regain his health. He is perhaps glad to be away from the sight of Walter courting me. Charles Marsden sailed for England in July. His father is sending him to study to be a doctor. (Charles is less than enthusiastic as he would much rather be a farmer.) Mr Kendall from the Church Mission in New Zealand has also sailed for England to see about the publication of his *Grammar and Vocabulary of New Zealand Language.*

Soon our friends the Hoskings will be going back to England, too. I will miss good Mrs Hosking very much. When they came, years ago, to take over the Female Orphan School, it was a disgraceful place and most of the girls ended up as prostitutes, but the Hoskings have quite changed the character of the place so that at least some of their girls are making good marriages and leaving with a little dowry. Now that the Orphan School is here in Parramatta, I have been able to see Mrs Hosking every week at all the Methodist meetings.

More Maori students have come to the seminary and Mr Marsden has sixteen of them there now. He is busily building a handsome new seminary building for them on the north of the river and hopes it will soon be complete. The boys are not all happy here in Parramatta as many suffer from illness and most feel homesick. I suppose I'd miss my family, too, if I were as far from home as they are.

Our Maori friends, Tui and Titore, are away in England at the moment. Mr Marsden thought it would be good for them to see a great civilisation. What do they think of it? I wonder. Sometimes Tui has made some comments on our way of life that are unnervingly perceptive – he seems to see through things and exposes the weaknesses in some of our ways.

Dear Walter is working very hard. With Mr Leigh away, he has responsibility for all the country preaching tours, as well as supervising the building of the Windsor and Macquarie Street chapels and alterations in Princes Street. There are Class Meetings, committees (he is very enthusiastic about the Bible Society and the Methodist Sunday School in Sydney), chapel subscriptions to solicit, sermons to prepare and preach, new believers to encourage and condemned convicts to comfort. We don't see each other often, but we have a private pact.

Every day at one o'clock we always pause and say a prayer for each other. When we are together and alone, we always try to pray together, asking for God's guidance and blessing and thanking him for bringing us together. Our Lord is a very active Person with us as we dream and plan.

My Mr Lawry has a number of worries as he thinks about our future. He has written, perhaps not wisely, to the London Committee to explain that he intends to marry even before his probation period is over. He says: 'I told them before I left England that I came as a free man, not as a prisoner, and that if the useful chord of general discipline was hauled too tight in particular cases, it will be liable to snap!' (I fear my Walter may find himself in trouble some day.)

He doesn't seem to have the great respect for rules and regulations that Mr Leigh has, who wouldn't dream of stepping outside the bounds set by their far-distant but all-powerful Committee. Walter is worried about money, too. All the Methodist money is being poured into chapel building and, specially if he is marrying without permission, how could he draw on their funds to finance a house and furniture? And Walter thinks my dear Thomas won't approve of a Methodist brother-in-law, because Thomas will have become accustomed to higher society and genteel church connections, rather than an earthy Methodist Cornishman who is able to appeal to the working-class people.

Sydney, New South Wales: July, 1819

Last week, Walter and I travelled by long boat from Parramatta to Sydney for me to spend a few weeks with the Bowdens and say farewell to the Hoskings. (Mother and

Samuel were with us, but we barely noticed them.) The boat journey was so beautiful. We usually travel by road on horseback, in the chaise, carriage or by Watsford's coach. This time we joined the river boat at the wharf near our house in George Street.

Somehow, Walter contrived to sit beside me under the small sails as we sailed down the Parramatta River, between rocky banks green with bush until the river widened into the beautiful harbour. The winter sun on the vividly blue and silver water was dazzling. As I shaded my eyes from the glare, I watched a little group of Aborigines fishing from a rocky promontory and a canoe, loaded with another family, paddling across the harbour. A cool wind came off the water, giving me a reason to draw my shawl around me and lean more closely on Mr Lawry's arm. As we rounded a curve in the river, the neat lines of timber, brick and sandstone houses, the little gardens and the windmills of Sydney town came into view, with the masts and rigging of anchored vessels in the safety of Port Jackson. I do like Sydney. As we clambered out onto the wharf, I looked forward to a lovely visit.

Since we have been in Sydney, there have been so many things to do and friends to visit. It is so good to be nearer Walter for a little while, to be able to go with him to the Methodist services and meetings in Sydney, and to see the house being renovated for us next to the chapel being built in Macquarie Street. All the planning is a great excitement for me – and a great worry for poor Walter.

Walter likes my beautiful new straw bonnet, which has just arrived from Thomas in England. I have been wearing it as we visit friends. None of my young lady friends will believe that Thomas chose our bonnets ('They are the very *latest* style with such high crowns! We thought Thomas would be above thinking of fashion...'). In fact, I didn't feel quite comfortable with the new style as it seems too extreme for me. In any case the bonnets arrived rather crushed from packing, so as I'm quite good with my hands I have made the crowns lower. I have told Walter all about the things Thomas sent us: paintings, books, stuffed birds of paradise to go in a glass case, a paintbox and brushes for me and, most treasured of all, a little New Testament which I carry everywhere I go.

Wearing my new bonnet so that I don't look like a peasant from the country, I have been visiting all the shops, full of wonderful things from England, France and India. Captain Peter Dillon's shop has some exquisite French lace, most delicate muslins and sprigged silk and I am going to ask Father to buy me some. Our wedding date is not decided, but if I begin making my bridal gown perhaps it will come sooner! There are some of the softest little kid slippers, too, with their ribbons to tie and ker-chiefs, parasols... Father won't mind, I hope.

At Mr Eager's grand new house the other day, we met some of the Maoris. Tui and Titore had arrived back from England on the same ship as the Rev. Cross and the Rev. Hill, new clergy for the Anglican Church, and some new missionaries on their way to New Zealand. Tui had a new confidence and sophistication and, though he was friendly, he was almost condescending to me, a mere ignorant woman who had never been to England. He was dressed so grandly with fashionable blue jacket and new trousers, waistcoat and snowy cravat. Only the ornate tattoos on his face indicated his Maori race.

Titore is a nice lad, though Mr Marsden thinks he is not as promising as Tui, and was ecstatic to have received a letter from Thomas which he showed me.

As I wrote to Thomas: 'He loves you dearly. I thought he would never leave off shaking hands with me, I was quite ashamed...' Mr Marsden is soon travelling with an American brig, the *General Gates*, to New Zealand with a new party of missionaries, the Butler family, the Kemps and Francis Hall, the schoolmaster. Tui and Titore are go-ing home with him, with some of the other Maoris from the seminary. I wonder if I will ever see my Maori friends again.

At last, here in Sydney near my love, I have written

plainly to Thomas about Walter Lawry. In the past I have mentioned his name, but now I wrote from the heart with complete openness. Now it is becoming clear that, despite the obstacles, we will one day be man and wife.

I wrote: 'I tremble on the brink as I am just about to take a step which will either be my greatest happiness or greatest grief and misery through life... Pray for me more fervent than ever... I feel the deepest unworthiness of the station I am soon to fill, but hope the Lord will give me grace to do his will in all things, and fit me exactly for an helpmeet in all things to my dear love, not being a hindrance to his usefulness in the smallest matter, but a spur to it, and soother to his moments of solitude and may we bear each other's burdens and take up our cross daily following Christ in all things... I really do love him more than any other I know or did know or wish to be acquainted with. I am unworthy of such a pious good man as he is... My motives for this step are all centred in love; I have for him what I never had for another, unalienable affection. And his love for me is everything but unbounded! The name of my love is Lawry... it was under his instrumentality that I was convinced more clearly that salvation was freely given by grace through faith alone...'

Mrs Hosking is going to carry my letter when she sails. Surely Thomas will see that I am not being forced into marriage unwillingly.

Not only Walter and I are in love, and Jonathan and his dear Miss Mary Rouse, but Samuel is in the same state. Samuel had been courting Miss Anne Marsden quite seriously, but every time he even spoke to another girl she was upset and sometimes was quite rude to him. I don't think she meant to turn him away, but he didn't know how to interpret her and was hurt by the way she treated him.

Then Lucy Mileham came to stay at our house for some weeks after Dr Mileham remarried. Not only did she and I become special friends, but Samuel fell in love. Now he has been out to Windsor on visits and gained the permission of her father for them to be married.

Perhaps Samuel is taking life and the idea of marriage very seriously these days. He came close to losing his life in floods on the Nepean River in March. The river had risen dangerously, flooding across much of the Cowpasture farm land. Samuel went with a party of men in the public boat to rescue two settlers up to their armpits in water, but as they tried to row to higher ground the boat was staved on a tree, broke up and sank, forcing Samuel and the others deep under the floodwaters. One, Constable Salter, was drowned and the others tore off their heavy clothes and swam desperately to safety through the turbulent waters. Poor Samuel was very shaken by it. It would have been terrible for my brother to have ended his days drowned on someone's stubble paddock.

Parramatta, New South Wales: October, 1819

It may be as well that our wedding date has finally been fixed for next month. We are being married at St John's Church, Parramatta, on November 22, in a big family party with Samuel and Lucy, Jonathan and Mary. We hope our old friend Mr Marsden will be back from New Zealand in time to marry us. Walter has been working as hard as ever, but he says he finds it difficult to concentrate. He showed me his diary and the poor dear had written: 'Courtship is by no means profitable for the soul. I am so deep in love as to be quite unfit for almost any other things... We love each other too well to part any more. But when we shall be married I don't know... The life of courtship I by no means admire. No man can be a true lover and at the same time quite happy...'

When I read those words, I turned on him. 'Aren't you happy? Whatever do you mean?'

'Not you, sweet Polly,' he said. 'But our marriage is all entangled with Methodist laws, which I'm about to break, and money, which I don't have enough of, and – please don't be angry – future parents-in-law who are Calvinist Dissenters. That is hard for a Methodist to swallow!'

He went out to 'Macquarie Grove' with me for a few days

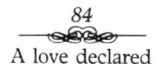
in September and each day we wandered through the springtime bushland. When I visited there in May with the Marsden girls, we spent almost all of our time riding so that by the end I was aching in every limb. Walter and I rode sometimes, but mostly walked together, exploring the sandstone rocks shelving to the river, the pebbly river beaches and the caves with ashes of Aboriginal camp fires.

Never again will I see crimson clusters of bottlebrush or the delicacy of a spray of minute bush orchids, clinging to the roughness of a treetrunk, without remembering the two of us, absorbed in each other, walking in the sun. From time to time I pointed out a flower, such as the fat candles of banksia like a giant floral candelabra, or a few bush violets hidden among ferns, but Walter wasn't really interested in flowers... It is well that our wedding day is very soon as he complains that his personal barometer seems stuck on warm to hot!

Everyone seems pleased about our marriage. Of course, everyone likes my Walter; he is a very popular man. Even people in Sydney society are congratulating him. He often dines with people of quality, although he finds the richest people are often less likely to become Christian than the most hardened convict — he says that they tend to embrace any scheme which offers an excuse for their conduct. But he told me with great pleasure how he had dined with the Governor and Mrs Macquarie and Sir John Jamison. Mrs Macquarie had said, 'As far as missionaries' wives are concerned, you may get who you like, I suppose, Mr Lawry, but I really think you could not have fixed upon one so suitable as Miss Hassall,' and the others had teased him and agreed.

Mr Leigh is back from New Zealand but the holiday doesn't seem to have done him much good. He told Walter that he was very pleased about our marriage plans, but I'm not sure. He has given Walter a great deal of extra work to do, though Walter is doing his best. It doesn't seem quite fair. Even his preaching isn't as good as it was. I think Walter feels that he managed better alone, without the misery of being out of harmony with his colleague. He told me that he once wrote to his father: 'I think having a roving commission like Lord Nelson is what best suits my talents and inclinations. I believe I am more fit to form plans than to execute those of other men...'

Both my Lawry and Mr Leigh were clearly very unhappy over several months. A week ago Walter went to Samuel Leigh and they had a good talk, trying to understand each other's problems. Walter told me later that he was very relieved to have been reconciled; they had been able to pray together and each felt as if he had found a new friend. The Governor has asked Mr Leigh to go to Newcastle for a while to visit the penal settlement there, so he'll be away at the time of our wedding. That may be as well.

Parramatta, New South Wales: November 22, 1819

The candle has been blown out and the room is shadowed and still. Rain is still dashing against the window, but I can faintly see the outline of my husband's head on my pillow. He is breathing quietly and his arms are around me. My husband!

Today Walter and I were married. Such a bald, unadorned statement. It sounds quite ordinary. But it is not, it is not! Today was the most wonderful day of my whole life and I lie here wide-awake beside my love, thinking about it all. How can he sleep?

There has been such a bustle and confusion around our home for weeks. Mother has been working to prepare our house so that it is scrubbed and polished and relentlessly spotless. There has been such preparation of cakes and pies, soups and meats, fruits and breads, pickles and sauces. The outside kitchen has been hot with the constant stoking of cooking-fires to prepare mountains of food for our guests. Inside there was the polishing of silver and brass and the gathering of sheaves of flowers. Lucy and Mary have visited me often in the past few weeks to work together on our wedding gowns, nightshifts and new dresses and my bridesmaid, Elizabeth Marsden, often

joined us to help with the sewing. We have each spent months on embroideries – I made pointlace – and have stitched our gowns with the daintiest of stitches. Poor Father tried to escape from the centre of things by announcing that he was going to compose a wedding hymn – and retreated to his room!

Just a week ago, one of the missionaries from Tahiti, Mr Orsmond, arrived in Port Jackson on the *Haweis*. Mrs Orsmond had died in Tahiti a year ago and he had been advised by the missionaries who knew Parramatta to come to propose marriage to *me*! When he discovered that he was too late for Lucy, Mary and me, he is supposed to have said, 'All the flowers have been picked'! I was very glad he was too late. Walter is the only man I wanted to marry, but in any case I don't think I'd like to be a missionary's wife and go to live among the heathen.

Walter arrived in Parramatta from his house in Sydney a few days ago. He came into the house looking so bleak and red around the eyes that I feared he had changed his mind and was regretting our plans to marry. His feelings tend to swing so high and so low – and so unexpectedly.

'Not marry you? Silly girl, I have every intention of marrying you,' he reassured me, holding me tight. 'But I admit that I have been feeling miserable all the way along the road. I suddenly realised how very far away my family is. I am marrying my beautiful Mary Cover Hassall and they have never even seen you. You will have all your family and friends around you, but I will be the stranger. I just wish my family were here, too.'

I think I can understand just a little. My dear brother Thomas wasn't with us today. I would dearly like to know whether he liked my husband and thought him as fine a man as I do.

Last night we were late to bed after finishing all the tasks. I had washed and brushed my hair – sometimes I wish it were curly, but it is long and gleamed like smoothest silk. Just before I slept, I looked again at my bridal gown, slender and soft with ribbons high under the bosom and the lace edging on the little puffed sleeves, my new flowery bonnet and the frilled parasol and gloves. I wanted to be as lovely as I could for Walter. I climbed into bed last night, knowing that it would be my last night as a maid and wondering what it would be like to be a married woman. I was not afraid. Walter and I have prayed about our marriage so much, and I trust him so deeply, that there was no room for fear — just a human curiosity about what our life together would mean.

When I awoke this morning, the sun was shining despite some clouds.

'It is going to rain,' Mother said anxiously.

By half-past-eight we were all at St John's Church, Lucy, Mary and I walking joyfully and proudly between the twin towers to join the men we loved. We stood together at the altar, feeling the warmth and the love surrounding us from our friends and family. Though we had kept hoping till the last minute, Mr Marsden wasn't back from New Zealand so the new minister, the Rev. John Cross, led us in our vows, calling first Walter and me, then Samuel and Lucy, then Jonathan and Mary. The promises are such great demanding promises, but I held tightly to Walter's hand and made my vows.

We came out of the church to a sprinkle of rain, but all our guests were whisked into carriages to come to my parents' house. Such a flurry of hugging and kissing, of whispered messages and teasing comments, of compliments on our gowns and appearance, of smiles and laughter and the hint of tears! We ate and drank, sang and listened to Mr Cross preach a wedding sermon, sang the wedding song composed by Father to the tune 'Adoration' and listened to his very energetic address to us.

Walter had chosen a hymn from Mr Wesley's Collection, No. 510: 'Thou God of truth and grace'. Somehow the words seemed specially true for us. We sang:

> Why hast thou cast our lot
> In the same age and place?

And why together brought
To see each other's face? ...
Didst thou not make us one
That we might one remain,
Together travel on
And bear each other's pain?
Till all thy utmost goodness prove
And rise renewed in perfect love.

I looked at Samuel born in Coventry, Jonathan born in Tahiti, Walter born in Cornwall and the other brides and I born in New South Wales and marvelled at how God had brought us together. I saw Father grasp Walter's hand and say 'Son Lawry', and knew that he had really accepted Walter as a very fine person whom he is proud to call his son. The lovely day concluded to the sound of rain drumming on the roof, with prayers as all of our family and friends asked God for his blessing on all six of us.

Quite late, our friends began to go home. Father looked out into the streaming darkness and announced, 'You certainly can't go driving off to Sydney in this – you must all spend the night here.' One by one we bade our guests farewell and saw them splashing off into the night. At last, Walter and I retired to my room and shut the door. In the quietness, we held each other very gently, not quite believing that we were alone, man and wife.

Walter spoke first. 'Mary, I have brought something for us. I hope you don't think it is wrong, but it seemed very important for us to share this.'

Hesitating in a way unlike his usual confident self, he produced a white napkin and unfolded it to reveal his pewter Communion plate, bread and wine.

'I wanted us to share Holy Communion – just us, not part of a crowd. I love you so much, darling Mary. I love you with my heart – and with my body as well. I want our love for each other to be in the circle of our love for our Lord.' And so, kneeling at our bridal bed, Walter and I received the body and blood of our Lord Jesus Christ.

Now I lie in the darkness, smiling. Inside the circle of love and safety, there is no fear and no shame. My body and Walter's are a gift from God and he has brought us together. Lying here in Walter's arms, I have a feeling of great freedom and thankfulness.

And our private service of Holy Communion? Perhaps, yet again, Walter has chosen to do the unconventional, even the unsuitable thing that would make many others (specially the clergy) raise their eyebrows in horrified disapproval. But I know that that secret moment of being in God's presence will remain in my memory as the most precious part of my wedding day.

A vale of tears

Macquarie Street, Sydney, New South Wales: February, 1820

As I wrote to Thomas, I wouldn't change my place for all the riches of Peru. My other self wrote in his diary, 'I wouldn't be unmarried again for all the world calls great and glorious.'

This morning Walter was in his study, surrounded by his beloved books and writing in his diary. (He has to send notes from his diary to the Methodist Committee in London to be published around England so that people can be informed about his work here.) I sat in the next room happily stitching, and I couldn't help singing aloud as I worked. I didn't want to interrupt, but I just wanted to be close to him. Dropping my needlework, I crept up behind him and wrapped my arms around his neck. He pretended to ignore me and went on writing – but there, in the middle of a serious account of our latest trip around the colony, his pen inscribed, 'My old Polly is leaning hard upon me, so that I cannot write. Banish her!'

'Now see what you have done, wicked girl,' he teased, abandoning his pen. 'There is yet another bit of my diary that I can't send to the Committee.'

I like living here in Sydney. From our house we can see the brilliant blue of the harbour at the foot of the hill. One day soon I hope dear Thomas will come into harbour and I'll be the first to greet him. Our Methodist friend, Mr Scott, has given this house – his own is next along Macquarie Street, with the new Methodist chapel being built between the two houses. Our cottage is very comfortable with an outside kitchen, verandah, a good garden and stables. Because he is still worried about money, Walter used his own private money to buy our furniture rather than call on Mission funds. I have been getting great pleasure from making the new cedar tables, chairs and sideboard gleam with polish.

Our house is directly over the road from Governor Macquarie's new buildings, the Rum Hospital, with its elegant long verandahs and classical columns upstairs and down and the newly opened Barracks with accommodation for the convicts. We see the men going out to work in the mornings and back at sunset, small work gangs going off under the supervision of the red-coated soldiers, some wearing the tell-tale yellow of newly arrived prisoners and others in the blues and browns of ticket-of-leave men. Beyond our street to the south is the big open paddock called Hyde Park (surely as a joke) where horseracing and cricket matches take place. On the far side of the Hospital and Barracks the land falls away down the hill to a branch of the harbour, thick with scrub where wicked men are said to lurk. It is not far to walk from our house to the nicest shops and I like to look at all the pretty things. They say that Mrs Rickard's Fashionable Repository has as fine a stock of lovely things as the smartest shops in Bond Street, London, but of course they are very expensive. With Walter's feelings about money, I usually just look. Yes, I really do like living in Sydney.

Since our wedding day, I have tried to go with Walter whenever I can and have been with him on his December and January tours into the country. It was beautiful riding along with him and the country looked wonderful. Of course, it was a good chance to visit my parents and my Parramatta and Windsor friends. Samuel and Lucy are settled out at 'Macquarie Grove', but Jonathan's Mary is staying with my parents while Jonathan finishes the job of felling trees and building them a little cottage on the land Father is giving them in the Cowpastures. They are calling it 'Matavai' after Jonathan's birthplace. (Lucy and Mary and I have had some private giggles; we think our triple wedding may be going to produce three grandchildren at once!)

Walter enjoys being a real part of our family, a son and brother, and certainly he is teased and treated like that. On our January visit, all the summer fruit was in season and Walter ate so much of it that he was quite ill – he got little sympathy from his new brothers and sisters. 'What do you expect if you gobble such mountains of peaches and apricots, mulberries and melons, pears, nectarines, figs, oranges? It serves you right!'

Walter says that our family is making up a little for the loss of his dear Cornish family, though he doesn't forget them. He often speaks about them and I try to think of them as my own family, too. When he says that my cooking is making him fatter, he says, 'One day I'll probably be stout – and bald – like my father, but I think you will always be slim, just like my mother.'

He is writing to his father to send with the next mail and showed me where he had written of a hoped-for day when we will both go to England and meet his family, and he will 'introduce to your notice and embraces a daughter, Mary Lawry, whose extraordinary sweetness of temper, modesty of character, depth of piety and firmness of attachment would I am sure greatly cheer and delight you.' In a letter to Thomas in which he introduced himself, he wrote: 'My heart rejoices in what I have done. . . the person of my choice greatly adds to my domestic and religious comfort; of the sincerity and strength of our mutual attachment it will be difficult for me to give you any just notion. As Jonathan's soul clave unto David, so (and more so) do ours to each other.' My darling seems to be as satisfied with his bargain as I am with mine!

Sydney, New South Wales: March, 1820

Samuel Leigh sailed for England late last month on the *Admiral Cockburn*. It is very difficult to know how to understand our friend, Samuel Leigh. Sometimes he is confident, full of great visions and strong faith; at other times he is despondent and pessimistic. The poor man has been very ill, of course, so perhaps his bodily weakness is making it hard for him to be the person he can be. I'm afraid Walter was quite glad to see him go, as the two of them kept rubbing each other up the wrong way.

His plan to work at the Newcastle settlement just before our wedding was short-lived as he was ill and had to take ship back to Sydney almost straightaway. Then, early last month, he decided to go to Tahiti. He even had his baggage on board the *Haweis* ready to sail, but at the last minute lost courage and took his things off again. Dr Redfern has been looking after his health and came to the conclusion that the only solution for his persistent ill health was for him to take the sea-trip back to England.

One person was specially sad to see him go. A nice Methodist young lady, one of my friends, cried for days after he left, poor dear. She told me privately that Mr Leigh had been courting her since early last year and they had decided to become engaged to be married. (I admit I was very relieved to hear it, because I had worried about whether Mr Leigh might still be angry with Walter for marrying me.) However, when Samuel Leigh was so very ill, he had told her that she should feel free to marry someone else as he thought he could even die on the voyage back to England. She doesn't want to do that as she really cares for him and says she wants to wait, just in case he recovers and comes back to her. The poor thing. . .

Walter doesn't think he will survive long. He wrote to his father about Mr Leigh: 'I expect he will totter along for several months and then lie down and die. I cannot say he has been judicious in his labours. Had he been, he would probably have not been so ill and yet have been more useful; however I suppose he followed his best judgement.

The Lord will accept him for his many sufferings...'

I think Walter is a bit hard on poor Samuel. When Samuel Leigh first came, he was forced to choose between abandoning the remote settlements to their ignorance or making very exhausting journeys into the interior, where there was often no welcome and very little in the way of comfort for a weary traveller. Maybe Samuel has been unwise in the amount he has attempted to do, but he has done it very sincerely for the Lord. It is just a pity that his physical ailments have affected his temper.

Samuel Leigh took a lot of letters to England for us – from me and my family to our Thomas and letters to Walter's family in Cornwall, as well as letters to the Committee. Walter has taken great care to write his report as wisely as possible, because he knows it will probably be published in the *Methodist Magazine* and be circulated around the world, even back here. Sometimes it annoys him to think that the British Methodist public think that the mission in New South Wales, among convicts and settlers, is not as romantic and exciting as a mission among island savages. But still he wrote to his father: 'How careful I must be in all my statements that nothing will be said that will admit of contradiction or injure the cause I wish to forward.'

Among his letters to the Committee, he mentioned the rapidly growing population, the encouragements of some conversions among the young men, ideas for a ministry among the aboriginal population and added: 'The Rev. S. Marsden has pressed your sending missionaries to the Friendly Islands which would be a mission of great promise if funds would allow its formation.' In another note that month, he wrote of the inclination of the people of the Friendly Islands and the Marquesas towards conversion to Christianity (or so he had been told by men from whalers): 'the mission of New South Wales would be much refreshed thereby, whose missionaries might, after spending much time in New Holland, go there and renew the glorious toil. For such an expedition I always stand prepared – but without anxiety...'

Sydney, New South Wales: May, 1820

Ever since the day when Walter rushed in with a letter,
yelling 'Ben Carvosso is coming!' he has been looking
forward to today. The first hint that the Rev. Benjamin
Carvosso might come to New South Wales was in a letter
from his mother, early in the year. Walter waited
anxiously for official word to come from the Committee.
When it came, he was ecstatic.

'We've been asking and pleading for more ministers for
New South Wales – any good men to share the work, so
that we can have resident ministers living in Sydney,
Windsor and Parramatta, and then for the settlement in
Van Dieman's Land. And I've been saying that we also
should have another man to work particularly with the
Aborigines and, after that, to follow up the great need for
the gospel in new fields like New Zealand and the Friendly
Islands. *Any* good man... But Benjamin Carvosso! He is
just like my brother,' Walter said, still not quite believing
it.

'He is Cornish – of course. His father, old Mr William
Carvosso, is one of the most amazing Christian men I have
ever met, a man who has walked from end to end of Cornwall winning the most unlikely people to Christ. My
Cornish family and I have always loved him. Ben and I
were students together in Plymouth, went out preaching
together, knew the same Cornish roads across the moors
and the same rocky coastlines, saw the same spiritual
revivals, loved the same people...'

Today Benjamin and his young bride Deborah arrived
and Walter is alight with joy. It is true, they are just like
brothers in their speech, their style, their sense of humour
and their zeal for God. I am seeing a new Walter, a Walter
who can't stop laughing, talking and sighing as he talks
about his family with one who knows and loves Mr and
Mrs Lawry, Anna and Emma and talks about his home and
his country with one who shares his memories. How he
must have been missing that!

'How are our Methodist preachers? Do you remember

preaching at Liskeard and Redruth? Remember preaching from that immense pulpit in Falmouth!... the wonderful Cornish Methodist singing... Do they still sometimes dance with the joy of the Lord in the meetings? How I miss the power and the atmosphere of the revival services...'

I like Deborah Carvosso and think she and I will find it easy to be good friends.

After the pain that was always there – under the surface – when Walter tried to work with Samuel Leigh, it is good to picture these two, Walter and Benjamin – with another man, Ralph Mansfield, who is expected in a few months – being able to work together with love and energy. Already, they are making plans for their first trip together around the colony. Walter intends for them to live at Windsor, where we have bought a house for the Mission.

Walter was less enthusiastic about the arrival of two other clergy earlier this month. When two Roman Catholic priests landed, he was really quite upset. He does not approve of Roman Catholics. We have never had a priest working in New South Wales in a normal way, though there have been a few priests here as Irish political prisoners, who have worked with the Catholics of our community in a limited way. I have no very strong feelings about them. We will see if they are as bad as Walter fears.

Sydney, New South Wales: July, 1820

It is strange indeed to be the wife of a minister. All my life, the wives of the clergy have been contemporary with my mother, mature women with families who have considerable respect and prestige in the social scale. Mrs Marsden in particular has been like a second mother to us all, despite being partly paralysed from a stroke ever since her youngest daughter was born. It is hard to live up to my idea of what a minister's wife should be like.

Some things about it are quite unexpected. Sometimes I have to stop myself from giggling when I see the preacher, the Rev. Walter Lawry, standing before his flock in his best suit and with his holy Sunday face, cravat arranged so neatly under his chin. In my mind I can also see him dishevelled, unshaven, relaxed, irritable, passionate or asleep – all the normal humanness of being a man rather than the minister.

There is a new element to sitting in the pew these days. Everything the preacher says and does is observed carefully by his wife. I sit there, so proud of my man, delighted when he preaches powerfully and anxious if ever there seems to be a wall between him and his hearers. Walter sometimes says unconventional, funny things from the pulpit. They are mostly accepted with good humour, but I am always hoping he won't offend anyone. A few Sundays ago, for example, a woman was in chapel with a crying baby who wept and howled on and on, interrupting Walter's preaching. In the end, he turned to the mother and said, 'My dear sister, it is like a toothache. There is only one thing for it – you must have it out!' The woman gathered her child and scuttled out, but she and everyone else was laughing, much to my relief!

There is change, too, in the relationship between myself and my former Sunday School teaching and between myself and my father. Because we are living in Sydney now, I had to resign from the Parramatta Sunday School. That made me really sad because I have always been part of it and I hated to give it up. At least now I have a new class of young children here in the Methodist Sunday School in Sydney. I also had to stand by my husband when he disagreed with my father on the question of whether it would be a good idea for the Calvinist Dissenters, the Methodists and the Independents to build themselves a chapel to share in Parramatta.

'It would never work!' Walter insisted. 'There are too many strong characters with too many differences of attitude and theology. Instead of building up the work of Christ, we'd end up fighting over who might use the chapel at what time and be destructive.' At least Father and Walter remain very good friends, despite their differences.

One thing I am learning is how much Walter worries

about money. His family in Cornwall is not poor – they are quite comfortable in farming – but Walter hates to be in debt to the Methodist Committee, or to commit the Methodist Society to spending money they don't have. He has an orderly mind and likes things to be done properly. However, I sometimes think he is paying for things out of his own personal pocket rather than wait for the Committee. He goes around calling on wealthy members of colonial society asking for subscriptions for his new chapels, but he never seems to have quite enough and the London Committee is so very far away.

The care he gives to convicts, specially those condemned to hanging, weighs very heavily on his mind, too. Some evenings he comes home to me looking grey with exhaustion and tells of the agony of being with poor, terrified men in their last hour, trying to bring them comfort and hope. On days like that he can't bear to look out of our front windows across the road to the convict barracks, to see the parties of workmen going back through the gates at sunset. Sometimes he spends hours with condemned highwaymen, pickpockets and murderers who go to the gallows quite unrepentant. Recently he came home shaken but profoundly moved after he had been with three convicts who had turned to God in their last week of life. Before they climbed the scaffold, they knelt together on the grass and prayed and then each man made a moving speech to the 6,000 convicts and military men there to witness their hanging, pleading with them to take the saving gospel of Jesus Christ seriously. He said there were many tears as his three friends went to their deaths singing a hymn. Even then, the rope broke on one of them and the poor victim had to wait another agonising twenty minutes while they found another rope. The man had the strength to wait calmly, still thanking God for his mercy.

People in society tend to like Walter and, of course, my family has always been well-known in Sydney, so we are sometimes invited to dine out at fine houses. This is fun as I love to visit my friends. The Campbell's place used to be the finest in Sydney. As a child I used to be astonished to visit their harbourside home with peacocks strutting in the garden. I still love to watch clever Mrs Sophia Campbell perched on her stool, painting Sydney street scenes with her watercolours. These days the grandest parties are at Captain John Piper's mansion at Point Eliza, near Rose Bay. We have sometimes been to magnificent afternoon parties there, with elegant food in the gardens, looking across the harbour. They say he keeps one hundred servants!

Yes, it is really very nice to be a married lady in Sydney society, sharing in the work of the Methodist Society with my darling husband and enjoying the pleasures of a big town. My dear family in Parramatta often calls to see me, and Susannah or Anne often come to stay for a few weeks. The girls stitch their samplers and I have been stitching baby clothes.

I have been watching our fruit trees and the wattles in the bush where Mrs Macquarie likes to walk at the foot of our hill. I have never really looked so closely before at the tiny tight bundles of blossom and new leaves on seemingly bare branches. That is how I have felt this winter: closely wrapped, enclosed, keeping my promise of new life safely tucked in until the spring. And soon, when the spring comes, the fruit blossoms will unfold, the tight wattle blossoms will open into a million tiny suns – and my beautiful baby will be born.

Sydney, New South Wales: September, 1820

Walter has written a letter to his parents, telling them of our troubles of the past month. Writing of me, he said, 'Mary is a perfect pattern of passive piety.' Dear Walter. He doesn't understand...

Walter and I had been finding great joy in loving each other and in sharing our home and our life with people. As we looked forward to our baby, it seemed that we had everything one could possibly want for contentment. Even Father said of us, 'There was never a pair lived more happy in the best things as well as the affairs of life.' Then came the influenza epidemic.

It was late winter, a cold bright winter of clear sunny days and bitter nights with sharp frosts that killed some of my young plants, another winter of drought after a number of dry years. Father was again anxious about his crops. In my happiness, the sunshine in a sheltered corner facing north had been a natural background to my contented days. At night we stayed by our fireside, unless there was a chapel meeting to attend. As winter wore on, people began to feel unwell. At first it seemed that many had caught cold, but soon we realised that people were seriously ill, so much so that it became a news item in the *Gazette*. Rumours were circulating that some people had even died of it.

Then came our last happy morning. Mother was here visiting and we had a lovely family time sharing Walter's delight at a long letter just arrived from his mother. We sat out on the verandah in the sun without any sense of what was to come. That afternoon I began to feel ill — miserably ill with aching head and throat and body, streaming nose and a cough that tore me apart. Mother put me to bed and Walter did his best to make me comfortable.

Out of my general wretchedness that night, a distinct and alarming pain separated itself from the general weariness of my body and I knew that my labour had begun. 'Walter, the baby... But it is too soon, much too soon... Oh, God help me...'

I remember very little of the next days, except a mist of pain and fear. Walter has told me since that I was in labour for thirty-six hours and, because I have helped at the delivery of other women's babies, I can imagine it all. I recall hearing his voice, in those first moments of peace after the long struggle, calling my name. Opening my eyes, I saw him standing there by me, haggard and dishevelled.

'We have a little girl,' he said, 'and she is so beautiful — our daughter...' Then suddenly he was on his knees by my bed with his face buried in the pillow close to my own, whispering, 'Oh my darling — I couldn't have borne to have lost you...'

Our beautiful daughter, Elizabeth. Walter insisted that she was just like me. She was so tiny and exquisite and so fragile. At first she did well, premature but healthy. The worst of my influenza was over, but I still coughed a lot and felt very weak. All my thoughts were centred on my baby.

Walter came to me one morning while I was feeding Elizabeth, cradling her in my arms. He said, 'Lucy and Samuel's baby was born last night. A little boy... he is not very strong. They want to call him Rowland after his grandfather. And your father — he's ill. He has caught the influenza. The family want me to go to Parramatta to see him.'

I heard his words with only part of my mind because of my preoccupation with my own child. I didn't even notice the strain on his face. I couldn't imagine that my father was in any danger — that was unthinkable. Father had always been there, would always be there; he was security, stability, the unchangeable centre of our family. He might have a nasty cough and even be reduced to bed for a week or so, but it was impossible to think of anything worse than that. And Lucy's baby. Lucy and Jonathan's Mary and I had all been so happily pregnant together. She and Samuel must be as happy as we were, but of course our little darling was so delicate.

Walter was away all day and, while he was absent, baby Elizabeth became very ill. All the familiar signs of influenza were there in our premature infant only days old and she was shaken with violent convulsions. I was terrified for her and, as soon as I heard Walter's mare come cantering into the yard that night, I rushed out to him. Even now I can't understand why I didn't ask about my father, but all I wanted was for Walter to be with me and Elizabeth.

It was only much later that night, when Elizabeth was resting a little more easily, that Walter held me very gently and said, 'Mary, I must tell you news of your family. Two things – one good and one very hard. Jonathan and Mary's baby was born today, a healthy boy they are calling Rowland James. And your dear father died this evening. . .'

With a sense of complete disbelief I listened to Walter's voice talking about the severe illness and the peaceful death of my father. It didn't make any sense. How could my world continue without Father? My generous, hard-working, loving, stern, stubborn, faithful, trustworthy, conservative, Calvinist, God-fearing, ill-educated, success-ful father, the man I loved from my earliest memories. He couldn't be gone – he hadn't even seen our Elizabeth.

For the next three days, our baby clung to life and I didn't leave her side. In Parramatta, my father was buried on Wednesday evening, August 30, in the cemetery near St John's Church. His friend Samuel Marsden was away in New Zealand with the *Dromedary*, but they say that a great crowd of respectable people were there to honour him and to remember a good life.

With part of my mind I grieved unbelievingly for my father, but most of my emotions were concentrated on Elizabeth who grew weaker and weaker. Some of our friends were with us watching by her cradle when we recognised at last that she was no longer sleeping quietly, but that life was gone. She was only thirteen days old. On our knees around her cradle, we prayed, 'The Lord gave and the Lord hath taken away; blessed be the name of the Lord,' our voices thickened and wavering.

On Saturday, kind Captain John Piper sent us his long boat and crew to take us and the small coffin by river to Parramatta. (Some unreligious people are wonderfully good and kind and Captain Piper is like that.) The river journey of seventeen miles was silent and bleak, the quiet splash of the oars a background for our brokenness. Mrs Marsden had sent her coach to the wharf to meet us and take us to my mother's house. Mother and I couldn't talk to each other, only hold each other tight in recognition of our mutual pain. My sisters and brothers all looked for the first and last time on our baby and then we all went up the hill to the cemetery.

The loose earth heaped to one side of the grave, I realised in a daze, was close beside the headstone of Father's missionary friend, William Shelley. The tiny casket was gently lowered onto the large one, the granddaughter joining the grandfather who had so much looked forward to having grandchildren around his table, but had seen none of the three born in the week of his death. I clung to Walter's arm as the service flowed around me, my face aching with the effort of controlling my heartbreak in front of all our friends. People spoke to me afterwards, but I had no words. Walter tried to tell me that God wanted her, but so did I.

Only two days after we buried my little darling, our family stood for a third time at the graveside for the burial of Samuel and Lucy's baby son, Rowland, aged twelve days. This time I stood stonily behind the crowd. With the irrelevance of grief, my eyes stared down at the wild yellow daisies studded on the ground at my feet and I thought, 'My little girl will never thread a daisy chain.' And then I cried – weeping for Samuel and Lucy's grief, weeping for my father, weeping for my Elizabeth, weeping for myself.

Oh Lord, I don't understand. Did you have to take three of our family? Why didn't I die, too? It hurts too much to live. Oh, it isn't *fair*. Dear Jesus, I want to love you, but I don't understand you at all.

Parramatta, New South Wales: December, 1820

One doesn't forget, but gradually life begins to flow on again. For weeks rain has been falling, flooding the outlying districts and seeming to fit my mood. My sense of loss continues and the reality of that loss has become clearer since the first numbness wore off. Only days after that terrible September 1 when Elizabeth died, I wrote a brokenhearted letter to Thomas. Now, after time for reflection, I am writing again. I wrote:

'I can say the God of Jacob hath been better to me than I am able to conceive. . . and not allowed me to murmur, but to see the hand of a great and glorious God in all this. It is a pleasure to reflect and say that our loss is their gain, but ah! there seems an aching void. When I go to Mother's, there is something very particular wanting. The place looks empty. When I make little improvements in my house or garden, I wonder whether my father will approve and be pleased. But alas! a second thought, and he is no more. He shall not see these trifles; nobler joys are his. When employed at my kneedle, what shall I make for my little one? When walking and meet[ing] a fond mother with the suckling in her arms, this arises fresh thoughts. Mine might be much finer and healthier than this. . . Oh that I was all he would have me be, but I find the flesh is still keeping up a war with the spirit.'

Poor Thomas. He has had sad letters from us all. Even Samuel wrote a long painful letter during the hours when Lucy was in labour and he couldn't find ease in any other task. I wonder if Thomas will come home soon to help Mother as her eldest son. After a time at Cambridge, he was advised by Dr Simeon to study in Wales and is now near the end of his studies. As well as our own letters, we sent Thomas the *Sydney Gazette* with Father's obituary notice where, after a long introduction about his former missionary labours, they wrote: '. . . society has lost a most pious and benevolent member, and his large and young family a tender husband, a kind father and a good man. His life was a continual example of genuine religion and piety, extensive benevolence and hospitality. He never lost sight of his original designation as a missionary and continued to the latest period of his life zealously to perform the duties of one, by preaching the gospel in almost all parts of the colony. . .'

Some things have changed. A fourth Methodist missionary, the Rev. Ralph Mansfield and his wife Lydia, arrived soon after our Elizabeth died, so Walter and I have moved to live in Parramatta while they are in Macquarie Street,

Sydney. It is good to be nearer Mother as we help each other. Mr Marsden came back to Sydney some weeks later and was very sad about Father. I feel very sorry for Mr Marsden. He is having a lot of disappointments lately. Things are not going well with his staff in the New Zealand mission who, they say, are always at odds with each other and rumour has it that there are scandals among them. And the Maori Tui who lived near us for several years and of whom Mr Marsden had such high hopes has gone back to being a complete pagan again. It is as if his time in Sydney and London were just dreams, while reality for him is his life as a young chief. At this time, the loss of one of his closest friends must be a sad loss for Mr Marsden.

Walter went on a long journey to Bathurst in early November with brother Samuel, while I stayed with Mother. He came back very excited about the fine country on the far side of the mountains and has great visions of Australia one day being a prosperous country like America or India. The road Mr Cox is building over the mountains is very rough, with great chunks of rock like giant stairs, thick bush everywhere, fine waterfalls and superb views. He says it was very hard riding on horseback, but thinks it will be even more difficult for anyone travelling by wagon with a team or taking their family over to the new land. Walter was very delighted to preach at a Methodist service in Bathurst to 200 men. He is the very first minister to go there, although my father had preached there several times.

Walter wrote to his father that, if he were to leave the ministry and go into farming, he could make a profit of five thousand pounds each year for the first five years and then a thousand pounds a year after that. He told his father to encourage good Cornishmen to migrate to the colony as the affairs of the place are 'on the improving side of middling'.

Father's will has been read. At the time of his death he owned 2,360 acres, consisting of a number of farms with livestock. Each of us has received a portion. Walter is rather embarrassed about it. Father had planned for me to

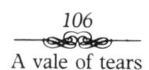
receive his big Parramatta orchard, a house, 200 acres at Pennant Hills with three mares, fifty cattle, ten pigs and 583 sheep, and the great riches of three hundred pounds a year. Of course, as a married woman I cannot inherit directly and so it is in my husband's name. But Walter says a Methodist missionary is not allowed to own property like that and should live on his stipend.

Mother would be very hurt and upset if my portion didn't come to me, so I said to Walter, 'We can use some of the income for all kinds of useful things for the Methodist Society like chapels — it will be all right in the end.' In any case, I am very happy to think that Father's orchard is mine. I have many special memories associated with it. Walter and I walked around it the other day and found no less than nineteen varieties of fruit tree, many stone fruits, citrus, figs, grapes, berries and twenty-seven peach trees! Walter is afraid that our new riches will be a problem to him — surely not!

So we go on with our lives. Walter and I are even closer to each other than ever. (He wrote to his father that 'the companion of my bosom and wife of my youth is such an one as conduces to make life glide sweetly along...' He calls me sometimes Polly and sometimes 'my little Mary Cover Lawry'.) We have had to struggle with our questions and feelings about the loss of our child, trying to accept it from the hand of God and wanting to go on in faith, trusting him.

Walter is very well, perhaps the most healthy he has ever been since I knew him. I tease him about his thinning hair and the odd grey hairs. He wrote to his sister that he will soon be 'partly hoary and partly bald'! He teases me for feeding him so well that he is getting slightly stout. It is good to live in Parramatta so close to my family. My youngest sisters Susannah and Anne come every day for Walter to teach them geography, because he is still fascinated with his globe and atlas and thinks they should be, too.

Perhaps Walter enjoys my sisters because he misses his

own sisters, Emma and Anna. We write to them both, but Walter tends to write rather stern, improving letters. When last I wrote to Emma, I told her about how she had been an aunt so briefly, asked about her schooling and added: 'It is an excellent thing to be accomplished, but my dear Emma, will you also take Jesus for your friend. Yes! I think you will not deprive yourself of such a worthy friend.'

Parramatta, New South Wales: February, 1821

We had heard nothing directly of Samuel Leigh since he left a year ago. Some of the Anglican clergy have had letters, but perhaps he didn't want to write to us. Walter had written him such a nice, loving letter last year, too, saying among other things: 'Do all you can, my dear brother, to get a mission established in Van Dieman's Land and, if it be possible, one also at the Friendly Islands... I feel unmixed and growing love towards you and long to hear how you are. If you come out, bring me aplenty of black cloth. Mrs Lawry sends her love '

Then the bundle of *Methodist Magazine* arrived from England with the regular section 'Missionary Notices'. There, among letters from Methodist missionaries in Africa, Ceylon and the West Indies, was a paragraph over Mr Leigh's name.

Why does there always have to be such tension between Walter and Mr Leigh? Walter was upset as soon as he read it and even more so after someone who read it announced that 'Missionary stories are a mess of cunningly devised fables'! He sat straight down and wrote a letter to say that he had not felt he could distribute the magazines until he had cut out the offending pages. Mr Leigh had greatly exaggerated the real numbers of Methodist members and chapels in the colony. I don't think the Committee will be very pleased.

They say that Mr Leigh's letters refer to seven new missionaries coming out with him. That is very good. As Walter said in a letter to his father, 'Tongataboo, the

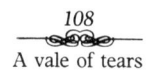
Marquesas and New Zealand to which they are destined need them much.'

Parramatta, New South Wales: March, 1821

A year ago, the future seemed to lie ahead, neat and predictable. Now everything is disintegrating and nothing is sure any more. A year ago, I thought that in 1821 Lucy, Mary and I would be watching our babies learn to sit and crawl and walk together. But my baby is dead and so is Lucy's. I thought that Walter and I would often visit Father and Mother, and Father and Walter would go on with their earnest but amiable arguments about doctrine and church practice. But Father is dead, too.

I thought that Governor Macquarie would always be our Governor, or at least for years and years. But now, since Commissioner Bigge's Report on the colony, there are strong rumours that he will resign soon and his place will be taken by a new man. For several years he has been in conflict with many colonists on several fronts, including the civil rights of people who were formerly convicts and the question of high expenditure on grand and perhaps over-elaborate building schemes.

Even Mr Marsden's seminary for Maori students has closed because so many of the boys were ill, died, or were too homesick to work as he had hoped.

And I thought that Walter and I would work on here in the colony, building chapels, winning converts, teaching children, comforting those in need and strengthening the work over the years. But even that may change.

Today Walter burst into the house, clutching a letter and white with shock. 'That rotten man! He can't bear to have me in the colony. I have just collected this letter from Mother. She says that the Methodist Conference of 1820, at the suggestion of Mr Leigh, has appointed me to Tonga!'

A hard decision

Parramatta, New South Wales: April, 1821

It is true, of course. At first Walter thought that perhaps his mother had misunderstood news from the Methodist Conference — London is a long way from Cornwall, he said — and perhaps they meant that we would have enough missionaries to begin a new work in Tonga soon. Or that some new missionaries had been chosen to pioneer that work, as he had recommended for a long time, and maybe Walter was to superintend it.

But no, the official station sheet for 1820 has arrived in the colony and Walter's name is marked down quite clearly: 'New Zealand, S. Leigh. One more to be sent. Friendly Islands: W. Lawry. One more to be sent. Two others are to be sent to the South Seas, whose particular appointment is yet to be determined.'

'Leigh to New Zealand? Me to Tonga? What does it all mean?' Walter demanded.

While he was still in a state of shock, he sat down and wrote an emotional letter to his parents: 'I never offered myself for the Friendly Islands, nor have I ever considered myself called to leave my present station. My labours are blessed and everything turns out according to my reasonable hopes. Why am I then appointed by Conference to another place? I can account for it thus: Mr Leigh paid his address to my dear Mary before I arrived in the colony.

She would not have him. His sweet heart has been sour ever since. As Mr Leigh is a person of great credit among us, I used to pay great deference to his judgement, until I discovered in him most glaring deficiencies and inconsistencies. Of these I used faithfully and affectionately to apprise him. He turned sulky and from that day has treated our continued kindness with haughtiness and disdain. In this spirit he went home, and see the result. He has told an untruth and I and my family must be transported out of the way!!!

'This is to me a very painful providence, but I have no doubt it will be fully sanctified; it is a link in the chain that works for our good. However I shall not think of going from my present station until I have a clear call, in which I shall include a strong inclination in my own mind – a passiveness at least on the part of my family and the approbation of my brethren here... I shall, I think, consider myself perfectly free to follow my own mind, notwithstanding my Conference appointment, which I consider has no right to send me from my regular station without my consent... I thank God for a disposition fully to follow his will in the intimation of providence, but I will not be dragooned, though the best men in the world are made tools of the work.'

As he laid down his pen, he said, 'I'm glad I said that to my parents. But perhaps it was too strong. Polly, my love, tomorrow we are going to drive out to Windsor in the chaise and talk it over with Ben and Deborah Carvosso.'

'What are we going to do, Polly?' he asked as we drove, the wheels of the chaise circling through the dust of a long summer. I had no answer.

At the Carvosso's home, which they have repaired and decorated with such good taste, we were welcomed and our friends listened to our story.

'But you have been writing letters about the importance of opening up a mission in Tonga or New Zealand, or both, for years,' Benjamin pointed out. 'Have you changed your mind?'

'No. But I hate the way this has been done. I don't think I should be forced to go without consultation. Any man being asked to pioneer a foreign mission field is always asked whether he and his family is willing. He is not just ordered to go. And there is no sign of planning — no party of pioneers to work together, no suggestion as to how I travel 2,000 miles to Tonga, no mention of supplies or links with Sydney. Just: "Friendly Islands, W. Lawry. One more to be sent." And *that* usually just means that they would like to send someone, if they had someone, which they haven't.'

'What about Mary?' Deborah looked at me anxiously. She and I have been comparing notes on our new pregnancies, she suffering miserably with morning sickness and I with my usual blooming health. She is specially sensitive to how I might be feeling.

'I don't think Mary should go to Tonga. If I go, and I'm not at all sure that I will, she must stay in Parramatta with her mother.'

Sitting there, my hands tightly knotted in my lap, all sorts of pictures passed through my mind, none of them good. Should I go to Tonga, facing isolation and danger and leaving my dear family behind? Should I let Walter go alone to a frightening unknown, not knowing whether he would ever return, and attempt to live without my beloved other self? Or was it right to disobey the Committee who were already cross with Walter over marrying without permission and not giving away my inheritance, among other things.

Walter went on: 'The whole point of wanting to go to the Friendly Islands with the gospel is because there are no Christians there among a wild and warlike people. It is certainly no place to take a lady. Don't you remember, Mary, the stories your father told of his friend, William Shelley, and the others arriving in Sydney after being rescued from Tonga more than twenty years ago — how they arrived in tatters, looking like slaves, with everything they possessed gone and glad to escape with their lives? And the massacre

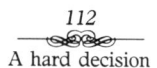
of most of the crew of the *Port au Prince* a few years later
– and recent stories of whaling crews who have been lured
there by false friendliness and then killed. No, Mary must
not go – but how can I go without her?'

What are we to do? Benjamin Carvosso thinks Walter
should go in obedience to the Committee. Ralph Mansfield
thinks he should not go, because of the danger and the fact
that he would have no colleague. Most people say I should
not go. Would I be prepared to risk the life of my second
child?

Parramatta, New South Wales: May, 1821

It is so confusing. How can we know the will of God about
Tonga? Could it really be God's will for him to abandon a
lively, hopeful but immature work just when things are beginning to grow and become established? He has been feeling that, perhaps, the London Committee isn't satisfied
with his work, that he is useless in New South Wales. Just
when he was feeling most discouraged last month, he had
some letters from some men who became Christians under
his preaching last year: soldiers with the 48th Regiment,
now in Hobart Town, Van Dieman's Land.

Corporal Waddy wrote of the Methodist soldiers leading
Class Meetings in their crowded meeting room and added:
'I have to thank God that I ever saw your face, for God has
made use of me to proclaim pardon to poor perishing sin-
ners by Christ Jesus... Dear brother, you have to praise
God much for his benefits towards you, for it is by your
converts that the church is established at Hobart Town. I
thank God that he ever sent you to Sydney and I believe
a great many more have reason to do so.'

Of course, that letter cheered Walter up a great deal, but
he asked: 'Does that mean that God can use me as an evan-
gelist to the heathen, or that he wants me to stay with my
ministry to the pagans of New South Wales?'

Our lovely little chapel is finished in Macquarie Street,
Parramatta. It was opened on Good Friday, April 21, with
Walter, Mr Mansfield and Mr Carvosso preaching at morn-

ing, afternoon and evening services. Walter preached on Isaiah 53:11. We have been so involved in paying for the chapels at Windsor and Macquarie Street, Sydney (which is turning out to be grander but much more costly than we had expected) that Walter and I paid over three hundred pounds from my legacy for the Parramatta chapel so that it wouldn't be in debt. It is exciting to see it well-filled with people who come because they really want to hear the gospel and not because they are paraded into chapel by soldiers.

A few weeks ago, Walter and I came home after the evening meeting there and I couldn't help hugging him.

'It is worth it, it really is! What a lovely congregation there was tonight. I was sitting in chapel, just looking around at all those dear people and thinking it would have been worth it to pay for this building, even if we had been forced to live on a crust! Or even to live in a tumbledown hut ourselves.'

Walter had been laughing with me, but became subdued. 'You don't know *what* you may be living in, or living on, if we go to Tonga — and we may see little good for it either.'

On top of everything else, now Walter has upset Mr Marsden, not to mention Anne and Elizabeth Marsden. I can see their reasons for being upset. It was our family Sunday School before the Marsdens took an interest in it, but Walter is quite sure that he has done the right thing and he probably has.

Recently, a former convict, Mr Bradley, who was converted under Walter's preaching, asked Walter if he could begin a Sunday School, using our Parramatta chapel. The Sunday School at St John's, where I taught for a number of years, isn't as good as it was when brother Thomas was in charge. Walter doesn't agree with some of the doctrine they are teaching in their catechism and some of the teachers think it ought to be a secular school instead of being attached to the church. Anyway, Walter thinks that the new young clergyman who is assisting Mr Marsden with the Sunday School would much rather hunt kangaroos than worry about Sunday Schools! So he encouraged Bradley to begin a Methodist Sunday School in Parramatta on the understanding that the children be collected from the streets and cottages of the village, not 'stolen' from the Anglican school, and that at the end of Sunday School all the children should be marched across the road to St John's for church service. (Walter himself is always away very early on Sunday mornings for his preaching tours, so wasn't expecting to be involved directly, but was delighted when they started off with seventy to eighty children, mostly boys and girls who were completely unchurched.)

Unfortunately, Mr Marsden is very angry and feels we have started in direct opposition to his work. Some few children have changed Sunday Schools, it is true. But perhaps the deeper problem is that Mr Marsden has a long-standing mistrust of former convicts in any case, and of our Mr Bradley in particular. Bradley received a full pardon for whatever may have been his crime and Mr Marsden was very angry to lose a lawsuit against him recently.

Mr Marsden and the other clergy are also angry with Walter and his colleagues for starting chapel services at the same time as church and serving Holy Communion in the Anglican parishes. They say that Mr Leigh was never in competition with them and always made sure that Methodists respected the Church of England as the mother church, returned to church for Communion and had their meetings outside church times. Walter and his friends insist that this is a very outdated attitude and say that in Cornwall and elsewhere in England the Methodists have been a completely separated church, with independent hours and opportunities for Communion for more than twenty years. In any case, he pointed out that there are far more people in the colony than can fit into the Anglican church buildings, so we are just giving more people a chance to attend worship! So he and the others have planned their preaching times to suit the people and we have Communion regularly.

As far as Communion is concerned, it is nearly a year

since the Anglican clergy last offered Communion in Parramatta, so Walter feels no guilt about it. We have our own Missionary Society raising funds for new missionary work, a number of our characteristic small-group Class Meetings and our lovely, lively Love Feasts. (Our first Parramatta Love Feast recently was a wonderful occasion, with twenty-two of us sharing a meal and our testimonies of God's working in our lives, and praying and rejoicing together.)

Mr Carvosso has many new and independent ideas, too. With the enthusiastic encouragement of Walter and Mr Mansfield, they have begun a whole new Christian magazine, *The Australian Magazine,* which our friend, young Mr Robert Howe, is printing for us. Robert has taken over the printing of the *Sydney Gazette* since his father's death last year; he worked beside his father from childhood and is now one of our new Christians. Robert and our men are very excited about their new magazine as it is the first non-Government publication in Australia – certainly the only Christian publication. They have sent off some copies to England for the Committee.

Another of Benjamin's ideas is that we should start a ministry to seamen who come into Sydney Harbour – a sort of floating chapel. And there is strong Methodist involvement in the Benevolent Society, the Bible Society and all the other things which are working to bring some spiritual health to the people of this colony, where most influences turn them away from God. There is so much good that could be done in New South Wales that it is hard to think of relinquishing it.

Parramatta, New South Wales: June 1, 1821

It would be so good if I could talk over our questionings about the mission to Tonga with brother Thomas. I have been writing to him, with news of many friends, thanks for beautiful new straw bonnets which he asked Mrs Hosking to choose for us, news of our brothers and sisters – Samuel's Lucy is expecting a baby any day and Jonathan's son is thriving with two teeth – and of our mother's rheumatism and the way she is coping better than I expected with widowhood, though we all miss dear Father so much. Folded into the pages of the letter I added a long, silky twist of my hair to show Thomas how long I have grown it. I admitted to him my fear that perhaps the baby I am carrying may not live.

Then I wrote about our plans. I said: 'We are expecting Mr Leigh with eight more missionaries every day when new changes will take place. It is likely we then, according to our appointment, will leave this [place] for Tongataboo, tho' it is not proposed by us but [due to] a misunderstanding of Mr Leigh's. Neither did we at all like the thought of it or intend to go, notwithstanding appointment when we first heard, but after more deliberation and prayer and the way of providence opening more clear we shall, if God will, proceed on our way with our lives in our hands. My greatest trial, I think, will be not seeing you once more according to my expectation; still this seems not too great a sacrifice for God. I view all the dark sides possible and very many there are, but when my heart a little fails me again I think: well, the gospel appears to be received almost everywhere and why not among the poor benighted people of Tongataboo? If the Lord be for you, who can be against you? Mother does not seem to feel it much; she *very* seldom mentions a word concerning it. Most people say don't go, let someone else go...'

I think I have seen Walter gradually turning to the idea of going to the Tonga appointment. The other day I was sure. He came home with a shy young Island lad and said: 'Mary, this is young Macanoe. He is off a ship coming from the Marquesas Islands. I want him to stay with us – he can help you in the house and go to school to learn to read here in Parramatta. Then later, I hope he can help me with learning the language, when I go to Tonga.'

There is nothing we can do until Mr Leigh comes with all the new missionaries. He will surely bring further instructions from London. We look forward to their coming, but perhaps not with the same intensity as the young lady in the colony who is hoping, now that Mr Leigh is well enough to return, that she may become Mrs Leigh. She has heard nothing from him, but that doesn't stop her from hoping.

Parramatta, New South Wales: October, 1821

What a series of dramas the last two months have been! It began in August when I was reading the new copy of the *Sydney Gazette* and discovered a tiny paragraph under the shipping information. It read: 'Notice of arrival at Hobart Town of the *Brixton*. On board are the Reverend Mr Leigh and Mrs Leigh, Rev. and Mrs William Horton, Rev. William White and Rev. William Walker.'

'Walter! The missionaries have arrived in Hobart. . . but there don't seem to be nearly as many as we had expected. And it says "Rev. Mr Leigh *and Mrs Leigh*"! My little hopeful friend is going to be bitterly disappointed.'

At least we were warned. When the *Brixton* anchored in Sydney Harbour a month later and we all went on board to welcome the new missionaries, our faces were suitably composed and welcoming and nothing was said at first of my friend who has spent the past weeks in weeping. We discovered that the Rev. and Mrs Horton have stayed on in Hobart Town to begin the Methodist work there, Mr White is to go to New Zealand and Mr Walker is designated to be the first missionary to give all his time to work among the Aborigines of the colony. The Rev. Erskine is to come from Ceylon to Van Dieman's Land, but we don't know when that will be. So if Leighs go to New Zealand and we go to Tonga, there will still only be two men left to look after Sydney, Parramatta, Windsor, Liverpool and all the settlements between.

The new Mrs Leigh, Catherine, is a very gracious and charming woman and so it seems a bit sad that she should have to begin her time in the colony with an undercurrent of resentment at her presence. Even more sad, to me, is the unfortunate way in which Walter and Samuel Leigh had barely greeted each other before they had locked horns. Walter went rushing in as the champion of my disappointed friend, accusing Samuel of betraying a sacred promise and stirring up a lot of bitterness and embarrassment for everyone – including my poor friend, who has been tearfully explaining to kind Mr Mansfield that it was not Samuel's fault and in fact the engagement had been broken before he left in early 1820. It was just that she hadn't given up hope that he would come back to her.

From Samuel Leigh's point of view, he has come back to a colony with a party of Methodists who are doing the very thing he has so carefully avoided, working independently of the Church of England, and he feels this is a big mistake. Their first Quarterly Meeting together was not the happy, harmonious affair it has been recently because Mr Leigh was unhappy about so many of the things they have been doing in his absence: spending so much on the Macquarie Street Chapel in Sydney with its handsome, dressed stone and much greater size than our other simple brick chapels; the new Parramatta Sunday School and services in church times; our independent Communion services; Walter still caring for my legacy of flocks and herds instead of disposing of them. In addition, Mr Leigh brought a letter of criticism of our Methodist work from the London Committee, commanding that the Methodists keep clear of all Anglican church times and Sunday Schools and avoid separate Communion services. It also suggested that our men spent too much time in the townships and should be always out in the little settlements.

Walter came home from the Quarterly Meeting feeling very agitated about everything. As he kicked off his boots, he told me that there are now new instructions from the Committee who say that Walter should go to New Zealand for a year with Samuel Leigh, as a preparation for Tonga, and then go to Tonga.

'We all thought that it was a stupid idea,' he said. 'What is the point of spending a year in New Zealand before going to Tonga? The language is different, the people are different – what would we learn that we couldn't learn better in Tonga, if we are to go there at all. And if Leigh needs a colleague in New Zealand, why not appoint one properly?'

There was more to it than that, I felt sure. Walter went on with a sheepish look on his face. 'And, I must admit, Benjamin and Ralph and even our new friend William Walker said that they felt that it would be lunacy to set up a new, isolated, pioneer work anywhere and man it with the combination of Leigh and Lawry! Even Leigh agreed to that. I don't *want* things to be this way, but Samuel and I seem to react to each other like tinder to fireworks – explosively!'

He is quite right, of course. His imagery reminded me of the farewell tour Governor Macquarie made through the colony recently when every home put a lamp in their window and we had great bonfires and lots of fireworks. The fireworks were colourful, noisy, sometimes frightening and potentially destructive, but always shortlived. If that is a true picture of what happens when these two good men are together, I agree that it would be better for them to work apart. But it is one more occasion when Walter seems to be about to do the opposite to the instructions of the Committee.

Not all our dramatic moments over recent months have been difficult ones, of course. There was the opening of the large new chapel in Macquarie Street, Sydney, on August 21, with a good crowd and the pleasure of seeing an excellent chapel in that street of fine buildings. Walter is very worried about the financial side of that. We have had a very large loan from Mr Edward Eager, who has recently gone to England with the petition signed by many emancipists demanding their civil rights. Walter doesn't know how we are going to repay it.

Then there was the happy day when Mr Leigh baptised the Carvosso's new baby son. I felt sorry for poor Mrs Mansfield that day. She has had one miscarriage after another and has had to spend most of the time she has been in the colony in bed because of ill health. Walter says that

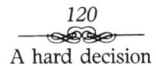
missionaries shouldn't bring out delicate London ladies to a place like this, but he is probably being rather hard. He expects all wives to cope with pregnancy with as little trouble as I do. Not that this pregnancy has been entirely without complication; I think I must have made a mistake in my calculations. I was sure I should have had my baby by now, but I am still waiting.

Another lovely day was on October 1 when we had our very first anniversary of the Methodist Missionary Society and had a most exciting meeting. The Ladies Auxiliary had raised twice as much as the men during the year – we worked hard, of course – and together we raised nearly three hundred pounds for missionary work. Everyone was very moved when Mr John Lees, an excellent layman from Castlereagh out in the country, insisted on giving a very generous donation, far more than anyone could expect from a struggling settler. He assured us that he truly wanted to give a great gift to his Lord for all his many blessings.

Yet even as these good things have been happening, there seems to be a clear division forming, with Walter and the other Methodist missionaries on one side and Mr Leigh with the Anglican clergy on the other. Walter wrote: 'There is great harmony among the brethren, excepting Mr Leigh.' And Benjamin Carvosso told us that he has written to the Committee to defend 'our beloved brother Lawry', adding: 'His disagreement with Bro. Leigh we sincerely regret. They are naturally unfitted for agreement in all the affairs of life; but without trespassing on your time by unnecessary minuteness allow us merely to state that, in our opinion, Bro. Lawry is not more to be blamed than Bro. Leigh.'

We have been told, too, though he did not show it to the other missionaries, that Mr Leigh has written a strong letter of criticism of us to the Committee. What has he said? What will the Committee think about it? They are so desperately far away from New South Wales and, whatever they think or whoever they believe, we won't know their answer for perhaps another year from now.

Parramatta, New South Wales: November, 1821

The missionaries, John and Mary Williams, are back in the colony from the Society Islands. When we last saw them, I was only seventeen and single; they seemed to me to be very heroic and wonderful as they set off on their great adventure. Now they are back, with their little Johnny four years old and me a married lady expecting my second child any day.

Both John and Mary have been very ill, John with elephantiasis which seems to be a common tropical complaint and Mary with general ill health. The poor girl looks so weary and thin, her face beginning to show the lines of anxiety and strain even though she is still only in her mid-twenties. For their health's sake, they had expected to travel back to England, but the *Westmoreland* was passing their mission on Raiatea in the Leeward group of the Society Islands on its way to New South Wales. They decided to come here instead, to see if they could recover enough to go back to their work. They say that the people of their island are very anxious for them to return.

Walter and I asked them both to come to our house to spend some time with us. Missionaries to the Pacific are no longer interesting curiosities to us, but people in whom we take a most active and ardent interest and whose words have great significance for us. They came today and we talked and talked: of their arrival in the well-established mission on Tahiti, of their period on nearby Huahine and their main work on Raiatea. Perhaps I am now more confused than ever.

Our conversation began as I served tea in our little parlour and Mary Williams commented on the pleasure of being able to buy tea quite easily in the colony. 'We always cherished our cups of tea,' she said. 'In moments of strain it always comforted me to put the kettle on the fire and make tea!'

Walter was very direct. 'We have been told to go to Tonga and begin a new work. Our group has decided to disregard the Committee's order to go first to New Zealand for a year. If you were me, John, would you go? Would you go alone? Would you take your wife and child?'

John Williams thought about it. Then he said, 'Yes. And no. Yes, I would go. The whole field of the Pacific is opening up and every new group of islands offers another opportunity to bring the gospel to a new people. What could be a greater or more satisfying work? But no, I wouldn't go alone. That would be stupidity. I believe that every mission station should have at least two families – more than that in a completely new, uncontacted country. Men have tried to manage alone, but the pressure is impossible and the people of the islands give little respect or credence to one lone stranger, however good a man he may be.

'You may remember, Mary,' he added, looking at me, 'Mr Crook who lived in Parramatta for some years and is now in Tahiti. He tried to work alone in the Marquesas but, even with the help and protection of a good chief, it was all he could do to survive as a man and a Christian without trying to preach the gospel effectively. He was very thankful indeed when Captain Fanning rescued him. He speaks very convincingly of the need for a missionary party, not a lone man. In any case, you would need some men with good practical skills to go with you as you would have no house, no food garden, perhaps no boat, and you can't count on the Tongans being willing to help you.'

He looked at his wife, Mary, and then at me. 'Yes, I would take my wife. It is not easy for a woman and it is asking a lot of her, but I couldn't have managed alone. I need my wife beside me in all sorts of ways. I need her calmness to temper my restlessness, her ability to put up with things to tone down my impatience. And among other things, I value her as the maker of our home. As I said in a letter home, my dear Mary is a famous cook. I'm sure I don't know what a poor man would do by himself in such a place as that! But if you take Mary to Tonga, Walter, don't underestimate what you are asking of her.'

'Did you find the work in the Society Islands as you expected?' we asked.

'No, I was very disappointed. Don't misunderstand,' he added hastily. 'It was not that I was disappointed in the way so many of the Tahitians had become Christians! In fact we arrived at the time of the greatest growth and zeal in the church, a high point when many were turning to God and before some of the falling away that has happened since. I was disappointed because it seemed that all the most challenging work was already done and I was too late to share it! I wanted to win people to Christ, not just maintain well-established churches.

'Another thing that really disappointed me was that I had been led to believe that there were many thousands of people in these islands with great opportunity for planting new churches. But in our first years there I found only about 4,000 people in that island group where we were. Once they became Christian, as they were doing very quickly, what was I to do? I even wrote a letter to the directors asking them to transfer me to a larger field while I was still young and mobile, with just the one child.'

'And *are* you moving from Raiatea?' we asked.

'No. Although we were ready to leave for England because of ill health and frustration on my part, God has been showing us his wider plan. He can use our strong, new congregation on Raiatea as a focus for sending out missionaries — islander missionaries, new converts — to take the gospel to group after group.'

Walter's atlas was quickly opened and together we gazed at the map of the Pacific as John Williams traced out his vision for us. His plan did not begin from Sydney as Walter had once imagined, but rippled out from an obscure island, using the related languages, culture and customs of other islanders who could say with authority, 'We too have worshipped the gods of wood and feathers and cane, we too have sacrificed and eaten people, we too have been terrified of the spirits of the dead — but we have met Jesus Christ, Son of God, and now we have found a new freedom where we can live in peace.'

We heard John tell the story of a canoe-load of people

from the southern island of Rurutu who were trying to escape from an epidemic on their island. Storm-driven, they were at sea for weeks and at last were cast ashore on Raiatea. They were so amazed at the transformation of the Raiatean people, with their idols and places of sacrifice destroyed and a neat new village with a huge church in their place, that they begged for some Raiatean Christians to go home with them, to share the news of the Jesus way with their people.

John Williams and Lancelot Threlkeld asked the local people and two of their best men offered to go. Only months later a Raiatean party returned home with some of the rejected gods of Rurutu, excited indeed by the success of their first venture into missionary outreach. On their way to New South Wales, the Williams have left another couple of good island Christians in the Hervey Islands and hope to go back to see how they are getting on when they return to Raiatea.

'For a long time I thought that it would be better to work on a large continent where I could move on to new fields quite easily. I cannot be content within the narrow limits of a single reef.'

'My John can never sit still,' muttered Mary.

'But now I have a vision for a Pacific-wide work. We need careful planning: ships to transport our island evangelists, local converts as missionaries, the use of local languages and idioms, translation of the scriptures, people taught to read with books to distribute so that God's word can speak to them directly, printing presses, self-help and self-support by new congregations – always looking to new fields, new places of need. Can't you see it!'

Walter was lit up with enthusiasm with what he saw. Mary Williams and I left them together, brooding over a plan for co-ordinated voyages of first-contact and discovery into every island group across the Pacific from New Guinea to Tonga to the Marquesas, to discover which areas were most promising for missionary work. They saw grand co-operation between Church Missionary Society, Methodist

Missionary Society and London Missionary Society, with
men like Marsden and Leigh strongly involved, shared
reporting and each mission being responsible for a broad
language area. A lovely idea...

Mary and I took little Johnny out into the garden for a
walk and, as we strolled along, I asked her the questions
that were most important to me.

'Please, Mary, be honest. What is it really like to be the
wife of a missionary?'

She was silent for a long while and at first I thought that
she would not answer. Then she said, 'A mixture... Some
parts are lovely. The islands are very beautiful – though
very hot, of course – and many of the people are very
friendly and loving. It is fun to make a home in such a
place, and my John has built us a truly beautiful house
near the beach, quite big with seven rooms and a verandah, all plastered with local lime and whitewashed and
with venetian blinds on the windows looking out over the
sea. He has laid out an elegant garden with flower beds and
gravel paths, built excellent furniture and set up a kitchen
garden and poultry yard. We wouldn't have had that at
home in the East End of London... Of course my husband
is convinced that anyone can do anything they put their
mind to, so long as they have a reasonably practical and
mechanical mind and have a book of instructions! He has
little tolerance for impractical men.'

She walked along the path a little, watching her child.
She continued: 'Of course, John loves his work and it is
nice to have a contented husband. There is nothing in the
world that could give him more joy than preaching the
gospel in a place which uses all his imagination and gives
him the chance to be inventive. So long as he is healthy,
he is totally happy in the islands.'

'Yes, but what about you? *Do you* like it? Are you contented? What about your child? What about... what about
having babies?'

Mary looked at me, seeing me not as a flippant young girl
but as a woman who has already lost a baby and whose

gown is even now straining over the curve of a child soon
to be born.

'Sometimes,' she said slowly, 'I'm afraid. When my
John Chauner Williams was born, we were still in Tahiti.
I was glad of the help of the other missionary women and
good Mr Threlkeld who has some medical training. We
were very new in the islands and so I was glad to be with
a large group of missionaries. That was in January, 1818.
Then last year I was expecting our second child and something awful happened. We were living on Raiatea by then
and a group of young men plotted to kill us. They came
into chapel one Sunday morning, reeling with drink, and
disrupted the service. That night they came back to our
house while we were eating our dinner and pounded on the
door, demanding to be let in. Providentially the door was
locked and our Raiatean servants were offended by their
rudeness, so wouldn't open it. At last they went away, but
we found out that twice they have made a plan to kill us.
I was terribly upset.

'Perhaps I should have been braver, but I hadn't been
well and went into premature labour. Our baby lived one
day. . . If it hadn't been for the help of our dear friends,
Mr and Mrs Threlkeld, I would have died, too. I was ill for
weeks. Then, of course, there was our friend Mrs
Orsmond in 1818 – she and her husband came to be with
us before her baby was due, to be near Mr Threlkeld. The
poor thing kept saying, "I'm going to die." And she did,
too, with her baby.'

Mary had a twinkle in her eye when she added, 'I did
suggest *your* name to Mr Orsmond as a nice girl for his second wife, but you had already made other plans.'

'Tell me about your life,' I asked hastily, as I didn't want
to pursue the idea of me as the second Mrs Orsmond, good
man though he is.

'John was always so busy. He started his day with two
hours of teaching people to read in the cool of the morning
– Mr Threlkeld taught the children and John taught the
adults, including a number of chiefs. Then he would go to

work on all kinds of practical things – boat building, inventing machinery for a home-made sugar mill, blacksmith work, building our home. He wanted our home and way of life to be a good model for the people. Quite soon our native neighbours began to admire our home with its cleanliness and convenience and, because it was all done with local material, John taught them how to build similar ones. He was not so interested in getting involved in business as some of the missionaries, but loved to teach the islanders things that would be practical and useful to them.

'I taught the women some of my own skills. They are very skilful with their hands, anyway, and I would sit with groups of women and girls teaching them how to sew gowns. I am quite a good spinstress and started to dress the local flax. John wants to buy or build me a loom. And you should have seen the lovely bonnets we made! We plaited beautiful bonnets from local fibres and all the ladies wore them to church with flowers.

'Of course, I go to all the church things. On Sunday mornings, hundreds of Raiateans crowd into our big chapel with its thatched roof. For our night meetings John made several big chandeliers with rings of coconut shells filled with coconut oil. They looked so wonderful. The warm glow of the little flames shining up into the darkness of the high thatched roof lit all the people sitting below them.

'The big meetings are always in their own language – John is very quick and clever with language, but I find it a lot harder. So I love the little meetings we have with our fellow-missionaries. We always share a meal and are free to talk in English, to pray together and study the Bible, and that was very important to us women. It would be awful if Mrs Threlkeld and I were not good friends, because we depend on each other and John enjoys Lancelot Threlkeld's quick wit and steady faith.'

As we walked, I watched her looking at her child. He seems to cling to her a lot; perhaps he is finding it difficult to come here to a strange place among strangers.

'What is it like for children?' I asked.

'When we first arrived in Tahiti,' she said, 'I remember being quite shocked by what I saw of the young children of the older missionaries. Some of them seemed to be allowed to run wild and spend most of their time with the native children, catching their diseases, picking up their coarse language, hearing all sorts of awful things. They have a tutor who is teaching some of the missionaries' children, but John says there should be a proper school for all of our children so that they won't grow up ignorant. It is not so hard when they are little – in fact, it is a good life for them and I'm not shocked now by the sight of native children playing with my child. But as John says, what future is there in the islands for our children when they are older?'

We moved slowly back to the house to join our men, I moving with the heavy sway of a woman in late pregnancy, very conscious of the unborn child. What should I do? Have we made the right decision?

Parramatta, New South Wales: New Year's Eve, 1821

The house is quiet and still and I have time to be alone and think about things. Walter has gone into Sydney to say goodbye to the Leighs. He planned to stay overnight for the Watchnight Service at Macquarie Street Chapel. Our beautiful baby, our sturdy Henry Hassall Lawry, has been fed and changed and settled back in his cradle. As I held him in my arms to drink, I marvelled at him: his strength and vigour, his healthy colour, the soft fuzz of his hair and the concentrated and single-minded way in which he tugged at my breast. He is seventeen days old now. I can't help thinking about our precious little Elizabeth, so fragile, who died after thirteen days of life. God protect my son.

I am glad to be alone tonight. It would have been good to go to see Samuel and Catherine Leigh leave for New Zealand, but it is too soon after Henry's birth to think of driving fifteen miles into Sydney. Henry was born the day after the special farewell service for the Leighs in the big

Sydney chapel. I was sorry to miss it, but Walter told me
that it was a wonderful service and Samuel preached a
very fine and powerful sermon — wouldn't it be wonderful
if the atmosphere of that service could go on between our
men! Walter said that the latest news of New Zealand has
just come and it is not good; there is news of tribal fightings
and violence.

Catherine Leigh was the one who was most sure that they
should still go. She is a woman of great strength and I
respect her for her faith and confidence, but I'm not sure
that I'd be willing to sail, knowing that there was that kind
of trouble ahead. Catherine gives her strength to Samuel.
He is certainly no coward and has proved that many times
in New South Wales, but his physical strength is not as
great as his dreams and I am glad he has Catherine beside
him. She must have been a great support in recent months
when problems between the Methodist staff made him a
very lonely man. They were expecting to embark before
dawn this morning and perhaps they are now out to sea,
on their way to uncharted new life. I pray for them, not
really knowing how to pray, just feeling a great sense of
awe at the step they are taking.

The silence of our house tonight has been a difficult but
creative silence. I brought Walter's Book of Methodist
Offices to bed with me as I think they will be using the
Covenant Service at the midnight Watchnight Service
tonight. It would be lovely to be with them all, sharing with
Walter and all our friends as they make their covenant with
God for the New Year, for the unknown 1822. By the time
I had settled Henry it was nearly midnight, so I am reading
the Covenant Service now, here at home in my own room,
knowing that Walter is saying it, too.

It is not easy. The words are beautiful, but I'm frightened
that they are too real, too immediate for comfort. And I am
comfortable here. What other comforts could I need? Happily married to a fine man, having a lovely baby, living in
the familiar town of my childhood near my mother and
brothers and sisters — and we hear that Thomas is on his

way home, too. We have all we need. Father's legacy has made it possible to pay for dreams like the Parramatta chapel and even some luxuries like a piano — Walter has advertised for a piano teacher. The Covenant Service reads: 'Thou hast comforted us with kindred and friends...'

Walter has been appointed to Tonga and wants to go, but I am not so sure whether I really want to go with him. The words of the service accuse me: 'Forgive us that so little of thy love has reached others through us, and that we have borne so lightly wrongs and sufferings that were not our own...'

People keep saying, don't go. I think I will, then I feel that it is impossible. How can I cut myself off from everything that is known and familiar, from everyone I love except my husband and child?

'Christ has many services to be done; some are easy, others are difficult; some bring honour, others bring reproach; some are suitable to our natural inclinations and temporal interests, others are contrary to both. In some we may please Christ and please ourselves, in others we cannot please Christ except by denying ourselves...'

They call them the Friendly Islands. I'm not at all sure about that. They are probably much like the Maoris who are fighting and killing right now. What if I don't like the Tongans? What if they don't like me! Mr Shelley's stories had some very disturbing parts, like the part about how his three friends were killed.

Perhaps Walter could go alone, just to see if it is safe. No, that is not what I want. Either we both go or we both stay. Yet I don't feel I should influence him to stay in New South Wales when he has been appointed to Tonga. I have no sense of call from God to go to Tonga, but I feel a strong sense of loyalty to Walter and I want to share his life even if it means going to Tonga. But I can't help feeling afraid. What if I am pregnant again? Will Henry be healthy? Could it be very dangerous? Catherine Leigh seems such a strong lady, with her ideas of sewing classes and reading classes

like Mary Williams. I think she will be an excellent missionary.

All I have to offer is my love for Walter, my inadequate, ill-educated love for people, specially young people, and – I think – my willingness to go where God wants me to go.

The candle has nearly guttered out, but I can still see to read the final prayer of the Covenant Service, the prayer I truly want to make my own. Lord, help me to make it true: 'I am no longer my own but thine. Put me to what thou wilt, rank me with whom thou wilt; put me to doing, put me to suffering; let me be employed for thee or laid aside for thee; let me be full, let me be empty; let me have all things, let me have nothing; I freely and heartily yield all things to thy pleasure and disposal.'

An awesome challenge

Parramatta, New South Wales: February, 1822.
Such excitement! Our dear brother Thomas Hassall has
come home from England. When news came to Parramatta
that his ship was in Sydney Harbour, our whole family was
all set to rush off to Sydney to greet him. My Walter was
away on a trip to Bathurst with brother James, so I had the
chance to be with Thomas first, before he met my husband. Thomas looks so well, so very handsome and more
mature, and such a lovely Christian gentleman. He has
come home a single man, so I hope he finds a very special
lady for a wife one day.

Thomas and I had a chance to talk. We recalled all kinds
of things about our childhood, about our dear father who
is not here to welcome home his son, about family news (he
tells me that he has kept all my letters to him while he was
away — I was the only one who told him all the little details
of news and he valued my letters) and he asked me about
my marriage.

'You look more grown-up, dear little sister,' he said,
'and prettier than ever! You are happy?'

'Oh, *yes*! You weren't quite sure about it, were you? I
remember that you wrote in a polite answer to Walter's
first letter to you that ''... were I to say no uneasy appre-
hensions darted across my mind when I heard it hinted to
whom she was to be united, it would be wrong, but that
confidence I have ever been enabled to place in my dear

sister enabled me soon to banish those fears and subsequent letters have tended to set my mind quite at ease upon the subject..." And you didn't know quite how to address him and wrote "my dear brother" and crossed it out. Then "my dear friend" and crossed it out – and finally put "my dear sir"! I do most sincerely hope that you and Walter will be truly friends and even brothers.'

Walter came home on January 28, exhausted and filthy after seven days of riding on horseback over the Blue Mountains out to the western plains and home again: 150 miles without having slept once in a house or had a chance to change his clothes. He saw brother Samuel's new property out there and preached in Bathurst at the courthouse – surely the Committee would see that as going to the outstations! It has been dreadfully hot, too, so he was thankful to be home. The next day we went together to introduce him to Thomas and, though they were a little shy of each other, he came home and said: 'I'm much better pleased with him than I feared I should be! I think he is a fine young man and I feel he will be a very good minister of the gospel here in New South Wales.'

Parramatta, New South Wales: April, 1822

To go to Tonga or not to go. To take me or leave me with Mother. To go for a short exploratory visit of three months or to plan to stay for several years. To go with a ship passing those islands, such as the *Westmoreland* which sailed in January, or to purchase a ship just for the purpose. All these have been possibilities over the past months.

Late last year Walter wrote to his parents: 'It is universally allowed here that a female would be in utmost danger among these savages...' But now we have finally decided on a plan. Walter has just purchased the ship *St Michael*, using my legacy and buying in equal shares with brother Jonathan and the Captain of the *St Michael*, Captain Beveridge. Jonathan and the Captain will use the ship for trading in pork, sandalwood and coconuts and Walter will use it as a missionary supply ship. (The *St Michael* used to belong to the trader Peter Dillon, but it was damaged after a fire on board last January, while it lay in Sydney Harbour. It has now been repaired and sold to us.)

I will go with him, with young Henry of course, and we will go for three months to see whether or not Tonga is a suitable place to begin a mission. If after three months we feel it is not the right time to begin, we will come back with the ship. In any case I expect I will come home then, even if Walter stays on for another few months. We will take with us our old servant Thomas Wright (he has permission to come even though his convict sentence is not yet completed), Macanoe the Marquesan boy who has been with us since last year, and maybe three young men who have become Christians under Walter's ministry – a number of them are very keen to go.

Walter has been very much influenced by his friend John Williams. In February we both attended the missionary anniversary here in Parramatta where John spoke. As he talked of the heathen things he had heard of or seen in the Society Islands – human sacrifices, torture, all sorts of barbarity – I was appalled and sickened. How could anyone go to such a place? Yet as he went on and spoke of the way people have become Christians and the wonderful changes that have happened there, I glanced sideways at Walter and knew that there was no question now about Walter going to Tonga. What man could resist the vision of being an instrument of change to bring a whole people from barbarity and fear into the light of Christ? Not my Walter!

John Williams was a great help to Walter over the past few months because he was working through many of the same problems. When John first came to New South Wales, he was disappointed that Mr Marsden was not able to help him with a missionary ship. Because he saw a ship as vital to his vision, he used a legacy received after the death of his beloved mother last year to buy on behalf of the London Missionary Society a new schooner of ninety tons, the *Endeavour*. He wants to call it by a native word, meaning *The Beginning*. When Walter was getting discouraged about ever finding a vessel going to Tonga, he decided to follow John's example and use our legacy to buy a ship, even though it is going to leave us rather short — it is no way to get rich and he worries constantly about money. He wrote a slightly offended letter to the Committee suggesting that perhaps they must be rather confused about the links between Sydney and Tonga as the only way a man could get to an appointment in Tonga was to buy his own ship!

Over the last few months, Walter and John Williams have spent a lot of time together, shopping for trade goods, organising stores to take to their respective missions, visiting the new governor, Governor Brisbane (Governor Macquarie left in December last year) and receiving gifts of livestock to take with them. Our share was seven sheep, seven cows and a bull.

At the beginning of the month, John and Mary Williams sailed for the Society Islands. They are both well again and happy to be going, though Mary remarked, 'In some ways it is harder to go back again than to go to the mission field in the first place.'

In about six weeks, it will be our turn to sail.

Port Jackson, New South Wales: June 16, 1822

Today I stood on the deck of the *St Michael*, fat little Henry on my hip, and gazed around me at Port Jackson, trying to fix it all in my mind. I know we expect to be home again in six months, but this voyage to Tonga is as strange and uncertain as a magical flight to the moon and I want to be able to remember that Sydney is real.

The bright winter sun was shining on the harbour, lighting the dark green of the bush and the grainy texture of sandstone rocks. Nearby lay the cluster of small buildings clinging to the hillside of the Rocks, with the usual movements of bullocks dragging their wagon loads along rutted, muddy roads and the colour of military red, convict yellow and blue drab going about their business. I could see the governor's house and other large buildings, the Rum

Hospital at the top of the hill and our large Macquarie Street Chapel with our first home just visible over the rise. Against the skyline swung the great arms of windmills and, down on the rocky shoreline which curved around this safe Sydney Cove within the harbour, was the road through the bush which I have often walked with Mrs Macquarie. Moving west through the town was the road to Parramatta.

A week ago we came along that road, with all my family and a cartload of our cargo, to board the *St Michael*, ready to sail when the time is right. Before we came away from Parramatta, I went to the burial ground near St John's Church and stood at the foot of our sacred family spot. A heavy slab of engraved sandstone now covers what was once a gaping grave. Under the names of our family and a description of my father's life, the stonemason had carved: 'Insatiate archer, could not one suffice? Thy shaft flew thrice and thrice our peace was lost...' Then I realised that I was staring at my own name, carved in stone: 'first born daughter of the Rev. Walter and *Mary Lawry*.' Trembling, I wondered: Will my real grave be here one day? In Tonga? Or even at sea...?

Driving away from Parramatta last week was harder than I had dreamed. As the carriage drove away and I had a last glimpse of our own home, my mother's home, our little Parramatta chapel, St John's Church where we were married and the familiar roads of home, I felt a tight knot of nerves in the pit of my stomach. Even the sight of a grubby urchin from our Sunday School waving a farewell was enough to bring me to tears. We drove along the well-known bends and hills through the bush of Parramatta Road. Even the over-elaborate tollgate on the outskirts of Sydney, the plain bulk of the Benevolent Asylum by the road and the dust of the brickworks seemed precious.

'I'm being silly!' I said to Mother with a sniff. 'Why am I being so emotional when I'll be home in a few months?'

Mother held my hand tightly. She sometimes finds it hard to say what she is feeling, but after a silence she said: 'I've been remembering. Even the filth of the Thames looked good to me the day the *Duff* sailed. Father and I didn't know what we were going to find either.'

Since we came on board, my family has been coming and going, most of them spending a few nights on board with us. As well as ourselves, we have on board Captain and Mrs Beveridge, young Mr Hall going to New Zealand and our own party for Tonga, including our servant Thomas Wright, our young artisan friends, George Lilley the carpenter and Charles Tindall the blacksmith, and our Island lad, Macanoe. (He is a good, gentle boy and we have become good friends from many months of working side-by-side in my kitchen – I think he is pleased to be going back to the Islands.) This morning when we had family prayers together, we had twenty-two people gathered around, including some of the eighteen sailors, so I feel the journey could be a happy time.

Walter has been writing a last letter to his parents to send with a ship going to England. Among other things, he wrote: 'Henry is positively the fattest child I ever saw. He grows pretty and is the astonishment of all who see him. . . We are almost certain of returning with the ship. . . A ship just arrived from Tonga brings most favourable accounts of their peace and strong desire to have *papalangi* (white people) living there. . . . The mission is a very great mission; probably there never was one more truly interesting. . . I feel no longing for home, no looking behind, no doubts or misgivings as to my path of duty. I most clearly see my way to Tonga and thither I go, not knowing the things which shall befall me there.' He also added that I was finding the parting from my family 'most painful' – and he is right!

A strong breeze has sprung up, the tide is right and we are ready to sail. One by one my dearest family, Mother and Thomas, Samuel, Jonathan and James, Eliza, Susannah and Anne, my dear friends the Marsden ladies and other people of the colony have said farewell and left the ship. (Brother Thomas was comforting Miss Anne Marsden with more than ordinary solicitude, but that is very understandable as he has recently received permission from Mr Marsden to marry Anne. They are very much in love and at last I have guessed that the reason why Anne was so cool to our Samuel while Thomas was away was probably because she loved Thomas all the time. The Rev. William Walker seemed to be standing particularly close to our sister Eliza, too – what does that mean?)

They are now only tiny dots in the distance as the wind fills our sails – now out of sight as we move away down the harbour. The bulk of the Heads yawns wide as we sail through into the open ocean and soon even our last sight of the South Head lighthouse is lost.

Suddenly I feel very cold and flee to the privacy of our cabin.

Bay of Islands, New Zealand: July 12, 1822

Once I stopped crying, the voyage wasn't so bad after all. It was my very first experience of the open sea and, after a few days of seasickness, I proved to be a good sailor – better than poor Walter – and began to enjoy the adventure. Henry was a very good baby, though at eight months he is very lively, wanting to wriggle and crawl away. After three weeks we were in sight of New Zealand where we were going first with stores for the Leighs, but for another week we were forced to beat up and down not able to make harbour. Walter used some of the time in rereading William Mariner's book about his experiences when he was shipwrecked in Tonga some years ago and read aloud one passage which has clung to my mind in a disturbing way.

Mariner was describing how the London Missionary Society missionaries (Mr Shelley and friends) found an escaped convict already in Tonga when they arrived in 1797. After some serious disagreements between missionaries and convict, the convict tricked the Tongan chiefs into believing that the missionaries were 'sent out by the King of England to bring a pestilence upon the people of Tonga, and that they accordingly shut themselves up in their house to perform witchcraft and make incantations, which was the cause of the pestilence that then raged, and that all their books were witchcraft'. How could the Tongans believe that? Could they think like that about us and blame us for anything that went wrong? I hadn't thought of that.

We anchored at last in the Bay of Islands, off Rangihoua. From the *St Michael* we saw canoes coming out from the shore. The settlement in the distance seemed to be clinging to a hillside: little cottages clustered above the beach, each with its strong timber fence. As the canoes came nearer, I held tightly to Walter's arm and tried to look confident. Of course, I have met Maoris before, many of them in Parramatta, but here they were in their native place, moving swiftly towards us over the water, wrapped in feather cloaks and looking frightening with tattoos.

A canoe-load clambered up over the rail onto the deck. One tall Maori, his face disfigured with the swirls of tattoo marks, a greenstone necklace and earplugs and feathers in his hair, moved straight to me. I shrank back against Walter, but the fearful figure called 'Miss Hassall!' in a delighted voice and greeted me in excited broken English. It was Titore, our old friend from Parramatta, one who had gone to England for his education. He seemed very pleased to see me, but where were his English manners, his education? He seems to be completely pagan and to have gone back to his savage ways.

We went ashore today. In this alien place, Walter and Samuel Leigh greeted each other as dear brothers and all the irritations and sorrows of the past seemed to be forgotten. The difficulties they are experiencing now, and the uncertainties we are facing ourselves, seemed so much more important than the things that have divided them in the past. Catherine Leigh was so pleased to see me, a woman she had known in a more civilised setting. She is a very nice woman and very good for Samuel who is still not a very healthy man. They are still living here with the Church Missionary Society people, although they plan to move off to their own station at Whangaroa as soon as pos-

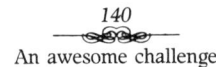
sible, on a bay some forty or fifty miles north of here. They had had another area in mind, but the powerful chief Hongi told them not to bother with that place as he intended to wipe that population out!

Walter thought that they should have begun their own separate mission by now, but I don't blame them for waiting. There is a security about staying here with the big group, with another group at Kerikeri only a few more miles inland along the Bay. That is one thing that sticks in my mind — when the Tahitian mission began, there were some thirty missionaries at Matavai, including five wives; when the New Zealand mission began, there was a party of twenty-five British people with seven wives. When we begin in Tonga, in conditions as uncertain, there will be four British men — and me!

Tonight we dined with Leighs and long-term Church missionaries, the Halls. After the meal, we women left the men to discuss the proposed new station at Whangaroa, the difficulties of language learning and the urgent need for a school to be established, while we women talked together.

Catherine Leigh was admiring our Henry. 'The Maoris didn't think much of me to begin with. They asked how many children I had and when I said "none", they announced that I was worthless and Samuel was a poor man!'

'Did the Williams family call here with the *Endeavour*?' I asked.

'Yes, they called here a few months ago on their way to Tahiti. John is so quick with languages. He said that this language was quite closely related to the language of the Society Islands, so he was able to make himself understood, after a fashion, within a few days. Samuel and I are struggling along with very small success. Samuel was so happy to have John Williams call here — he appreciates John very much and John has called my Samuel "an excellent man". I enjoyed seeing Mary Williams again and she gave me some advice about starting sewing classes for girls, like hers. Tomorrow I must show you what some of my girls are doing — they are not very good yet, and sometimes knot the thread to the needle's eye or turn their cloth into a nasty tangle, but they are clever little creatures. Surely a people who can carve so delicately and make such wonderful cloaks and garments of feathers or patchworked dog skin and woven flax will soon learn to sew. I make the girls wash and they hate that!'

She paused to pour us another cup of tea and then added: 'I must be honest. There have been times when I have wanted badly to go home. Sometimes the Maoris frighten me with their violence. They mostly leave us alone in peace, but they are so violent towards each other. And they can't stand any of us to interfere with their affairs, because they are always sure they know what is best for them. They don't mind us setting up businesses for them or bringing in wealth, but they don't want to listen to the gospel at all.

'There is something else that scares me. Samuel is a very fine man, but sometimes he – how can I put it – plays the part of a martyr when it isn't necessary. A few months ago, he deliberately visited the most dangerous part of the coast, where the ship *Boyd* was burned and all the crew and passengers massacred and eaten. He didn't *have* to go there, but he did – and only just escaped with his life. He was long overdue back here and I had despaired of seeing him again. When he finally reached our cottage again, I couldn't help crying with relief.

'Then another time he tried to stop a fight between two angry Maori groups by preaching to them and nearly got himself killed. He succeeded in annoying them so much that some of them pushed him down a steep hill in the mud – I saw it happen and rushed out to ask the chief what reconciliation payment he needed. He wanted a garment, so I snatched the big patchwork coverlet off our bed and presented it to him as a reconciliation gift. Off he went, beautifully draped in my coverlet with the battle satisfactorily resolved! Men,' she added confidentially, 'are so brave and daring, even reckless – but sometimes they don't see the *simple* solution to their problems.'

Bay of Islands, New Zealand: July 23, 1822

Tonight, when we were safely back on board the *St Michael*, I crept into Walter's bunk, wriggling down into the narrow space to the safety of his arms. Walter thought I wanted to make love – and that was true, too – but chiefly my need was to hold him and to be held by him. Later, in the darkness, I said, 'I'm glad we are not staying here.'

Walter was drowsy, but he mumbled sleepily, 'Mmm, awful weather – this miserable winter cold and rain and sleet. Surely Tonga will at least be warm. And I don't care much for the countryside I have visited over the past few weeks either. A dismal place...'

'I wasn't thinking of that,' I said.

'The Maoris? Probably the most unlikely people in the world to become Christians, don't you think? They are so sure of themselves and their customs – I don't think they will find it easy to turn to God. Samuel Leigh will have his problems.'

'No, I was really thinking that I'm glad we are not staying here with this group of missionaries...'

Walter was silent, but he held me tensely and I think our thoughts were following the same paths.

Our friends in Parramatta had strongly discouraged Walter and Samuel Leigh from trying to work in co-operation in New Zealand, but their differences paled beside the troubles of the Church Missionary Society staff at Rangihoua and Kerikeri. Even when we first arrived, we sensed that all was not well with them. Nothing was said at first while they all made us welcome but, after a few days, the painful truth began to come out. The conflict and unease we sensed was not because the missionaries were in fear of the Maoris. The conflict was within; they were at odds with each other.

Some blamed Marsden for remaining their authority at a distance, while all those on the spot were commanded to be equal. They said that there were continuing struggles for ascendancy, arguments over property, divisions of opinion. Some said of others that they were lazy, that they were proud and ungovernable, that they were only there to set up businesses and make money, that they didn't care for the heathen. Some whispered of brethren with fiery bad tempers who could easily turn to violence, or others of missionaries who were prepared to put quantities of muskets and gunpowder in the hands of the warlike Maoris for gain, even though they had promised not to trade in firearms. Some talked of the young single men who had taken Maori girls and abandoned them to become prostitutes.

The thing that hurt me most of all was the sad story of the Kendalls. I lay for a long time tonight, staring into the darkness and feeling the gentle motion of the ship at anchor, but aware of physical distress in my body as if we were caught in a storm. The faces of Mr and Mrs Kendall were there before me: the young, eager faces of the couple I had known years ago in Parramatta merged into the older faces – the angry, defiant face of Kendall staring past the bleak, faded face of his wife. How could this have happened? Was anything or anyone to be blamed? Was there any hope for them now? Over and over I heard the words of accusation which we had first heard one night when we had dined ashore with Leighs and Halls.

Mr Hall had made it quite clear that he couldn't abide Kendall and the feeling seemed to be mutual. 'If they had known what that man was really like, they would no more have ordained him than his bootblack!' he said. 'I could tell you absolute facts that would make the hair lift your hat off your head' – and he proceeded to do so.

It was a sad, tangled story. A brilliant man, quick to learn the Maori language; a thoughtless husband who left his large family to fend for themselves while he went to England to publish his grammar; Mrs Kendall seeking comfort, but finding disgrace through having a child by another man during her husband's absence; a deeper and deeper involvement in Maori culture till Kendall's mind was full of pagan thought; a beautiful and intelligent Maori chief's daughter available to advise on matters of culture;

temptation, adultery, defiance and refusal to repent; disappointment, disillusionment and destruction, not only for Mr and Mrs Kendall but also for their tiny community who did not know what to do with their skilled but sinful brother and his plaintive, little wife.

Lying in the dark, I thought: is this the real danger of going to a strange people? Is this what is real – not the fine words spoken in a crowded missionary meeting in Sydney or in London, when people speak of taking the light to dark places? I remember Samuel Marsden preaching about the mission in Tahiti and speaking of 'Satan's dark dominions' and how the missionaries 'surrounded his city, blew their rams' horns and the walls of Tahitian Jericho fell... the habitations of cruelty were illuminated by the morning star, which indicated the speedy rising of the Sun of Righteousness, with healing in his wings...' It sounded so fine. But do we bring our own darkness with us? I have always thought that the missionaries I have known were special people, who might have some very mild imperfections when they live in their homeland but who surely must be protected, shielded, perfected when they go among the heathen. But it is not true.

I am seeing the terrifying truth that we carry our weaknesses and sinfulness with us when we go to a strange country. Being away from home and friends won't make me stronger – perhaps I will be weaker, more vulnerable, more complaining, more in need of forgiveness, more distant from God. Could my Walter be tempted by a lovely native girl? Could... could I feel drawn to one of the young men of our party? God help us! Dear Lord, protect us – I didn't know, I didn't even imagine that this could be part of our missionary experience.

Walter has woken, startled to find me clinging to him fiercely and soaking his nightshirt with my tears.

St Michael, off New Zealand: July 28, 1822

On the deck of the *St Michael* today I didn't know whether I was going to be sick or faint, but a fearful fascination kept me there staring across at the beach in the distance and the ghastly activity there. (We left the Bay of Islands yesterday on the sabbath, much to the distress of Walter and me who tried to encourage Captain Beveridge to wait till Monday — he is proving to be a pig-headed man whose Christian attitudes take second place to his authority over his ship.) There is war between several Maori tribes and the people of Hongi have been triumphing. Their great war canoes were passing by our ship, so close that I could see the spiralling details of the carved figureheads, with protruding tongues on faces of awful ferocity and the tall sweep of carved timber towering high over the stern. They were close enough for me to see the terrified faces of prisoners as they passed; with eighty to one hundred people on board, they were three times as many as we on the *St Michael*.

A canoe came alongside, its sleek lines longer and perhaps more elegant than the bulk of the *St Michael*. They were not threatening us in any way — I think they just wanted to show off their many captives. Almost without thinking, Walter tossed down a tin of ship's biscuit as a gift for the chief (a gift for safe passage?) and we were startled to see the chief grab one of the captives, a lad, and thrust him up over the ship's rail as a return gift!

The boy, whose name appears to be Manihera, has been crouching on deck ever since, staring out across the water to the beach. We, too, can see the war canoes beached; we can hear with him the screams as his fellow captives, his family, are being slaughtered and prepared for a cannibal feast. We can see the line of severed heads, impaled on poles on the beach.

Manihera is trembling, moaning a very small sound of despair and terror as our ship moves on, away from the horror of the beach. I find I am shaking, too, so that my feet fumble with the steps of the ladder leading down into our cabin and the sanity of a fat baby waking from his nap and needing a change of linen.

St Michael, at sea on route to Tonga: August, 1822

Seasickness I expected, though I've proved a good sailor. Weeks out of sight of land was something I was prepared to accept. I looked forward to the sight of whales and leaping porpoises. What I had not expected was the misery of being cooped up in a small ship with Captain and Mrs Beveridge.

Before we left Sydney, Walter was very impressed with Captain Beveridge and thought Mrs Beveridge a charming woman. On board ship, things have changed. The Captain has become rude and domineering and Walter has reacted by trying in his somewhat tactless way to object to his behaviour. The result is that Beveridges and we are not speaking. The worst thing is that Captain and Mrs Beveridge have been indulging heavily in their stock of rum. That terrible stuff has done more harm in our colony than anything else. I enjoy a glass of wine and brew our own beer — but rum! After the Captain had been drinking heavily recently, he made a mistake in his navigating and we will have to travel 200 miles further than we should.

I whispered to Walter today, 'I'll be so glad to get off this ship. I *hate* living like this. I don't care what Tonga is like — I think I'd rather be there than here!'

St Michael, off Tongatapu: August 17, 1822

For two months we have been on the way to Tonga, always with those islands somewhere in the future, not yet real, a place and a people with almost the quality of a dream. Today the dream has taken on flesh and blood, colour and aroma; today the imagined has become real.

Just two weeks ago, Walter celebrated his twenty-ninth birthday. I teased him. 'You are nearly thirty! Quite old — no wonder you have a few grey hairs.' He was quick to point out that, as a mere child of twenty-two, I owed him more respect. Looking around at our little missionary group, I realised that we are all quite young. Apart from Walter's servant Thomas Wright, who is a middle-aged man, Charles Tindall is in his twenties, George Lilley is only nineteen and Macanoe, the Marquesan boy, is even younger. We also have the Maori lad, Manihera, with us as our responsibility and he is little more than a child. Our Tongan enterprise is putting a lot of responsibility on Walter's shoulders.

As we come to the real beginning of our contact with the people of Tonga, we are praising God for his help. Already he has shown that we are safely in his hands and he is providing for our needs.

The first sign of this, though we did not immediately recognise it, was that the Lord stopped us from landing on the first land we had seen since we left New Zealand. Captain Beveridge, now speaking to Walter again though rather grumpily, had pointed out the steep, heavily wooded island which he said was 'Eua and said that we would land there. For several days we tacked to and fro before the island, but couldn't get close enough to land. Captain Beveridge said, somewhat abruptly: 'Watch your child! If he falls overboard here, he'll be falling into some of the deepest waters in the world.' I found myself clinging to Henry, scared to let him away from my grasp.

As we looked across at 'Eua, we could see great waves boiling up against cliff faces. I was quite relieved when the Captain decided to sail on to attempt a landing on the island of Tongatapu, about twelve miles further on and the main island to the south of the Friendly Islands group. As we beat north to round Tongatapu, we could see a ring of coral reef encircling the island, a frill of white surf breaking on the reef and the dramatic colour change from the dark blue of the deep waters to clear turquoise green as the water became suddenly shallow within the reef. Beyond, we could see a narrow line of white beach and the darker line of land and bush, unbroken by cliff or mountain.

We came to anchor yesterday in what Captain Beveridge called Port Maria, just off the north coast, and almost immediately lines of canoes began to move out from the shore to meet us. I stood by Walter on deck, keeping Henry firmly in my arms, and watched the canoes skim closer, hundreds of people in small and large canoes, hundreds of strangers. Friends or enemies?

Then the second sign of God's care was shown. We had expected to be completely isolated as none of us knew anything of the Tongan language, but to our amazement one of the first canoes to reach us drew alongside and a white man came clambering over the rail. He was dressed as the Tongans were, barechested with an island fabric wrapped in long layers around him and knotted at the waist, but he was certainly a white man. He introduced himself as Singleton, a man who had survived the destruction of the *Port-au-Prince* in the northern islands of this group, some sixteen years ago. He has lived on Tongatapu ever since. His use of English is a little awkward, from long lack of practice, but he evidently speaks the Tongan language fluently. He was immediately friendly and welcoming. What a wonderful bridge he will be between us and the Tongans.

Soon after Singleton arrived, another canoe came alongside and, amid general excitement from the Tongans, a *huge* man came up on deck. I have never seen a man more massively built, as big as two ordinary Englishmen. He was the object of great respect, it was clear, and yet I thought he had very kind, friendly dark eyes and spoke to us with courtesy. With the help of Singleton, Walter talked to our stately guest. He explained how we wanted to visit the Friendly Islands, to find a place to stay on Tongatapu or perhaps in the Ha'apai or the Vava'u groups of islands, to see if we would be welcomed to teach the people the true religion so that they could become wiser.

The vast chief spoke rapidly in reply, his words flowing along without any meaning for us and we had to wait for Singleton to interpret. At length, Singleton said: 'The chief's name is Fatu. He says he wants you to live in his area. He says don't go to the Ha'apai group or to Vava'u; stay with him. He says he would keep you safe in time of war.'

'War?'

'No war just now. No war for two years here on Tongatapu. But there is war on 'Eua. Only two moons ago the whaler *Ceres* landed on 'Eua and six men were killed – others escaped. Not a good place to land.'

So that was why God didn't let us land there. Already we are thankful for his mercies.

Today, Walter went ashore. It was all very well to be safely on board the *St Michael*, even when surrounded by canoes. But to see him go ashore, alone. I saw him go down into the ship's boat, holding him with my eyes until all I could see was his hat rising oddly among the dark heads. As they moved towards the landing place across the water in the distance, I could see men wading out through shallow water and I thought I could see Walter being hoisted onto the back of a very tall man and carried, pick-a-back, to the shore. Then he was swallowed up into a great, moving crowd of people and I could see him no more.

It would be a lie if I said that today was an easy day for me. Henry, bless him, was not in the least uneasy and he was happily entertained by the many canoes which came out to the ship, fifty or sixty of them, trading in pigs and sennit rope. They are quite familiar with white people calling in their islands. Fifty years ago Captain Cook made three visits in these parts, and gave them their name of 'Friendly Islands', Captain Bligh's crew on the *Bounty* mutinied in the northern islands of the group, London Missionary Society missionaries like Mr Shelley lived here about twenty-five years ago, various escaped convicts and beachcombers have lived here, and whaling ships and traders call in from time to time.

They seem quite accustomed to coming to a ship and trading, though I think Henry may be the first white baby they have seen. Fortunately, he is a friendly child and is not at all overawed by all the attention he is getting. People brought him bananas and Henry was charmed by them, squashing ripe banana in his fingers and displaying all four of his teeth. As I watched the Tongans on the ship, I looked anxiously for signs of treachery, but all I saw was laughter,

friendly faces and superb physiques. Are they *really* the Friendly Islands? I wondered. Will Walter come back safely? If they are so friendly, what is the meaning of stories we know to be true of ships cut off, of sailors killed?

In the evening, the ship's boat returned with Walter, safe. Our relief – *my* relief – to have him back was great, and to find him quite unharmed and excited about his day. After he had disappeared into the crowd, the chief had ordered the people to form themselves into a ring, seated on the ground, and Walter was told to sit between Chief Fatu and Chief Taufa while a strange drink called *kava* was prepared and presented to them. Walter said he didn't like it much! They gave him a great bunch of bananas. When he asked to walk into the countryside, the chief sent his son with Walter and they walked for several miles.

'It is beautiful!' Walter said. 'Very different from New South Wales or England, but very rich and fertile. William Singleton came with us and told me about the things we saw. Everywhere we went we were surrounded by people, who watched everything I did. They seemed interested in my plaid jacket and sniffed it, felt it and even put a fold of it in their mouths. I am very hopeful that we will be welcomed here.'

In a strange land

Mu'a, Tongatapu: September 3, 1822

Rightly or wrongly, we have chosen our place and are
sleeping ashore tonight. The *St Michael* is in sight across
the bay.

Since he first landed, Walter has been more and more
drawn to Fatu's land at Mu'a on the great lagoon which
curves into the heart of the island of Tongatapu. He first
saw Mu'a when he landed the livestock there: the seven
sheep, seven cows and a bull donated by Governor Brisbane. (The Tongans were very impressed with them.) He
says we are now near the only safe anchorage available on
the island as the rest of Tongatapu is completely circled by
reef and shallow water. Around Mu'a, he says, are the
homes of several chiefs, including our friend Fatu, as well
as some sacred places which are like the ancient cities of
refuge where anyone can flee to safety.

The first time I went ashore was on August 27. By that
time we had met so many Tongans on the ship, Walter had
been ashore a number of times and Chief Fatu was so welcoming to us that I looked forward to going ashore with real
excitement and confidence.

Because the lagoon quickly becomes shallow, the ship's
boat could only take us part of the way to the shore. I
found myself scooped up by two big Tongan men and carried between them through the knee-deep water and soft
wet sand up towards the grass at a place called Ma'ofanga.

(I find it hard to be sure of Tongan names and words.)
Young Henry was hoisted onto the shoulder of a lad and
rode laughing beside me.

'If only Mother, Thomas or the girls could see me now!
Or the Marsden girls — or any of the ladies of good society,'
I called delightedly to Walter as I clung to powerful, well-
oiled shoulders and tried to hold my dangling feet clear of
the water.

I have not been on land since we left New Zealand a
month ago and it was a pleasure to feel grass and firm
ground under my feet again. (How did my parents manage
seven months on board the *Duff?*) Despite Walter's
descriptions, I was not expecting the beauty I found all
around me. From the white sand of the little beach and the
dark roughness of the coral rocks we walked along a wide,
flat roadway under the arch of magnificent shady trees,
twined with flowering vines. I recognised the blue of morning glory, but there were other blooms that were new to me
and everything seemed to be breathing perfume. After the
fumes of the Captain's rum and the stuffiness of our little
cabin on the ship, the fragrance was a joy. On either side
of the road grew strange and beautiful trees which I had
never seen before. Singleton pointed out the tall leanness
of fronded coconut palms, shorter trees each leaning under
the weight of a great bunch of bananas, nutmeg trees,
breadfruit, enormous leaves of many kinds of vegetables —
everything seemed so much larger than normal.

We walked along the road to a fenced area enclosing the
places of refuge that Walter had described. I have never
seen anything like them, though Walter says they may be
a little like the ancient pyramids of Egypt. Great blocks of
coral stone, evenly cut like giant bricks, were built into
platforms, some laid in flat squares and some rising up
step-by-step for three or four layers, some steps nearly as
tall as I am. All around us were great trees overhanging and
giving shade; there were even trees growing on top of the
strange stone places.

The castaway Singleton pointed to the mighty stones and

said: 'This is where their ancestors are buried. They are very sacred and can be used for important occasions. People in trouble or danger can run to them and be safe.'

All around us as we approached were crowds and crowds of people, all cheerful and all watching us intently. I found, a little to my own surprise, that I was not at all afraid of them. Despite their curiosity, they were courteous and gentle and seemed to be treating us with respect. We were escorted up onto one of the stone platforms and into an airy house on top of it — really just a thatched roof on high poles, with matting on the floor. Under the roof we sat with seven chiefs, among them Fatu, Finau and Taufa, and all around the house crowded the people. Walter thought there might have been as many as five hundred.

With Singleton interpreting, Walter explained his purpose to the chiefs: of wishing to stay and teach them, to set up schools for their children and to tell them about our God. He brought greetings of goodwill from Britain and presented them with gifts of twenty chisels and two axes. They seemed delighted with the gifts and said they had never received gifts from Britain before. All the chiefs seemed interested and said that they would send 'thousands' of their children to our schools and even come themselves sometimes. They assured us that we would be safe. Just as we were preparing to leave, they brought out two roast pigs and a leafy basket of cooked yams for us to eat, apologising that they were not better prepared — if they had realised we were coming that day they would have killed fifty pigs!

As the men talked and we waited for interpretation, I sat and watched, fascinated with all I saw. The Tongan people are really beautiful. The men are tall and of impressive proportions; the women very fine with lovely, rounded limbs gleaming with scented oils, perfumed flowers in their long wavy black hair. Their skin is a warm coppery brown, lighter than the Aborigines around Sydney, and they wrap around themselves layers of fine, native cloth with woven matting tied over the top. The bare breasts of the women do not alarm or shock me as some of the London ladies have been shocked by the underclad Aboriginal people of Sydney — I have seen people in their simple native dress all my life and find myself admiring the beautiful shapeliness of some of the young girls and men. Their little children were running around in the crowd, mostly with neither a stitch nor a leaf of clothing. Our Henry wanted to crawl off my lap and wriggle over to inspect one of the chiefs, sitting on the mats with massive legs folded neatly in front of him. The child was accepted quite naturally and was soon enthroned on the chiefly lap, playing with the fine fringe of the mat around his waist.

As we left at last to go back to the *St Michael*, some of the chiefs took off part of their decorated native cloth and presented us with them. They seem to be so pleased to have us stay.

Since that day, Walter and I have been to look at Mu'a, the chief's place on the lagoon, and Walter has bought six acres of land there. It is a truly beautiful spot, looking across the wide lagoon and out to sea, with mangroves growing along the shoreline and a wonderful variety of fruit trees all around. We have great plans for a vegetable garden and a place for chickens and our other animals. I'm going to love it. Walter has bought a large house from the chief, a thatched roof with rounded woven walls at each end but no side walls, and with layers of matting on the floor. Today when we all arrived at Mu'a, Walter bought some big bales of the native cloth called *tapa*. We used it to partition the house into three areas, one end for the men, one end for us and the middle section for us to share.

So tonight here we are, all of our little party, settled in this simple house which will be our home till we have built something more permanent. When we joined together for our evening prayers, we did so with thankfulness to God and a strong sense of our need of him. As we bowed in prayer, we were being watched by some Tongans who had stayed with us all day, watching every move we made. I don't know what they thought about it.

Mu'a, Tongatapu: September, 1822

Everything seems to be starting off amazingly well. Only the day after we moved into this house, Chief Fatu sent for Walter to come to the sacred tombs nearby to hear the words of a man who claimed to have had a vision or a dream with a message from a dead ancestor. When Walter returned, he was very excited.

'The Lord is really opening up the way for us,' he said. 'Singleton explained that no-one can lie on those sacred places, so everyone has taken the vision very seriously. The vision was a warning to the chief to beware of danger to our ship and to us: that many wanted to cut the ship off, but that the chief must protect us; that those who had killed the white *papalangi* in the past were now all themselves dead, too; that the white people had come with good intentions — to teach — so why should they want to kill by their prayers? Can they teach the dead? Can they have conversations with coconut trees? The *papalangi* had come with gifts, not to kill. We should be recognised as human beings, not as dangerous spirits. And he even suggested that Fatu should send his son with the *St Michael* to Sydney as a guarantee of our safety! The other chiefs were very impressed and have promised to protect us. What a wonderful beginning!'

So we have been settling in with confidence. Since our first night in this house, all of us have been very busy. The men blocked up the doorway in their end of the house and use a main door in the side. We have built side walls, four feet high, leaving wide open the rest of the space to the thatched roof and the breezes come through. Singleton and his wife, a Tongan woman called Afu, have built themselves a little leafy shelter in a corner of the middle section of the house and are becoming part of our group, though Singleton himself has no strong Christian convictions. Our floor is well covered with good woven mats, Walter's shipboard bookshelf has become our cupboard and Charles has built us a fine big bedstead, with sennit bottom and mats under the bedding. I have made a valance of *tapa* cloth and

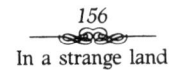
hung it all around the bed so that we can hide our boxes and things underneath.

The men and I have been busy planting our garden, because we need to have some of our own vegetables to add to the things we buy from the people. We have already planted pumpkins, melons, peas, beans, turnips, corn and cabbages. I am specially hoping that the wheat and maize we have planted will do well – when our stock of flour runs out, I will need it to make our bread.

Charles and George have been starting on work for our new, permanent house, but it is not at all easy to get timbers from the people. We may have to live in this very open house for quite some time.

The people are very friendly and kind to us, but I am finding it a bit of a strain to discover that they are always *there*! There never seems to be a moment when we are alone. From first thing in the morning till last thing at night there are people around our house, leaning on our walls and looking in, calling for us to come and barter with them for pigs or poultry or fruit, wanting to play with Henry, watching me wash or iron, poking into our things. Often groups of them come in to sit around on our floor and talk. I've caught them lifting up the valance around our bedstead to peep at the things hidden underneath, or fingering anything that takes their fancy. They are very generous, but they expect us to give them anything of ours that they admire and, if we don't, they are quite likely to take it anyway.

The chiefs often come to visit and we have been told that it is the custom that a guest must always be fed before he goes. I don't know what I would do without the help of young Macanoe; his Marquesan language proves to be completely unlike Tongan, but he is a wonderful help to me with cooking. Almost every day we find ourselves scraping and preparing mounds of root vegetables and pork, or the rather tough fowls, to fill my big cooking pots to feed the chiefs. They fancy my kind of cooking and my good bread and arrive with a retinue of friends – sometimes only eight or ten, but sometimes a crowd of fifty and even a hundred people have arrived and sat, waiting patiently while Macanoe and I have worked our way through a mountain of yams. At least they don't seem to be in a hurry! I suppose I'll get used to it, or they'll tire of pork and vegetable stews.

Mu'a, Tongatapu: October, 1822

The first time I said, 'Take me with you,' to Walter, he thought that I was afraid to stay at Mu'a without him when he went off to look at other parts of the island.

'Afraid? Nonsense, I'm not afraid to stay. I'd have Thomas and Macanoe and probably Charles and George here with me, anyway. No, I want to go with you — to be with you and to see things for myself. Henry will enjoy the outing, too.'

And so we have gone. Sometimes we have walked two or three miles across a narrow part of the island to lovely beaches on the ocean side — Walter and the other men love to swim as often as possible. (Like many Australian 'currency lasses', I enjoy the water, too, and swim with the women.) We have explored around the lagoon and visited villages in the far reaches. Now that the *St Michael* has gone off trading around the nearby islands, we have kept one of the ship's boats for our use and go out on the lagoon and sometimes out over the beautiful waters of the reef.

In the evenings, we sometimes go out for a walk around the area and visit the houses of the nearby chiefs. Women come to their chiefs with necklaces of sweet smelling flowers and the men bring gifts of fruit and baskets of food. Some girls hold torches to light the area while some prepare *kava* — healthy young people carefully biting the *kava* root and grinding it in their teeth, before fragments are mixed with water and strained through coconut fibre for the ceremonial serving. Others circle around the group, singing melodiously. After watching some delightful occasions like that, Walter wrote in his diary: "This dense population requires nothing more to make it happy, than an emancipation from the bonds of supersition by the introduction of genuine Christianity.'

One day in September, we went to see a great festival about ten miles from here up the bay. (They called it, I think, a Kartonga. Walter had his little notebook with him as usual, writing down all the Tongan words that he was learning, but it is very hard when you have no idea how to spell any of the words you are hearing and they seem to sound a little bit different every time you hear them. The language is very musical and pleasant to the ears, but they pronounce many words with a strange little catch in their voice which defies Walter's excellent spelling and, of course, my own spelling is uncertain at the best of times!)

As our boat was beached in sight of the festival, we were amazed to see the great crowds gathered. Walter thought there might have been 5,000 people – certainly there were a very great many. I kept close to Walter and we walked around among the crowds, absorbed into the brilliant patchwork of colour and movement, the odours of flowers, coconut oil and sweat, the sounds of singing and excited voices and the rhythm of drumming paddles, the vibration of hundreds of dancing feet, the flowing movement of the arms and hands of women performing their graceful sitting-down dances. Singleton explained that the festival was in honour of chiefs who had died. Some of the people showed their sorrow and respect by cutting their heads with paddles. We watched them preparing hundreds of hogs to be cooked in trenches in the ground, along with many yams, green bananas and other vegetables. For the most part our presence was ignored, apart from our usual little train of children looking at Henry, because the people were much too busy and involved with what they were doing to be bothered with us.

Early in the afternoon we had seen enough. We were hot and tired, my head was aching from the noise and Henry was starting to be irritable, so we went to our boat and set off for home. As we rowed across the bay, a canoe came after us with a gift of a pig and vegetables from Chief

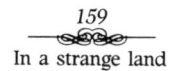
Taufa. It was very kind of him, but I said to Walter, 'I don't think we should eat the pig – it has only been heated in the hot stones and I think it is just warm and still almost raw.' Still, it is encouraging to think that we are welcome to visit the Tongan festivals and even be given a gift of food.

For another festival this month, I didn't have to leave home. Hundreds of canoes were beached on the sand flats near Mu'a and Henry and I were able to go out each day to see what was going on. We were told that this was a 'Mackee' festival – a time to present the first fruits of the crop to the gods. The festivities went on for nine days. On some days we saw great quantities of fruit and vegetables presented to the gods; on others we watched hundreds of men go singing along the road in their *tapa* cloth, wrapped up in their best mats and red leaves. We watched some mock battles, as great Tongan men pretended to attack each other with the stems of coconut leaves with high drama and enthusiasm. I think I might be the first white woman to have ever seen such things in Tonga. I do find it very interesting, indeed.

Henry loves the sand and the sea. We sat today on the beach in the shade of a great breadfruit tree, with the tide out and little groups of women and children wandering across the wet sand looking for shellfish. Henry crawled around my legs, burrowing into the softness of the grainy sand. Sometimes he stood up unsteadily on his fat little legs, then sat down abruptly on his round bottom. He is too lazy to walk yet, though he is nearly a year old. Perhaps he thinks he need not bother, with so many friends willing to carry him about.

Wherever we go, we always have a constant company of children fascinated with our Henry. They crowd around, always watching everything he does: admiring, laughing, cuddling him, taking him for little walks. Often they present him with a vivid flower or a shell for his pleasure, or sing him little songs. The children are charming and gay, their young naked bodies shiny with water as they run in and out of the sea. Tonga is a place where children

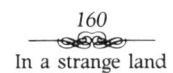
are cherished and treasured, so that every child seems to be secure in the knowledge that he or she belongs to a family of limitless 'mothers' and 'fathers', aunts, uncles and cousins, with endless arms to comfort, numberless houses to shelter and many cooking fires to provide food. Our Henry is a novelty, with his fair skin and fine brown hair, the only white child in these islands (though they say that Singleton has some children running around wild on one of the other islands). He is getting a share of the love these people give to their own precious children.

Chief Fatu has a baby son called Tungi, who is only a few months older than Henry. Today the chief's wife and I sat together on the sand, with Henry and Tungi tumbling over our knees and shouting for the right to the same banana. The chief has taken a special interest in Henry and calls him by the Tongan name, Tupou. He has even said that one of the many little islands in the bay belongs to Henry.

On the beach today, we found a shell of great beauty – delicate marking spiralling into a secret interior where a sea creature has been living. The children were showing it to Henry and, when he tired of it, they threw it aside and I picked it up. There was still the grittiness of wet sand on it and the smell of salt but, when I held it up to the light, the sun glowed through the thin curve of outer shell against the clear blue of wide sky. Shells like this lie tidily on parlour shelves in Sydney, torn from their place, robbed of sand and salt and reduced to mere curios, things to be dusted. Will it be possible to take a day like today – of blue and gold and carefree children – and carry the idea of it to Sydney whole, not losing its glow and its saltiness?

Coke Vernal, Mu'a, Tongatapu: October 30, 1822

The bay before us spreads wide, empty of sail. Early this morning the *St Michael* still rode easily at anchor, a visible link with the world and a means of escape. Escape? Why do I even think that word – I didn't mean it, surely. Now the ship has gone, not just for a few weeks of trading but back to Sydney.

With the ship have gone my letters to my family, and Walter's diaries and letters to his parents. In my letter to Thomas I used the new name for our mission place, 'Coke Vernal'. Walter and Samuel Leigh each had instructions from London that they must use the name of the founder of Wesleyan Missions, Dr Coke, and the name of the founder of Wesleyan Methodism, the Rev. John Wesley, respectively in their names for their missions. Mr Leigh had thought of using 'Wesleydale'. Walter said that 'Coke' was not at all a pretty word for such a place as Mu'a (he said it reminded him of sooty blackness, even though Dr Coke himself was a much respected man), so he softened it by adding 'Vernal' in honour of the freshness and beauty of this place.

I wrote to Thomas about the difficulties of our relationship with Captain and Mrs Beveridge and that 'that poisonous stuff Rum is his friend'. I added: 'This my dear brother I mention not as evil speaking – indeed it gives me pain so to speak of one who we hoped so much better of – and had it not been for this I sincerely think I should have returned to the colony, to have seen you all once more and take a more affectionate leave of my dear friends; however I trust all things will work together for the best...'

With Thomas I felt I had to be honest. I wrote: 'I like this place and the people much but O! my dear brother I have left you all to be a stranger in a strange land with not one female who can speak to, or understand me, no public means of grace, nay, I can no longer walk to the house of God with my dear friends and sweetly enjoy their conversation from time to time. I feel I should not dwell on these things lest I should repine and so rebel against my God, who is ten thousand times better to us that we deserve and very far better than we expected.'

I described our new home in detail, mentioning something which I would dearly love to know the truth of: 'I seem to think my dear that you are married; if you are, the Lord bless you and yours...'; and asked him to pack up some more plants and seeds for us to try to grow here in Tonga: '. . . we might try the hop plant, to bitter our beer.' I have been collecting some Tongan seeds and plants with their Tongan names to send to Sydney, but had to explain that it wasn't really the right time for collecting seeds. I remember all through my growing-up years how Mr Marsden was always collecting Australian native seeds to send to England and now I am doing the same. The whole tone of the letter suggested that I intended to stay in Tonga at least long enough to make it worth Thomas sending plants in another six months' time.

As well as all our letters and journals, the *St Michael* also took with it two Tongan men to visit Sydney and come back when the *St Michael* returned for us. One was the son of the chief, Futukava and the other, Tata, was a priest of their religion. Both are big and impressive men — I think they will make an interesting impression in Sydney. Walter has advised them to wear their own Tongan dress while in Sydney; they will look very handsome in it. In any case, I doubt whether they would find it easy to find trousers and shirts to fit them! The Maori boy, Manihera, has chosen to stay with us for the time being because he clings very much to Walter, but I expect we will take him with us to Sydney when we go home.

Before I went to sleep last night, Walter and I talked late. 'Are you *sure* that you want to stay, Mary?' Walter asked. He looked at me, willing me to meet his eyes and speak the truth. 'Are you quite sure you want to be here in Tonga and not safely back in Parramatta? There would be no shame in you sailing with the *St Michael*, even if I stay here.'

'I'm staying. You know I want to be here with you, Walter. I don't think I could bear going back with the Beveridges without you there. But I'm not trying to be heroic,' I assured him. 'It is just that I feel that everything will be well with us.'

Together we listed our reasons for staying. 'The people are so friendly and welcoming; the country is rich and fertile so that we can hardly starve to death; there have been no wars here for several years, they say, so it is a perfect time to come to introduce the gospel; George and Charles are such excellent young men and both are very keen to go on with what they have begun; the *St Michael* will be back in less than six months in any case; we are both thoroughly sick of sea travel and are happy to settle.'

'Sometimes,' Walter added, 'I'm afraid that I try to plan my life around what *I* want to do, and hope that that is God's will for me. This time I'm not afraid, because our decision to come here was certainly not what I wanted to do for selfish reasons, yet I'm certain that this is where God wants me to be.'

'And I want to be where you are – that is God's will for me.'

Even as I curled up on our bed beside Henry, Walter's shadow was thrown huge up the wall as he sat over his coconut oil lamp to write a final letter to send to Thomas. He wanted to explain why we were staying; probably my mother will be horrified if I don't go back with the ship, but I really want to stay.

That was last night. Now, this evening, the *St Michael* has sailed for Sydney and beyond the reef the horizon looks very empty indeed.

Longing for home

Mu'a, Tongatapu: December 1, 1822

Since the *St Michael* sailed, it has been almost as if we were all waiting for something to happen. Perhaps the general calm and acceptance of our presence seemed too easy, too good to be true, and without realising it we were waiting, listening, expecting trouble... When it came, I think Walter was almost relieved. Perhaps he thought that any mission that was not under attack by Satan must be so feeble and useless as to offer no threat to the powers of darkness. At any rate, he wrote in his diary: 'I have wondered that the old lion has not roared before. There is now some hope of our mission prospering.'

People are talking about dreams again and this time the dreams are not in our favour. A few days ago, Walter was with the men sitting at the *kava* ring, listening with the help of Singleton to the many speeches. One old man said that we were spies from England and that soon a large English force will arrive to take their islands from them. He told them that our prayers are magical formulas, speaking to our ancestors, just like the missionaries who were here in Mr Shelley's day.

'What happened then?' he demanded. 'Wars broke out, the old chiefs died and epidemics of disease killed the people – and that will happen again!'

Another chief told of a dream in which the ancestors had warned him about us and said, 'The white *papalangi* will

pray you all dead.' And the men in the *kava* ring believed it all.

When Walter came home with Singleton, they talked about it. It was as if history were repeating itself, an old story retold: the same misunderstandings, the same confusions, the same accusations which destroyed the beginnings of the London Missionary Society work here are rising up to trouble us, too. This is just like the story which Singleton's shipmate, William Mariner, wrote after he escaped from Tonga, had published and which Walter had read to me. Suddenly, not all the faces around us are smiling.

Then yesterday some of the Tongans had an argument with George and Macanoe as they worked with the pitsaw. They attacked our men and ran off with the saw. When Walter and Singleton tried to reason with them, they made such threatening signs to each other that our men decided to leave the matter before more damage was done. Chief Fatu is away from home, so we can't appeal to him. Not everyone behaves like that to us, of course, but it is not pleasant to think that some people dislike our presence so much.

Today, the Lord's day, Walter preached on 'We walk by faith and not by sight', and we clung to the promises of God. It is only a month since the *St Michael* sailed, but it seems much longer. We are all struggling with the strangeness of the language, being irritated by continual petty thefts, never free of onlookers, watching with little hope for a passing ship which just might carry news from home, facing daily hindrances in the practical work of building a better house. None of these things are so very big in themselves but, when they are put together, they begin to make life more difficult and less delightful than we first thought.

Other little things have been bothering us, too. Dogs killed our sheep and in this heat the meat only lasted about one day, so most of it was wasted. The house we live in, though light and airy and not really hard to keep clean, is very exposed to the public eye. Also its thatch and woven walls are a home for many cockroaches, fleas, beetles, centipedes, rats and lizards. Walter soon changed from his original view that this house was rather romantic and charming to deciding that 'our house is far inferior to the worst in which my father's bullocks lie.'

There is no escape, of course, from the flies and mosquitoes which are always with us. None of these problems are big – I know that – but they begin to annoy and undermine us all. Perhaps Satan works more effectively with a missionary by attacking with many mosquito bites than with a cannibal club.

Mu'a, Tongatapu: December 12, 1822

It was hard to believe that today was my birthday. Today I am twenty-three years old. I remember happy birthdays in my mother's house, with my brothers and sisters and friends, and I miss them so much. Quite soon, the *St Michael* should be arriving back in Port Jackson and my family will be expecting me to be on it – and I'm not. What will Mother think? She'll be thinking about my birthday, too, but I won't be there. I've never been away from my family on my birthday before and Walter noted in his journal which he is keeping for his parents: 'Mrs L. has been indulging in the luxury of tears while reflecting on her mother's house and family friends.'

This morning, birthday or not, I got up at first light and began my washing before the day grew too hot for such work. When I came back into the house to start lighting the fire for our breakfast tea and yams, I found Walter sitting up in bed in what he calls 'our hole of a bedroom' with his letter to his parents on his knees and a most offended look on his face. Several Tongans were there watching him in bed, casually suggesting that they had just called in to see what was to be seen. Walter was really cross!

'They'd have pushed their way in here just the same if you had still been in bed with me – can we have no privacy at all?' At least they were perfectly friendly and we are no longer under fear of attack. Fatu has come home and, when Walter told him about our problems with some people, he threatened to club the culprits to death. He would have done it, too, but fortunately they escaped to the place of refuge and have now been banished from this part of the island.

Later in the day, some men brought in the unexpected joy of a letter from the chief officer of a passing whaler. He was a man we have never met, he had no news to tell us as he has been at sea longer than we have been here, but it was a *letter* – a communication in English to reassure us that the rest of the world still exists. I do miss the pleasure of sending and receiving letters, and Walter misses his newspaper badly. He reads and rereads his collection of books as his way of retreating from Tonga, but he feels out of touch with contemporary news.

Perhaps the same whaler which sent us the letter also lost the whale which was beached last week. Walter and Charles took me and small Henry with them in the boat and we went to see it. For me it was like a special birthday outing as we set off early to explore a new part of the island, big Charles as usual carrying me out to the boat through the shallows. We went right out of the big lagoon, out past the place where there is good anchorage, and rowed for fifteen miles inside the reef that fringes the island. Henry sat on my lap and I held a parasol over us both to protect us from the sun as we floated over the transparent green of the reef waters. Below us in the shallow water was another world of extraordinary beauty: corals of all shapes and colours and textures, delicate branches, waving tendrils, engraved mounds, lacework in ivory, purples, pink and peach, red and yellow. Darting and flickering in and out, brilliant fish moved among the foliage of the coral forest with metallic greens and crimson or banded with stripes, trailing shadows over the patches of white sand between rock and living coral. If only one could paint it.

As we moved along, we began to notice the clarity of the water being fouled with oil and, long before we saw it, we could smell a strong odour. 'That is the whale!' said

Walter. We came at last to a great crowd of Tongans, excitedly appreciating the vast whale which had beached itself on their shores, a huge thing of perhaps eighty feet
without the tail and ten or fifteen feet through the middle.
Walter thought its oil would have fetched six or seven
hundred pounds in London. The Tongans were thanking
their gods for such a generous gift and will eat every bit of
it.

It will be Henry's first birthday in another two days. He
is a lovely fat child, still with only four teeth and not yet
walking. Walter insists that he is trying to talk, but I think
he knows he can get what he wants without language. Will
he speak Tongan or English first, I wonder? He is such a
heavy child for me to carry that kind Charles is making
him a little carriage at his blacksmith's shop. I think the
Tongans are quite surprised. It is easy to forget that they
are not used to things with wheels.

Mu'a, Tongatapu: Christmas Day, 1822

What a very strange Christmas. I think I understand now
the real meaning of the word 'homesickness'.

Until Christmas, I had thought that Sundays were the
worst. That was the time when great waves of homesickness rolled over me, threatening to drown me. If we were
home in New South Wales, Sunday would be full of lovely
things. Walter would be leading us in worship in the
chapel in Parramatta, crowded with our friends, all of us
in our best clothes in honour of the day, singing songs of
praise to God at the tops of our voices. I would be teaching
the children in my Sunday School class, telling them the
wonderful stories of the Bible. Or our whole family might
go to St John's for a service with the Rev. Samuel Marsden
or one of the other clergy. In the evening we would gather
again to praise and sing and pray, crowds of us encouraging each other, praying for each other, talking with each
other about the messages from God we had each received
through the reading of scripture or the preaching. Or
perhaps Walter may have set off early to ride to three or

four services in the country while I stayed with our Parramatta people and the thoughtful preaching of one of our laymen, going back to my mother's house with my sisters and brothers for a bountiful Sunday lunch.

If we were home...

We are not home. Here Sunday means nothing at all to the Tongans. The markers of their lives are the cycles of the moon, the tides and seasons, not weeks of seven days. They go on with their lives as if there were nothing at all special about the sabbath and even come demanding for me to barter for their vegetables when I am trying to make it a special day for God. None of them want to worship with us. Even Singleton prefers to find something else to do. Poor Walter would love to be able to preach to them and he tries so hard, but the limits of the language he has learned tie his tongue in knots. The Tongans have said to him, 'Your religion is good for you, and ours is good for us,' so he becomes more and more discouraged in trying to communicate. They are not interested and he hasn't enough language.

So the only ones he can preach to are us. Even though Walter prepares very careful, good messages for our little group from scripture, sometimes I feel rebellious and don't want to listen. Though I feel desperate to hear God's voice, he seems as remote as Sydney. We try to sing, but our voices sound so thin when we sing some of Walter's favourite Wesleyan hymns. How can we do justice to 'O for a thousand tongues to sing my great Redeemer's praise' or 'Love Divine, all loves excelling' with six voices of mixed quality?

It sounds embarrassingly silly to even think it, but I miss the chance to dress up. How can I dress in my Sunday-best to walk from our bedroom through the curtain into the open middle area of our house where we cook and eat, wash and iron – and worship? Even our prayer times feel difficult and strained, because we are conscious of people observing us over the wall who suspect that we will 'pray them all dead'.

Years ago, I remember Mr Marsden pointing out a solitary dead tree on a hillside of his 'Mamre' property west of Sydney. He said at the time: 'That dead tree reminds me of some of the missionaries. It used to be surrounded by timber and was tall and healthy – then I cleared the rest of the timber away and that healthy tree was exposed to wind and weather. It couldn't survive the lack of support, the isolation.'

All the feelings of separation from everything that is familiar which I have felt on Sundays have been even worse during the Christmas season. Almost *nothing* has been like a real Christmas and only our reckoning of the calendar tells us that this sacred time has come.

For Walter, the extreme heat worries him. He says it can't really be Christmas if he is melting away in the heat. (Of course, a hot summer Christmas Day is perfectly natural to someone who was born in Parramatta.) When he tries to write in his journal, his hand sticks damply to the paper and he has been complaining that his work on learning the language has been almost impossible in the heat. When his heavy British cloth trousers began to wear out, I cut up one of my cotton gowns and made him a pair of light trousers. He had been threatening to wear nothing but a shirt, but the thin trousers keep him cooler and at least decent!

For all of us, Christmas in the past has meant special food. Here I did my best, but I missed being able to go to the stores to buy raisins and cinnamon, apples and oranges, suet for the pudding and herbs for the stuffing. We certainly didn't go hungry, because we always have plenty of pork and Walter has been buying up many local birds for our new poultry yard: ducks, geese and hens. There were plenty of fine vegetables, coconut cream for our chicken, greens and good seafood. I used some of our stock of flour and sugar to make a cake. There were tropical fruits, too: pineapple, banana and pawpaw, but Walter says he would give up all the tropical fruit of Tonga for one good apple. (Poor Walter has always had a rather ticklish digestion and finds the steady diet of pork, taro, yams and breadfruit rather hard on his system.) We even drank some of our tiny store of coffee with our Christmas meal to-day. But we all remembered our families together around tables loaded with turkey, white potatoes, mince pies and Christmas puddings stiff with dried fruit soaked in brandy.

But it is not just the food that we miss. We miss being able to buy little gifts for each other. We miss being able to visit and be visited by our dear families on Christmas Day. We miss the joy of greeting all our dear friends as we join in Christmas services of worship. We miss the carol singers and the special songs of Christmas in church. We miss the crowded church full of people. Today, our Tongan neighbours were very excited about some sorcery which has been threatened by enemies and had not the least interest in the Child, the Christ of God. Three days ago, on Sunday evening, we had a lovely service of the Lord's Supper after the evening preaching. It meant a great deal to me, perhaps the most precious part of a Christmas season which seems to have been deprived.

Yesterday, on Christmas Eve, Walter and I went for a walk along the beach with George, Charles and Macanoe in the early evening. The heat was oppressive, but a bank of thunder clouds had built up and, as we walked, the rain started to pour.

'We might as well have our swim – we are wet anyway,' the men said and, stripping off their things, they ran into the water and swam a long way out. I stood under the trees, watching their heads bobbing around and hoping there were neither sharks nor stinging bluebottles out there – they have had trouble with both in the past. The rain streamed down over me, glueing my gown to my body in an almost indecent way and turning Walter's little pile of shirt and trousers, shoes and hat into a sodden bundle. I thought at least his clothes will be cool to walk home in. And I thought about home on Christmas Eve: of my mother preparing the stuffing for the birds for tomorrow, of Eliza and Susannah and Anne giggling over the gifts they are hiding for each other, of Walter's description of carol singers coming through Cornish snow to sing for his family beside blazing fires, of Australian carol singers coming to our house in the warm summer twilight – and I felt sick for home.

And, although I haven't told Walter yet, I felt a bit sick anyway. I am almost sure that I am going to have another baby and I am afraid to have it here in Tonga.

Mu'a, Tongatapu: January, 1823

It is my complete helplessness that hurts so much. I have been sitting by little Henry, holding his hand and gently brushing the damp wisps of hair off his forehead. It is too hot and sticky to cuddle him – it is much easier for him to lie on a sheet in the shade than to suffer the clamminess of my arms. His eyes are oozing with a nasty infection and his poor little bottom is raw from scalding stomach upsets. He has been crying, poor little lad, a sad fretful weeping, throwing his feverish head from side to side as if trying to escape from a pain. Is his head aching? Has he caught malaria? Is his illness some terrible tropical disease, or just the misery of infant teething? I don't even know what is wrong. Even if I knew, I wouldn't know how to help my son, nor do any of us know.

Walter is expressing his anxiety by being angry: not angry with me or the others, but angry with himself. 'I'm a fool, a thoughtless, stupid fool! What did I expect?' he mutters. 'Did I think we would all be kept safe from accident or disease without taking any precautions at all? We need a doctor – or at least someone who knows something about medicine. What use is our little box of potions and bandages when we don't even know how to use them properly? What good are they, even if they impress the Tongans as good magic? It was too late to write asking for a surgeon after we had arrived here. I'm such a fool...' and he marches off along the beach, kicking up bursts of sand.

There is a lump of misery knotting itself somewhere under my ribs: a tight ball of tension and fear, of unshed tears and sheer homesickness. If only I could ask Mother what to do to help Henry — she has raised nine children and would know how to ease him. If only I could ask Eliza or Susannah to sit with him for a little so that I could rest. If only I could send Walter off on his horse to call Dr Balmain, Dr Bland or even old Dr Mileham.

It isn't only Henry who needs help, either. On the day after Christmas, both Macanoe and Charles became very ill and were ill for many days, though none of us knew what was the matter with them. Poor old Thomas has been suffering from a nasty crop of boils and skin infections which is making him very miserable. For a few months, Macanoe has not been really well and has been coughing a lot and losing weight. Recently he began vomiting blood and Walter says he is ill with consumption, poor lad. He probably won't live long, I fear. Walter himself has been suffering from very severe headaches. Sometimes in the afternoons we spread a woven mat out under a shady tree by the water and Walter and I take Henry down where we can all catch some cooling breezes off the water. Walter always takes a book with him, intending to read, but his headaches have been so bad that often he finds it easier to lie down and let me fan him gently to sleep.

I've not been feeling very well myself with early pregnancy, but that is just normal woman's trouble. The troubles which have been disturbing me have been more the problems of my heart and mind. At New Year our little group held a Love Feast, a time of sharing our spiritual needs, and I feel that it helped me a lot to talk to the others about how I was feeling. I discovered that I wasn't the only one who was struggling. They all admitted to being greatly shaken by our experiences here. We spent a lot of time praying for each other — I'm so thankful that our party is so loving and supportive, not at all like the agonies of our New Zealand friends. After the Love Feast, Walter wrote in his diary: 'My dear Mrs Lawry appeared to have been

passing through deep waters, arising out of her outward exposure, privations and solitude. But this evening the Lord lifted her up.'

More serious than that has been the problem that several of us have had bad attacks of influenza lately and, when some Tongans caught it, they blamed us. Now some elderly Tongans are very ill with it and people are saying: 'You see? They have come to destroy us!' Now our lives may be in danger. Walter wrote in his diary: 'It has recently been proposed, as a remedy for the complaint, to murder us and share out our property. God says, "Fear not, ye are of more value than many sparrows..." These savages are not so much in love with us as with our property. They are not to be restrained within bounds while we retain so many good things, of which they know they can possess themselves if they use their power.'

But for now I sit by my own sick child, watching his face and feeling the tense lump of anxiety which hasn't been unknotted in me for weeks. Charles tried to cheer me up by pointing out that the Tongans have no doctors, yet most of them seem to grow to healthy and magnificent manhood. That is all very well for them – I find I don't really care how an anonymous crowd of strangers copes. But, dear God, this tear-stained little one is my child, my Henry, and I don't know how to help him.

Mu'a, Tongatapu: February 15, 1823

When first I told him, Walter didn't understand.

'I'm bleeding,' I said, my voice quiet and toneless. He wasn't quite awake and mumbled some vague questions: Had I cut myself? Had I been scratching mosquito bites again?

It was no use getting excited and upsetting him. He already had more than enough to worry him and there was nothing at all we could do about it. But I knew that I was losing the baby I carried. Even before it was daylight today I had been lying awake, staring into the dark and knowing that something was wrong. Walter was sound asleep, even snoring a little, somehow remote from me as I faced the loss of the child. On the other side of me, Henry lay quietly, so much better now, thank God, and with several fine new teeth. Outside our room, with its walls open to the sky, I could hear the gentle swish, swish of coconut fronds rubbing in the wind and the occasional thud of a falling coconut. In the woven walls a lizard or perhaps a rat was rustling, the normal sounds of the night. As the sky lightened enough for me to see, I put my hand under my nightshift and drew it out, sticky and red. Yes, it was true, the thing I had known. I was miscarrying the baby.

Yesterday was so hot and I worked so hard. Perhaps that is why this is happening. I had a big pile of dirty washing: Henry's things, the clothing of all the men, my own things and the household linen. Even early in the morning the heat was intense. I struggled to fill the heavy buckets with water from the spring and carry them, brimming and splashing, into the shade of the house. I scrubbed and rubbed, watching our precious stock of soap melting away, dragged heavily water-logged sheets out to twist and wring them till my hands were raw, then stood in the sun to hang the things out to dry. In the afternoon I heated my flatirons on the fire and stood for several hours, with perspiration dripping saltily into my eyes as I ironed Walter's shirts and my gowns.

Walter is sometimes very cross that the Tongans rarely help me with laundry, though several young people are becoming very good friends and are very willing to help me with cooking. The Tongans keep their bodies beautifully clean, often bathing twice a day, but their own *tapa* cloth or matting garments are not washable and so they probably see no point in washing our things, either. Of course, I don't think it would occur to Walter that he could help by carrying the water tubs himself, or even help me at the end as I was straining to tip the great wash tubs to drain away the dirty water. He was absorbed in his books, in language study, in conversations with the people, in men's work.

As I lay there this morning, I thought of poor Lydia Mans-

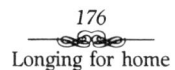
field in Sydney. The poor girl has had one miscarriage after
another and spends months lying down, resting. I don't
want to be like that – I've always been so strong and I want
to be able to do things.

A very wicked thought was going through my mind as I
lay there this morning. It was not just because I didn't
want to distress Walter that I was accepting a miscarriage
so quietly. I'm ashamed even to think it and I couldn't tell
Walter, but I was secretly relieved. Ever since I knew I was
pregnant, I have been afraid of giving birth here in Tonga.
Who could help me? What if I had another difficult labour
like the first one? No, a miscarriage at three months isn't
such a terrible thing, perhaps. Even so, when Walter at last
understood what I was saying and tried to help me in my
need, he had to use his handkerchief (clean and ironed, of
course) to wipe away my tears.

Mu'a, Tongatapu: March, 1823

I have come to a surprising conclusion about missionaries.
I think it may be easier for a woman to be a missionary
than for a man.

In the months since we came here, Walter has become
more and more discouraged and depressed while, despite
the many times I have been troubled or miserable, Walter
could write quite truly in a letter to his parents: 'Both Mrs
Lawry and little Henry seem to glide through it, dreary and
solitary as it is, much better than I can presume to do.'

Many times in his long letter to his parents (now sent off
on the ship *Kent* which called briefly in January) and in his
diary he has written of the struggles he has been experiencing. He has written such things as: 'I have felt sorely tried
during my residence in Tonga. No tongue can express the
sorrow which my soul has passed through in this dreary,
comfortless land . . .'; 'my heart is overwhelmed with per-
plexity and sickness at the sight of insurmountable difficulties'; 'I seem to have done nothing for the conversion of the
heathen . . . I look up and the dark cloud impedes me'; 'it
is peculiarly trying to live among the heathen without being

able to speak with them about concerns of the soul'; 'I feel just able to walk by faith, but have no strength to spare for those who lack. My mind is much drawn out in prayer and, though often violently attacked by Satan, it is generally resigned to the will of God. I verily believe that I am one of the most unworthy and useless missionaries that the great Head of the Church ever chose to honour with so many opportunities for glorifying him.'

Walter talks and writes often about death, his own probable death in these islands and says he would be quite happy to go: 'nevertheless I feel inexpressibly grateful to the Lord for giving me a beloved wife, every way just such as I require for a helpmate, and a darling boy, and numerous friends whom I should be glad to see . . .' He often says that even if he lives, he doesn't expect to stay more than three years here at the most and then pass the work on to others.

Why is he finding it so difficult? Why do I 'glide' through it more easily? It seems to me that each of us, and this includes Charles, George and Thomas, has had a place and a work in society in New South Wales and in that work we knew what was expected of us and who we were. For me, I am able to come to Tonga and bring my work, the shape of my days, with me almost unaltered. The bundle may have been rearranged, a little lumpy in places, but the same elements are still there. I am still a wife to love and care for my husband, a mother to cherish and nurture my child, a housewife to create a loving home with good food and clean clothes for the people I love. I am still Mary Cover Lawry of Parramatta, even though I live in a foreign and alien environment. With my efforts of sweeping and cleaning, cooking and sewing, gardening and arranging fresh flowers, I am creating a protective shell around me and mine, my way of saying: 'In this tiny area, it is all right to be ourselves as we have been, to speak our language, to eat our food, to wear our clothes. In this small space we need not strain to be anything but ourselves.'

For Walter, it is much more difficult. In a way, his work

as a minister in the known and understood way has disintegrated. The high point of his week, preaching in his own language to a number of congregations and knowing that it was being used by God, has dwindled to preaching to the five of us. There are no Christian homes to visit, no committees to attend, no Class Meetings, no Bible study groups, no Sunday School children, no convicts to pastor, no church building funds to raise. He can't preach because he doesn't yet know enough language (and Singleton has been becoming more and more distant from us and unwilling to help interpret spiritual things). He can supervise the building of our house, but Charles and George know more about that than he does and only need encouragement. In any case, the house is nearly ready for us to move in.

Walter tries to spend a lot of time with the people, learning their ways and trying to communicate something of the gospel to them, but the people don't want to hear and often ignore him. Day after day there are clashes between Walter and the people. They see things one way and insist 'This is our custom', while Walter feels strongly that their way is wrong and tries to tell them so. He can't teach a school until the supplies come. When we first came, we didn't bring school books or equipment because we were not even sure whether it would be safe to stay here at all. Though he sent a request for all the things needed for a school, he must wait for them till the *St Michael* returns. That will surely be very soon and then he will be free to start his schools.

When the time comes, I will be teaching in the new schools, too, and I look forward to that. Our instructions from the London Committee say, among other things, that we are to erect a school building and that 'the brethren and their wives are directly to adopt such methods of instruction as they may, on mutual consultation, judge most suitable, and that they themselves act as teachers'. Walter will probably teach the older children to read and write. Maybe he will hope to introduce them to things like his favourite geography, though I don't suppose Latin or Greek would be very useful, and I'll enjoy working with the little ones as I have done in Sydney.

Because so many of the tasks which he used to do are no longer available to him, Walter spends a lot of time studying his Bible and other books and at prayer. He says that he has felt a real growth of his own spirituality and closeness to God, far greater than was possible in the busy rush of life in New South Wales. This is very good, but he still feels that he should be *doing* something, which the London Committee would approve as a sufficiently spiritual activity for a missionary. Even though he spends a lot of time with the people, listening to and learning their language and becoming familiar with their customs, it doesn't seem to him to be real work, and I think poor Walter feels that he has almost stopped being a real missionary.

Even learning the language seems to be a bit easier for me. Not, of course, that I am cleverer. But while Walter sits with lists of words, trying to unlock the key to how the language works and how to spell it, I just chat to people. Some lovely young Tongans come to our house often – a fine young man called Tama Nau, another called Malungahu and a beautiful chief's daughter whom we have been calling Eliza Ann – and, as we hear them talk to each other and to Henry, I listen and try to mimic them. We say very simple things – about cooking, the baby or the weather – and it is getting easier and easier to recognise and understand the words. I don't attempt to discover how to spell them properly, but enjoy talking to my young friends, even if they laugh at the odd way I use their flowing language.

Walter, of course, must take the language much more seriously and learn to say everything correctly, as well as finding the words for ideas about religion, which is much harder than chatting about fishing or pigs. He says he keeps finding out the meaning of rude words, which is no help at all! And, although Walter says we can't trust *my* spelling, I have almost convinced him that he should be spelling the name of our friendly chief 'Fatu' or maybe

'Parlu', 'Falu' or even 'Paloo', instead of 'Palau' as he has been doing. I suppose he knows best.

Learning about the customs of the people is even a little easier in some ways for me. When I have finished my housework, I often put Henry in his little carriage and push him around the two villages here at Mu'a: Tatakamotonga and Labaha. We visit the old tree where the people say Captain Cook sat when he visited here many years ago. We go up and down among the enclosures, visiting people, watching women collect shellfish in the wet sand, sitting on the grass with the women and watching the flicker of clever fingers as they weave beautiful patterned mats with the finest of narrow strips of cream or brown-dyed pandanus leaves, the loose ends curling and twirling over their busy hands. Henry loves to sit beside the line of women as they beat out a steady rhythm with their mallets, beating the bark of the paper-bark mulberry tree into sheets of soft cloth. The women laugh and gently move him away from their work when they have spread great long carpets of their *tapa* cloth along the grass to paint on the traditional decorations, in case he should smudge their work or knock over their little containers of vegetable dyes. We watch and enjoy the very skilful and ornamental work of the women. I learn how important Tongan women are in their society: how much influence the senior women have over their people and how the most important women will often be the most gifted artists because they don't have to spend so much time in their gardens. I can wander around and enjoy the people, teaching them some of my own skills of sewing, but Walter doesn't feel he has that freedom because he should be 'working'.

Mu'a, Tongatapu: May, 1823

Walking along the beach at low tide today, a set of tiny footprints in the sand frightened me. Our beautiful Henry, now eighteen months old and walking well, had walked beside me, clinging to my finger as he ploughed along in the sand which sank a little under his feet with every step he took. We walked slowly, gently, my eyes watching the horizon as always, hoping to see the longed-for sail of the *St Michael,* and then turned back towards home. It was then that the line of tiny footprints overwhelmed me.

Where are we leading those trusting vulnerable feet? I thought. He has had no choice in coming here; he is here because we brought him. The new child I am carrying, to be born in November, has had even less choice. Have we done a terrible thing to them?

Could Henry be killed in a tribal battle? No, I don't think so. The people here love children too much to hurt them. But *we* could be killed. We know that the people still sometimes discuss whether they would do better to kill us now and take our things or wait till the *St Michael* comes back when they will get still more. Sometimes the people are very cross with us, specially when Walter tries to argue with them over things like hacking off a child's finger joint as a sacrifice, or refuses to give gifts which they say are their custom. We know that former missionaries here were killed. Even in the last few months a chief from 'Eua boasted in front of us of pretending friendship to men who had gone ashore for water, from a whaler. After several weeks of generosity, he had had them thrown over the steep cliffs of 'Eua into the surf.

Walter wrote recently of signs of insult, violence and theft 'leaving us with the graves of our predecessors before our eyes, to conjecture how these things will end'. Though many of our neighbours here at Mu'a have become good friends, we hear rumours of an invasion of tribal groups from the northern Ha'apai group of islands. They would have no hesitation in attacking us while they attacked our protectors. Recently I have learned that I am not the first white woman to live on Tongatapu. Some twenty years ago, the crew of a passing ship was killed and a white woman who had been on board was taken as an extra wife for a chief, till she escaped on another ship two years later. The thought of that happening appalls me!

Could Henry or the new child suffer from illness? Cer-

tainly, he could catch any of their diseases and we have no medical knowledge to help them. Even now, though very healthy at the moment, Henry has a badly sunburned nose and often suffers from infected bites or prickly heat. (The weather has become much cooler now and we are all thankful.)

But it is not physical harm to his fat little body which I fear. It is damage to his mind, his personality, his spirit.

What if we stay here for years? What if the *St Michael* never comes back and we wait and wait? Will Henry be confused about his identity if he stays here a long time? Will he feel that he is Tongan and be miserable in New South Wales? Will he become so accustomed to Tongan culture that he will take all their values as his own, good and bad? Will he listen to so many stories about ghosts and evil spirits, sorcery and magic that he will wake up in the night with nightmares as I know other missionaries' children have done? Sorcerers and soothsayers are so much part of Tongan life, and often their magic and their predictions so convincing, that any child would be easily impressed by their power. Neither Walter nor I can think of any easy explanations for some of the strange stories of supernatural power and knowledge we have heard. Or will he grow up to feel that he has been deprived of his true heritage as a child in a comfortable, secure home in New South Wales or Cornwall, and come to hate his parents' God, who made them bring him to such a pagan place?

I used to be very shocked by Sarah Henry and her wild brothers, and by some of the stories I heard of wicked behaviour of some other missionaries' children in Tahiti. I thought that their parents must have been very careless in their upbringing and ought never to have let it happen. But I am learning that it is not as simple as that.

They, and we, have brought our children to a foreign place because we truly believe that God has called us to bring the gospel here. Our children are surrounded by people of another race, another language, another way of seeing things. Much of it is beautiful. Our Henry is almost

swamped with love and affection from the people. He is
perfectly happy now, enjoying a wonderful babyhood
where he is free to wander from family to family, from
friend to friend, cared for by each one. He grows fatter and
fatter because everyone gives him food and he always
seems to have a banana or a chunk of pineapple or some
cooked yam clutched in his sticky little fist. He is learning
to say 'Mama' and 'No!' in English and responds to 'Come
to me' and 'Don't do that' in Tongan; he will probably
learn to speak both languages well. He likes to be free of
clothes, like the young Tongans, and in this climate who
can blame him? His dearest friends are our missionary
party, Chief Fatu and some of the Tongan women and children, specially the small, lively Tungi. If he stays here till
he is older, it will be much easier for him to learn fishing
and sailing than to have an education in books. He will
probably learn to accept the slower tropical pace of life as
the best, rather than forcing himself to work long hours –
and who could expect anything else? As his father has said:
'The people are not really lazy. Why should they tire themselves out in a hot climate to make or buy things for which
they have no use?'

So what can I do for my child? How can I let him appreciate all that is good and beautiful about the Tongan way of
life, but protect him from its dangers? Perhaps the only
thing I can do is to keep on praying the prayer I have
prayed for a long time, that our Lord will build a wall of
safety around our son, protecting him from anything that
could damage his personality and his spirit.

Mu'a, Tongatapu: May 27, 1823
The skyline where the open ocean blends into the blue distance is as empty as ever. When will the *St Michael* come?
Ever since October, when it sailed, Walter has been doing
calculations to see when we might expect to see it back
again.

'If they have a good voyage straight to Port Jackson,' he
said, 'they should be there by the middle of December –

a month to buy our school supplies and stocks of provisions, maybe find a surgeon and a printer as we requested, and teachers – then back here again. Perhaps by the end of February we could see them back here...'

All through January and February the men worked particularly hard trying to complete the new house because we were hoping for more staff and wanted to be ready to welcome them. But the house is finished and we have moved in (without Singleton, who chose to leave us and stay with his 'wife') and there is no sign of the ship. Earlier this month a ship passed by the far end of the island and sent messages for us to say that we should not expect the *St Michael* for at least another two months! There was news from New Zealand from Mr Hall. Mr Leigh *still* hasn't moved to the proposed new Methodist mission station and is said to be a sick man. Also they are expecting new Methodist staff to go to New Zealand with the *St Michael*. There is no news of any help for us.

Walking along a beach recently, I watched the scalloped edge of the water running up the sand with frilled and dimpled texture, white on white. It reminded me of the dainty, whitework embroidery of my bridal undergarments. My things then were so pretty, fresh and crisp with starch, edged with lace and touched with embroidery. Not any more. Piece by piece my things are spoiling, rotted by seawater, stained with sweat. Edges of lace are fraying, torn by undergrowth, rubbed ragged by constant scrubbing. I try so hard to keep our things clean and mended, but we have run right out of soap and my thread is in very short supply. Walter didn't bring a lot of clothes and now is almost completely without shoes or hats. We have been using some of my old clothes in exchange for vegetables or pigs, because many of the women don't mind a shabby dress if they like the colour. Their favourite fabrics are vivid florals, specially with reds and blues, but we have nearly finished the bolts of fabric we brought for trade.

If only they didn't steal from us all the time. We came here with what seemed to be a lot of things to use for trade and for gifts, but in the months that we have been here we have used many of them up. The people become very annoyed with us if we don't give them everything they want. It is so irritating to hang my washing on the line and then, when I come to collect and fold it, to discover that another of Walter's shirts is missing, a gown of mine or a towel. We dare not leave a spade or hammer lying by our own door while we pause for lunch – it won't be there when we go back to take it up again. We will soon have run right out of trade goods at this rate.

In 1820 when Mr Leigh went to England and urged the Wesleyan Methodist Committee to start new work in New Zealand and Tonga, they assured him that it was a financial impossibility for them as they were already in debt for other worldwide mission work. So he asked permission to travel around the manufacturing towns of England, asking for donations of trade goods. He finally arrived back in Sydney with crates of spades and shovels, hammers and chisels, saws, axes, knives, scissors, thousands of fish hooks and even a collection of one hundred wedding rings! These goods were divided between the New Zealand work and us in Tonga and have certainly been a very great help. The Tongans highly value all metal tools and have been happy to trade with us. But now Mr Leigh's fish hooks are beginning to run low and what we haven't used have been stolen. What will we do when they are all gone?

Walter will just have to bear eating only Tongan foods until the *St Michael* comes. We planned our food with three to six months in mind, but we left home eleven months ago and have been in Tonga nine months already. Our sugar ran out several months ago. Though we enjoy the sweetness of sticks of juicy sugar cane or the tropical fruits, it doesn't do much for a cup of tea! My bags of flour were getting staler and staler before they ran out and I had to sift out the weevils before I baked a loaf. The bread tasted stale even while it was still hot from the camp oven. We sometimes dream of the delights of a slice of fresh bread, thick with butter and homemade apricot or straw-

berry jam, of scones with cream, of roast lamb and new potatoes and mint sauce . . .

Most of the time we have been very happy with the young men we brought with us, I'm thankful to say, but the one time I heard Walter really angry with them was as long ago as January when they went across the island to make contact with a passing ship. They came back without asking the captain for help with such things as bread, soap, ale and port wine of which we were already very short.

No, we won't starve while we wait for the ship and it doesn't really matter if we have few clothes. But there still remains the possibility of danger. And I am thinking about November and the new baby. Will the *St Michael* come in time for me to go home and have my baby?

Mu'a, Tongatapu: July 11, 1823

We are still waiting. There has been no word, no sign of a sail for the past two months, though we are weary of watching. We should be thankful that things have been so peaceful here.

This evening Walter came in very happily.

'I have just been having a most interesting time with a group of men,' he said. 'We came from a number of different places: two from Fiji, two from the Navigator Islands, one from Samoa and three Tongans with myself. We were all speaking in Tongan, even me! I found I could understand a lot of what they were saying, which was a great encouragement, and could make myself understood fairly well. We talked about their island homes, their gods and the problems of their places. They seemed to be very interested in what I was saying about our God, the Creator and Lord, though they complained that they couldn't understand all that I was trying to say because of my bad Tongan. They are not like some of the British convicts who are so hardened against the gospel that they are almost impossible to reach — they are very interested in things about power, the supernatural and comparing gods. I really have a lot of hope for the future with these people.'

Later this evening, when he was completing his diary for the day, I saw he had written: 'They seemed glad to be instructed in the truth and joined heartily in lamenting the ignorance of their several countries. For a considerable time I have observed a change for the better among the natives. They are become more kind to us, and promise well to become fine subjects for religious instruction.'

If only we were not in such need of supplies and I were not hoping to return to Sydney for the baby, I think we would be encouraged to stay on here for some years, whether or not the ship came. Over the past two months, things have been much more peaceful around here, though there are rumours of wars coming from the northern islands. The Tongans have had years of small wars, with awful destruction of property and crops and horrible massacres of people as certain chiefs have been struggling to take over religious and civil leadership in the country. They say there used to be one spiritual ruler called the Tu'i Tonga and another civil ruler called the Tu'i Kanokupolu who ruled over the whole of these islands. For a few years these positions have not been filled and there has been a lot of fighting between the chiefs over who is the true ruler.

I think they may be getting sick of the misery and fear of all the fighting, and wish for a more peaceful way. Perhaps they hope that we may be able to bring them the peace they need. At any rate, when Walter complained to two of the chiefs that some of the people had been acting roughly towards us and stealing our things, and that perhaps we would move to another area, they pleaded with us to stay with them.

For whatever reason, the people have been very good to us lately. We have been free to travel widely over the island, Walter in particular, though I have been with him on some very interesting trips. He has been taking note of the location of all the villages and the numbers of people who live there and has worked out that there are three key places to place mission staff when more people arrive to help us; here at Mu'a, in the middle of the island at Pea

and on the far coast at Hihifo. After that, he would like to put missionaries on the island of 'Eua and then on the northern island groups.

Walter has these wonderful visions of many missionaries, lots of churches, many schools with hundreds of school children, thousands of Christian Tongans... At the moment it seems an unlikely dream, because all that there is to show for our time here so far is our little group of missionaries, most of us just helpers, a house, a blacksmith's shop and carpenter's workshop, a good garden and a big poultry yard with some livestock. We have no churches, no schools and certainly no Christians. Still, we are all working hard on the language, earning the trust of the people and trusting God for the future.

A few weeks ago, Henry and I went with Walter on a visit to Hihifo. It was another time of hope for our mission. We took the boat and went outside the bay, following the coast around inside the reef, steering in and out through the coral. Walter thought we might have travelled as much as forty miles, though it is only about twenty miles across the island.

When at last we arrived at the fortress of Hihifo, with its strong fence and protective moat, the chief Ata seemed very pleased to see us come to his place. But, after his first greetings, he ignored us and went on with the more important matters of talking with his people in the *kava* ring. After nearly a whole day out on the water, we were very tired and would have been glad of something to eat and drink and somewhere to sleep. Fortunately, I had packed some cold chicken and yams for us and we were able to find a native house which was available for us to sleep in. We were all so exhausted that we just lay down on the mats after our meal and dropped off to sleep.

It was dark, I don't know how late at night, when we were woken by people arriving with food. The chief had decided, belatedly, to offer some hospitality and a procession of people spread before us three palmfrond baskets of fowl and yam, a large turtle and then twenty more big yams and two pigs! Rather sleepily and very full of food, Walter tried to talk to the people about the gospel and the reason why we had come to these islands, but no-one seemed to understand what he was talking about or care either.

We stayed at Hihifo for two more days before we started off for home again. By the time we were ready to leave, Ata had decided that he was more interested in what Walter had to say. As we were leaving, he said to Walter, 'Make marks to Britain; tell them to send white men to come to live here with me.' Walter has promised to write to the Committee about it and is very encouraged indeed. The chief's wife gave us a huge bale of *ngatu*, their fine *tapa* cloth, which I think is beautiful. After our exhausting trip to Hihifo, we decided to return in two stages. At sunset we rested overnight in a house built on stilts over the water, with the tide moving beneath us; it was a quiet village called Nuku'alofa. We rose before dawn and travelled the rest of the way home in the cool of the day. I'm glad I went with Walter – the inconveniences of it didn't trouble me much and I really enjoyed seeing another part of the island. I hope we will be able to make many more trips like that together. It may even be a way of showing the chiefs that Walter comes in peace if he brings his wife and child with him.

So we look forward to the work that we believe that God has for us here. Walter believes that his job is to preach the gospel, not to start by setting up businesses for the people in order to introduce them to civilisation through trade – as has been the pattern in Tahiti and New Zealand. He has great hopes for the church here.

We have decided that when the *St Michael* comes, which it must surely do very soon, I will travel with it back to Sydney to have the baby. I am really scared of staying here with no-one who would know how to help me. Walter will stay and go on with the work, and I will return to him when the ship comes back to Tonga with the next load of supplies. Macanoe will go with me back to Sydney to see whether there is anything the doctors can do for him, but my shy and gentle friend is a very sick boy indeed and I'm afraid they will be able to do nothing.

Deep trouble

Mu'a, Tongatapu: July 12, 1823

At first, I didn't believe it. Perhaps I did not even really *see* what was before my eyes.

Today the people have been gathered here at Mu'a for a great festival in honour of the chief's daughter, who is a person of great importance in their society. Since before dawn people have been coming with their pigs, their mountains of yams and piles of vegetables. Henry and I had been trying to cover our ears to block out the screams of hundreds of pigs being slaughtered, maybe five or six hundred of them, but we couldn't help wanting to watch what was going on. Somehow, the scene reminded me of some of the paintings which I have seen of Sydney in the past few years, where the artist has set out the things he or she has seen: the roads, the buildings, the windmills, the shipping in the harbour, the people going about their business. As one stares at the painting, one sees more and more details to be discovered in the distance. I was just wondering what an artist would make of the vivid scene before me, of Tongans all absorbed in the complications of their own customs, when at last I noticed one of those little details in the background, a sail. . .

A sail! A ship was coming over the horizon towards harbour.

'Walter!' I shrieked. 'Look! A ship.'

I clung to him, babbling with excitement, and with

Thomas and Charles, George and Macanoe we watched in awe and thanksgiving as the *St Michael* moved closer and closer, to anchor in sight of Mu'a.

All around us the Tongans went on with their own affairs. The arrival of the ship was, to them, less important than their festival. Even as we watched the ship in the distance, they were placing the chief's daughter high on a heap of beautifully decorated bundles of *tapa* cloth, her face painted red and wearing her best ornaments and feathers. Even though Walter suggested to them that they should save some of the vast amount of pork to trade with the ship, they were more interested in their traditions than in trade.

I didn't really care what they did. The ship has come at last. We have been watching for it since February and now it is here. There will be mail from home, sugar, flour, maybe some new missionaries, supplies of all kinds, and a way for me to go home to Sydney to have our baby. Walter hopes they have sent newspapers and more books, and I hope our friends have sent us lots of letters with news of home and encouragement in our work here. Some encouragement will mean a lot to Walter as he has had so many times of depression, though he has done his best in very discouraging circumstances.

Mu'a, Tongatapu: July 26, 1823

So much for encouragement from home! I have been swinging between tears, mirthless laughter and blind rage. The stupidity, the lack of sense, the complete lack of understanding and feeling of some people, the *unfairness* of it all... How can they be so cruel to my Walter, after he has worked so hard with high hopes and dreams? And the hardest part is that this comes just when the Tongans were beginning to respond and show an interest in the gospel.

The *St Michael* has come, certainly, but when Walter went on board eagerly looking for new staff, Captain Beveridge looked blank.

'New missionaries? Oh no, none for Tonga,' Captain Beveridge said. 'I took the Reverend William White to New

Zealand to work with Mr Leigh, but there were none to come here.'

Walter came back with the first of the stores and with the precious bundles of letters and newspapers. For a while I rushed around, trying to get my fresh stocks of foodstuffs stored away safely and to see what wonderful things had come, at the same time longing to read every letter at once. Walter emptied the bundles of mail out onto the table and we sorted it: letters from my family, from friends in New South Wales, some from England for Walter and our servant Thomas, a separate heap of bulky letters from the Missionary Committee in London and copies of the *Sydney Gazette*. Even to hold the letters and see the handwriting of Mother and Thomas, of dear Samuel, Jonathan and James, of my dear sisters Eliza, Susannah and Anne was enough to bring me close to tears. There was so much mail there that we knew it would take us days, perhaps even weeks, to read it all and we looked forward to it all with happy anticipation. That was before we realised the pain some of it would bring.

We began with some of the family letters and discovered first of all some lovely family news. They all wrote to tell of a joyful family wedding only a few months after we left Sydney: Thomas has married Miss Anne Marsden and Anne was expecting a baby in May, just when the *St Michael* left Sydney. Probably I have a new nephew or niece and Mr and Mrs Marsden are grandparents for the first time. Another family romance was that of Eliza, betrothed to the Rev. William Walker, the Methodist missionary to the Aborigines. They were to be married in May — our family will have three ministers in it! Father would have been pleased, even if two of them are Methodists. There were many delightful pieces of news about the family, of colonial affairs, of the Sunday Schools with my dear brother Thomas in his position as Anglican clergyman, chairing missionary anniversaries and Sunday School anniversaries and examinations, both Anglican and Wesleyan, and other public functions.

Mother wrote of how she is carrying on Father's management of our family property and how she received a good
price for her wool this year. My brothers wrote of how all
of them have applied to Governor Brisbane for grants of
land over the Blue Mountains and how James had taken
William Walker with him on a trip to Bathurst. There was
news of other friends, such as the wedding of Anna Blaxland, and I told Walter about the time years ago when the
Blaxland girls used to collect mulberry leaves from our tree
for her silkworms. Now she is a married lady and wore a
beautiful embroidered, fringed silk scarf for her wedding
– from her own silk. Letters from Benjamin Carvosso told
how he had read aloud from Walter's Tongan diary (the
first few months before the *St Michael* left us last October)
in chapel in Macquarie Street, Sydney, and how very
moved and attentive everyone had been.

While we were so eagerly looking at our mail, the Tongans were very happy to have their two men home from
Sydney. I think they had thought of Futukava and Tata as
hostages for our safety and had not been quite sure
whether or not they would see them again. There was great
excitement a few days after they arrived when great
crowds sat in the *kava* ring to hear the stories they had to
tell of Sydney. Walter went to listen and came home full
of hope.

'I have never felt more confident about our mission,' he
said. 'The Tongan men have spoken so highly of what they
saw in Sydney and of the excellent way in which Governor
Brisbane showed them respect. He showed them all
around his town, from his kitchen to the observatory, to
watch soldiers drilling, to see all the tall buildings – which
astonished them, of course – and everything else. The
people here were amazed. They have been describing
horses – which they think are *huge* because they have no
animals as large – the variety of fruits, the shops full of
things for "barter", the harbour full of ships and the country stretching so far in every direction – unlike their own
small island. Also the kindness of the Sydney people –

their own people are tremendously impressed by what they are hearing. I think they thought we were telling lies about our own place, but they believe their own brothers. Now Futukava has told them about Sydney schools and Sunday Schools and that until they also have schools and learn about such things, they will never be wise.

'And the chiefs are agreeing with them! They have begun talking about the schools we promised and which we can start now that the *St Michael* is here. I hope that our school supplies are on board. Never before have the people been so open to us or so ready to listen to the gospel. The atmosphere today was electrifying, exciting – they are eager to learn.'

Captain and Mrs Beveridge came ashore the other day and dined with us. After nine months of seeing no other white woman, even Mrs Beveridge seemed a most charming and delightful person. I was able to show her my home and our garden and all the improvements we have been making. She was astonished to see how much Henry had grown and took an interest in the sewing I have been doing for him and for the new baby. I was just a little embarrassed to realise how shabby my clothes had become, but I can't help that. Walter thinks that he should be everything I need in a companion – certainly he is my most precious and beloved husband – but some things which are important to me are not even slightly interesting to him. I was so glad to have a woman with me again who could speak my language and know the things that are part of my life.

While the Beveridges were with us, Walter wanted to know why the ship had been delayed so long. It was a long story. First, the ship had travelled by way of New Zealand to collect a further load of timber and that had delayed their return to New South Wales. Then they were asked to wait for the new Methodist missionaries for New Zealand, two newly ordained Englishmen. One, the Rev. William White, had been waiting in New South Wales with his stores but the second, the Rev. Nathaniel Turner, was waiting in Van Dieman's Land with a sick wife. In the end, the *St Michael* sailed for New Zealand without him in April. The trip took a tedious five weeks and then the *St Michael* was used to help the Methodists settle at the new station which they had been meaning to move to for months. Until June this year, Samuel and Catherine Leigh have still been at the Church Missionary Society place at Rangihoa.

'We took Mr and Mrs Leigh, Mr White and the laymen Stack and Wade with some Church missionaries who had come to help and sailed south to a place called Whangarei,' said Captain Beveridge. 'But there had been serious tribal wars and many signs of cannibalism at Whangarei, so we turned back and sailed north to Whangaroa. There is a good harbour there, but there is also the serious disadvantage that at that place, some years ago, the ship *Boyd* was destroyed with nearly all the crew in revenge for insults to Maori chiefs by white men. That black day has never been forgotten, neither by the whites, nor by other Maori tribes who suffered as a result of the crime of their fellows. But Mr Leigh feels that Whangaroa is the right place to start his work. That is where I left them, about forty miles north of the Church mission, just starting to build a house to replace the leaking tent in which they were living.'

I thought about Catherine Leigh in a damp and leaking tent in a New Zealand winter and felt for her. Despite our various difficulties, we had much to be thankful for in our Tongan work and far more signs of hope for our mission than Mr Leigh must be finding just now, at the very beginning of his new work. And he is still a sick man, Captain Beveridge says.

But thoughts of hope for our Tongan work were before we had finished opening all our mail, before the dark cloud had descended upon our heads.

Untruths, fabrications and part-truths have been circulating about us. First, we heard that rumours had been started in New Zealand by the crew of the *St Michael*, on their way home from here last year, saying that Walter was obtaining a lot of gold and silver here in Tonga, under cover of establishing a mission. Gold and silver, for goodness' sake! Our Tongan friends don't appear to have minerals of any kind as part of their lives. The nearest we might be to gold or silver would be in the wreck of the *Port-au-Prince*, somewhere under the ocean in the northern islands. Walter hasn't even started any kind of trading enterprise in coconuts, pigs or land. He only bought six acres of land for a mission property, when his London Committee had suggested he might buy up to 500 acres. On Tonga, that would have been impossible anyway, but certainly he has not been using his missionary work to make himself rich!

When we turned to copies of the *Sydney Gazette* we found he had not done right in the eyes of some Sydney people, either. They seemed to think that he had forced me to stay here with him. After a colourful article referring to Captain Beveridge picking up survivors from the massacre of the *Ceres* last year and the report of a shipwrecked mariner rescued by the *Governor Macquarie* from the islands, the writer went on to sound very shocked that we had not all, or at least me and Henry, returned to Sydney last year with the *St Michael*. He wrote: '. . . it must have been nothing less than a most powerful and flattering opening that could have induced Mr Lawry to embosom his family, and little retinue, amongst thousands and tens of thousands of those benighted creatures who exist amid the habitations of cruelty.'

At first the article just seemed ridiculous, too highly coloured and extreme. I looked up from the newspaper to watch Nau laughing with friends as he poked sticks under our cooking fire, Eliza Ann trying to practise a simple stitch on the sampler I had begun for her, her intelligent face wrinkled with concentration, and several small boys with shaven heads and little topknots of hair rolling around on our mats in fits of giggles with Henry. They didn't look any of them like benighted creatures, though we know that the Tongans can be cruel when they choose. But after being amused by the article, I realised that Walter was hurt by

it, as it suggested that he was probably risking our lives in a cause which was probably hopeless anyway.

But the thing which has hurt Walter most desperately has been the letters from his Missionary Committee in London. He started to read the letters this evening, hoping perhaps to find some kind words of encouragement, some pastoral concern from his 'fathers in Christ'. There was a pile of them, the accumulation of over a year, and as he sorted them into dates he found that some were written early last year, nearly a year-and-a-half ago.

He started reading cheerfully, saying, 'I'd better wade through this lot.' Soon his tone had changed and I was startled to hear him groan, a noise of pain and shock. At last he turned, very pale, and said, 'Oh Mary. I'm in deep, deep trouble. I've been ordered to go to Van Dieman's Land to await the Committee's pleasure, either dismissal, removal or recall.'

I went to him quickly. 'But *why*? Why?'

He couldn't answer. I held his head against me and he clung to me, the two of us silent, my mind full of questions and his mind full of unspoken pain. After a long time he moved away, his cheeks wet, and blew his nose vigorously. 'You'd better read the letters,' he said.

The first thing I realised was that the letters were going over problems which went back years, to things which had happened in 1820 and 1821, two and three years ago. There was a long, long list of criticisms, most of them based on things Samuel Leigh had written from Sydney late in 1821 at a time when he was at odds with Walter in particular and also Benjamin Carvosso and Ralph Mansfield. They had a particularly difficult and unhappy meeting in October 1821, shortly after Mr Leigh had returned from England. I remember that there was a lot of tension about the way Walter and his friends had carried on the work in Leigh's absence and what Leigh saw as their disobedience to the instructions of the Missionary Committee. Leigh wrote letters of criticism to London at that time and now, nearly two years later, we are reading their reply.

The letters were written in December 1821 and April and July 1822.

They are angry with Walter, Carvosso and Mansfield, but see Walter as 'foremost in irregularity and disobedience to our rules'. He is specially blamed for administering the Lord's Supper, for a spirit of opposition to the colonial Anglican clergy and for following the local Sydney committee's decision for him to go direct to Tonga instead of to New Zealand with Leigh. He is supposed to have been disrespectful to the London Committee and opposed to their authority, established Methodist services in Anglican Church hours, and begun a Parramatta Methodist Sunday School without consulting Marsden (who wasn't even in the colony at the time). He is accused of 'extravagance and profusion of expenditure', 'indulging in personal ease and pleasure' and 'doing less (the three of them) in their combined exertions than Mr Leigh when alone'. (Well, we *did* spend a lot — my legacy from Father to pay for our furniture, and the Parramatta chapel, and to buy our share in a ship to get us to our missionary appointment.) All three are accused of confusion of the Society's accounts, of overspending and drawing unauthorised bills for the Macquarie Street Chapel — that terrible muddle which Walter agonised over at the time, with an unsatisfactory builder who had to be replaced when his business affairs collapsed, loss of time, rising costs once the work was well under way and people (particularly Edward Eager) demanding repayment early for loans of funds to the chapel.

For all these sins, Walter is said to be 'very blameable' and is ordered not to go to Tonga at all, but to a new appointment in Van Dieman's Land. It is rather late to hear this now! The Committee writes that his conduct 'has been so bad as to entirely forfeit their confidence and to their confidence he cannot again be restored without special acknowledgement of his own error and expressing his determination to act under their direction in future'. He is threatened with non-payment of bills and the publication of their censures in a general circular to all Wesleyan missions around the world, with a vote of censure in Conference against each of them. No wonder Walter is so crushed.

So I am angry. I'm sure every one of those faraway Committee men is fat and ugly, hairy and horrible, pouring out poisonous words, untrue words, unfair words against my beloved. Do they sit in a dark room in a London building, spinning their globe till they find the tiny dot that represents Tonga, or the mysterious bulk of Australia and stab it with a sharp pen point, saying: 'What was his name again? That Cornishman Lawry in Australia. Ah, yes, the disobedient one that Mr Leigh doesn't like. A few stern words will improve *his* manners'? As for Walter, he wrote in his diary tonight: 'I am at my wits' end — never was I in circumstances more painful.'

Mu'a, Tongatapu: August 16, 1823

What a tragic confusion. Ever since Walter read the letters from London, he has thought of little else. He has gone over every detail of the accusations and tried to answer them honestly, searching his heart and his memory of the events to see whether he may have made some serious mistakes. But he concludes that he has not. They have demanded that he must admit his faults before they will accept him back again, yet he says that he is still convinced that he did what was right in the eyes of God.

'I did *not* "seduce" the Parramatta children to come to our Sunday School. I offered Holy Communion to people who had not received it for long periods. The Anglicans had already changed their church times to clash with ours *before* we made our changes. You and I spent our own private money on equipping the church. We decided together, with Leigh present, that I should go direct to Tonga, not New Zealand, and wrote letters explaining our reasons to the Committee, but they evidently pay no attention to our letters.' Poor Walter, he keeps on talking about it.

In his diary he has written: 'I never felt any inward call

to go to any foreign station, more especially among savages after my marriage in New South Wales and, if anything did drop from my pen when writing to the Committee which they considered an offer to go myself to any of the South Sea Islands, they must have misunderstood my meaning. Or possibly (though I can hardly bring myself to believe it) I may when urging the Committee to send missionaries to the Friendly Islands have not only said I would not be afraid to go there, but I might in the warmth of my heart have said "If they appoint me I would go", though of any such offer I have not the least recollection.'

The thing which seems to wound him most deeply is that, just when he thought he was being obedient to the Committee, coming to Tonga even though he did not feel a strong sense of call, he is accused of many things but especially disobedience. And that the name of Mr Leigh keeps appearing as the man who is so right in the eyes of the Committee, yet Walter says: 'Leigh might as well have stayed in London instead of going to New Zealand. He has only just moved to his own Wesleyan station after a year-and-a-half, he has had no success in learning the Maori language and, as to anything else, he has not even attempted it. Yet I am censured and he is honoured.'

The *St Michael* has gone off trading among the northern islands of this group with promises to return in a month. By the time it returns, Walter must have made his mind up what to do next. He has struggled very desperately with the problem; whatever choice he might make seems to be wrong. He hates the thought of abandoning the new, infant work here in Tonga, just at a time when the people are beginning to show a real interest and when the two men who visited Sydney are providing a helpful bridge between their traditional world and the possibility of change. Yet, if he insists on staying here, the Committee will accuse him of multiplying his disobedience by not going to his appointment in Van Dieman's Land. If only by some miracle he could speak today directly to the men of the Committee and explain his own point of view man to man, and have permission to go on with this promising work. But that is an agonising fantasy. It would take months and months for him to travel from Tonga to England — the same time for a message to travel there — and more months to return to this work. By that time the ideal moment among the Tongans would be lost.

We gathered for worship in our communal meeting room here in our fine new house last Sunday. Our little group sat quietly, gloomily, feeling the uncertainty of our situation very deeply. Walter has been reading a lot in the writings of the prophets and I think he has been finding some comfort in feeling that they too struggled, asked unanswerable questions and watched while the powers of evil seemed to be triumphing. He read to us from the prophet Habakkuk. As he read, he pointed out that bedded in among words of doom and destruction, of heathen vengeance against the good, of injustice and shame, were words of shining hope. Not only did those beautiful hope words speak of local relief, but spoke of the whole earth being at last bathed in the light of God. He read from the second chapter: 'For *the earth shall be filled* with the knowledge of the glory of the Lord, as the waters cover the sea. But the Lord is in his holy temple: let *all the earth* keep silence before him.' So surely that means even us, here in Tonga.

Walter read to us the final words of the prophet Habakkuk and I have been clinging to those words ever since. Even in this time of deepest darkness for Walter and me, this word of scripture is profoundly true for us. He read:

'Although the fig tree shall not blossom, neither shall fruit be in the vines; the labour of the olive shall fail, and the fields shall yield no meat; the flocks shall be cut off from the fold, and there shall be no herd in the stalls:

'*Yet I will rejoice in the Lord*; I will joy in the God of my salvation.'

Mu'a, Tongatapu: September 30, 1823

The decision is made. Though it was so difficult to know what to do for the best, now that the choice has been made it seems that there really was no choice. The only thing Walter can do is to leave Tonga and obey the Committee, then try to go to England to clear his name with them. Until that is done, any ministry he attempts will be under a cloud. Writing letters seems to be useless, as we have all written many letters in the past to no good purpose. Walter assures me that the men of the Committee are not the evil and sinister hobgoblins that I picture. In calmer moments, I hope not! They are very good men, he says, fine leaders and deeply spiritual Christians. 'But they are so far away,' he says, 'I suppose we can't expect them to understand what it is like to be here, or even to be in New South Wales.'

So, when the *St Michael* returns from this trading trip, Walter and I will leave Tonga together – sadly and, to our surprise, rather reluctantly. George and Charles are willing to remain and look after things for us until more missionaries arrive. The chiefs, who are very fond of our good young men, have promised to look after and protect them from any harm. Walter feels that George and Charles will do as good a job as he might in caring for mission property until new staff arrives. There is no point in him going on with the language learning if he is being withdrawn from this work. And knowing that I am going back to New South Wales to have the baby has made him realise that he leans on me more than he has admitted. He wrote in his diary: 'I am by no means certain that I would have the nerve to bear up in the absence of my family, under the trials of my mission and the censure of the Committee.'

Our Tongan neighbours have reacted to the news of our departure with much more emotion than I thought possible. From morning to night they are crowded round our place, sitting on the verandah, filling the doorway and windows with faces. Our special young friends have been squatting on our floor, weeping dismally and pleading with us not to go away. They are asking us to come back again, if we must go, and 'bring some of your relations with you'! I really think they mean it. As I have been packing up the things which we will take with us – Henry's things, the tattered remains of our clothing, the gifts of *tapa* cloth we have been given, shell necklaces and beautiful mats – they have been hanging around the boxes, hoping for gifts but bewailing our departure. Perhaps they hope that, if we go and then return, they will receive more and better gifts than we can give now! Certainly there is very little left of any worth among our things. What there is we are leaving for the use of George and Charles.

We have offered to take two of the young men with us to Sydney and the chiefs have agreed. One will be our good friend Tama Nau, who has lived with us for some time and has been very helpful with cooking, specially in recent months since poor Macanoe has been so ill and has not been able to help me much. The other is a fine young man called Malungahu, who has also spent a lot of time at our house. They are both big, strong and impressive young men and I think it will be exciting to be able to show them all the wonders of Sydney. As we pack, they are preparing their own things to travel with us. Our young Maori friend, Manihera, will come with us to Sydney, too, and now that we hear that Mr Marsden is planning to begin his Maori seminary again, perhaps he can go to school there.

Even now, with most people weeping and wailing about us going away, some people have *still* been stealing things from us. Only the other day a man came and stole a lot of our yams. And, while they like our things, we can still not be sure whether they are to be trusted to leave us alive – we *think* so, but can't be certain. Their usual lives go on as ever, as if Walter had never told them even once about our great Lord who made them, loves them and died for them. Even in the last few days, we have seen the despair of a native funeral, revenge sorcery and the capture and sacrifice of a young girl (they really wanted to sacrifice a young man, but he escaped).

We even heard Fatu complaining that he had been told by Futukava that Governor Brisbane had warned of retribution if any harm came to us. The way Fatu spoke, it seemed that he thought that Governor Brisbane was just looking for an excuse to attack these islands. Fatu was by no means certain that he would want to protect us under those circumstances. How very uncertain everything is.

So we are ready to go. Our one big problem is that, while we wait, the *St Michael* still hasn't come back from Ha'apai. They promised to be back in four weeks, but nearly seven weeks have gone by and every delay brings us closer to the day of the delivery of our child. Unless I have miscounted again, as I did with Henry, this baby will be born in five or six weeks. Unless the ship comes very soon, I will give birth at sea.

St Michael, at sea: October 4, 1823

The very strange thing is that I think I felt the pangs of leaving Tonga today more bitterly than I felt leaving my home and Sydney fifteen months ago. When I left home, I had every hope of going home again, even though I was afraid of what was ahead of me. But over the last few days in Tonga, the thought was constantly in my mind: 'Mary, you will never see this place again. You will never eat yams or fresh sugar cane or pineapples again. You will never again watch women and children stooping along the shining wetness of the sand at low tide looking for shellfish, smell frangipani flowers or taste coconut cream. You will never again float over a rainbow reef, visit a family in an airy Tongan house, swim in a warm sea or hear their sweet singing. You will never sit with the Tongan women, listen to their language and laugh with them . . . this is the end.' And somehow, I couldn't bear it.

Yesterday, all our things were carried out to the ship which was anchored some seven or eight miles out, at the anchorage in sight of the bay. Crowds of people pressed around our home and many hands gathered up our luggage and carried it off. A year ago, I would have feared that I would never see it again, that the people would steal the lot, but yesterday we watched a string of canoes spread out over the bay, each carrying some of our things to the ship.

I stood for the last time on our verandah, looking across the villages nearby, the beautiful expanse of the bay before me with its little islands and the feathery tops of hundreds of coconut palms mixed with the spread of breadfruit and banana trees. I had taken my last walk around the garden I helped to plant and seen the thriving maize, cabbage, peas, beans, turnips, radishes, melons, tobacco, cotton and the fruit trees we planted – still young – and knew that I would never taste the fruit of those peaches, figs, pears, apples or loquats. On one side of the house were the carpenter's bench and smith's shop where George and Charles will go on working without us, still decorated with the bird cages of vivid parakeets and turtle doves they have hung from the trees. On the other side was the poultry yard with the two geese, the two muscovy ducks and other ducks and chickens which I have tended and fed, and the birds I had been fattening for a Christmas meal we won't now eat in Tonga. As we walked away from the house down to the beach, it felt as if I was leaving a part of my own body behind and the pain of it was bitter. I am very thankful that we are not leaving behind a grave of one of our beloved company – that would have been even more painful.

When we reached the beach, crowded about by our Tongan friends, Fatu was waiting for us, his face crumpled and damp with weeping. As we were ready to step into the boat to go out to the ship, Fatu stopped us and we realised that the whole crowd was forming into a vast ring, like the *kava* ring. To a chorus of sniffs and tearful snuffles, one of their most eloquent men spoke.

'We thank you for coming among us,' he said. 'Before you came, it was dark night in Tonga; now it begins to be light. Your friends in the foreign lands have sent for you. Go, and tell them that Tonga is a foolish land. Let them send us many teachers. Our hearts are sore, we are pained in our bellies, because you are going away from us...'

He burst into tears and so did everyone else. We fled into the boat, our own eyes streaming and our hands straining

to touch, to comfort, to farewell, as the boat was rowed out across the bay, away from a people who have frightened us, irritated us, ignored us, fleeced us and, at last, accepted and loved us. I find that the people of Tonga have become very precious and dear to me in a way I would not have thought possible.

Tonight we are under sail for Port Jackson – and home – and my feelings are very mixed. I am thankful to be on the way, hoping so much to get home to my mother before the baby is born. It is wonderful to think that I'm going home to everything that is familiar: to comfort, to safety, to family, to Christian friends and the joys of going to chapel. But I have come to love many of the people of Tonga – not *all* of them, of course – and I am going to miss their friendship very much. Walter and I are anxious about George and Charles. Will they really be safe until new missionaries come to join them?

Why did we go to Tonga? We thought we were doing the right thing at the time, but has the whole expedition proved to be pointless, a waste of time, a ridiculous bit of futility? Might we just as well have stayed home and saved our money and our effort? Did God have a purpose in bringing us to Tonga or did we just make a mistake?

Walter and I stood at the rail and watched the flat line of Tongatapu until it slipped over the horizon, trying to wrestle with our questions. After a while, Walter brought out his diary and showed me some reflections he had noted down, some of his own answers to the question 'Why did we have to go at all?' Among other things, he feels that we have proved that it is possible to establish a mission in the Friendly Islands and have paved the way for others to come after us. He sees himself as a pioneer who makes it possible for others to settle into a long-term work. He feels that we have proved that a regular supply ship is essential, with well-established links between the missionaries and their 'relatives' in Sydney to give the white men adequate prestige in the eyes of the Tongans.

We have left two fine young men who are very good with

the language and have real spiritual depth and concern for the conversion of the Tongans – they will be a great help to future missionaries. Walter has written that he didn't ever expect to stay for a lifetime, and that he wouldn't like to have to wait till he had seen his first convert before feeling free to go to England to visit his aging parents. He wrote:

'He who would see fruits of labours among the natives of Tonga must, without a miracle, wait until an accurate acquaintance with their language has been acquired, schools established, books printed and read and the influence of continued instruction has effectively enlightened the savage mind. For this business set down at least five or perhaps seven years. The missionaries were labouring seventeen years in Tahiti before anything like conversion appeared among the natives. The New Zealand mission has been established eleven years, but no fruit yet appeared. Patience and perseverance are necessary.'

Walter also wrote that he felt he could be very useful to the Committee in London by being able to correct many of the mistakes in trying to establish the work in the Pacific. He feels that the work in New Zealand was 'begun in the dark, with much expense and property misapplied,' and he would like to be able to advise others so that they can avoid such mistakes in the future.

So, was it all worth it for us to have gone to Tonga and gone through the year that we have just completed? Maybe. Perhaps we will never know.

St Michael, at sea: November 1, 1823

I had forgotten, in my anxiety to be safely on board the ship and on our way home, just how miserable a sea voyage can be. Wouldn't it be wonderful if one could be transported by magic and take wings from Tonga to Sydney and arrive on the same day as one left! As it is, we toss and plunge and roll on and on, week after week. Captain Beveridge told me rather sharply that we have two thousand miles to sail, so we'll just have to be patient.

For the first week or so, Walter and I were horribly sea-sick. For me, the discomfort of the motion of the ship was combined with the discomforts of late pregnancy and anxiety about the baby coming so soon. For us both, our physical distress was made worse by our confusion of mind over our departure from Tonga. We had gone there rather unwillingly, only intending to stay a few months, and had spent many difficult and worrying hours while we had been there. Why, then, were our feelings so mixed about leaving? Are we feeling that we are failures? Have we lost something very important to us, or are we discovering in ourselves a feeling for the Tongans which we did not rea-lise was there? Whatever the reason, we were a pair of dis-mal miseries. We lay on our bunks, green and pathetic and very sorry for ourselves. Maybe it is just as well that one can't travel as fast as I had dreamed, because I think we have needed the time to get used to the idea of leaving Tonga.

Just when we were beginning to feel a little better and prepared to face the hazards of dining at the ship's table, our ship was struck by a gale. It was fearsome to see the waves pile up, higher and higher, and watch wind-driven clouds stream across a darkened sky. Under orders from Captain Beveridge, the crew struck the royal and top gal-vanised masts and stripped the mizzen mast of all canvas, the main and fore topsail were close-reefed, and topsail and main storm sail were set to the wind. As the storm lashed around us, the *St Michael* rode the waves. Walter made me stay below, but he couldn't govern my imagi-nation.

'Do you remember the story of the awful journey Ralph and Lydia Mansfield had from England?' I asked anxious-ly. 'How they were caught in a storm — maybe like this — and their ship was holed? And do you remember how they stuffed a featherbed into the gaping space just above the waterline to keep enough water out until the storm eased and it could be repaired?' I was perching on my own feather mattress, clutching at its softness and trying to see

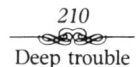
in my mind's eye how it could possibly keep out the sea.

Travelling with a lively child who is nearly two also has its own terrors. I have been very glad of the help of our Tongan friends – specially of the Maori lad, Manihera, in caring for small Henry. Ever since the day when Walter impulsively threw a gift of ship's biscuit to the Maori cannibal chief and was rewarded with Manihera, the boy has found comfort and healing of spirit in caring for our little one.

One day recently, when we had been at sea several weeks, something happened which has given me nightmares ever since. Henry had dropped off to sleep in a coil of rope on deck, with Manihera squatted nearby to watch him. In my chair further along the deck I sat, frozen, as an unexpected wave broke over my child. It all seemed to happen so slowly in my mind. I saw the wave, a flurry of limbs, the empty coil of rope unwinding. It was like watching a cup falling from a high shelf, bouncing down, knowing that the only end must be smashed fragments on the floor. I think I screamed.

Before I could move, Manihera was overboard and I saw two heads, one dark and one fair, bobbing together in the water. Then the Maori boy and Henry were being dragged dripping back on board and I was hugging them both in one warm, wet bundle of precious humanity. How I thank God for his mercy!

Walter is anxiously counting the days. Every day we are driven before the storm is another day of delay, making us later and later in the time we will reach Sydney. I find myself talking inwardly to the child who is yet to be born. 'Wait, little one, not yet. The time is not right. You are safe where you are. Please wait . . .'

I have been looking around the ship, imagining how it will be if the child is born on board. Even our tiny cabin is not private and, if I were to cry out – as I am sure I shall – the crew would hear me. Mrs Beveridge is on board, but I feel very uneasy with Mrs Beveridge who has been comforting herself with rum again. I think I'd even prefer one of the Tongan women to help me. (Captain B., as usual, is quite tyrannical on board his ship.) Poor Walter is so anxious. He watches me intently and, if ever I move restlessly trying to get comfortable, he is quick to ask, 'Are you in pain?'

We are both thinking of the story we have heard of the Rev. Samuel and Mrs Marsden, when they were young people first coming to New South Wales years ago. Their vessel was so close – just outside Sydney Heads – but a gale was blowing and Mrs Marsden was in labour with Anne, her first child. Mrs Marsden told me many years later how very nervous Mr Marsden was (though I find it hard to imagine him youthful and nervous) and how she herself had tried to stay calm to tell him how to help her. The ship was tossing so violently that her husband had to cling on to stay on his feet. Even as baby Anne was born, a wave broke over the quarterdeck and salt water splashed in through their porthole, wetting infant and bedlinen. And all in sight of Sydney Heads, so very close to harbour. Wait, little one.

We are watching Macanoe, too. The poor lad is very weak and ill. We try to encourage him with promises of help from Sydney doctors, but he, and we, know that he is dying. Walter has talked with him about his immortal soul and my shy young friend has been recalling things that he first heard in the Sunday School at Parramatta, when he first lived with us. I think he has a very real faith. The Tongan men, Tama Nau and Malungahu, are kind to him, but I think they are wondering whether they, too, might die far from home. I feel with them – I have been wondering the same thing.

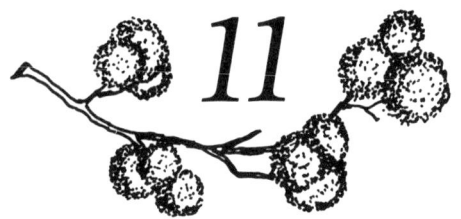

Loose ends

Port Jackson, New South Wales: November 7, 1823

The rocky arms of the Sydney Heads, the entrance to Port Jackson, were stretched out to the *St Michael* when I woke this morning. The crew and Captain Beveridge were working to bring the ship through the Heads in safety, with our little Henry watching in fascination from the vantage point of his father's arms. My eyes were not on the sailors, but on those outstretched arms of sandstone, the dear familiar rocks of my childhood, draped in the green-grey and olive of the eucalyptus scrub, coming nearer and nearer till the welcoming arms were around us, enclosing us, and the tossing waves of the open sea were gentled to the easy motion of safe harbour.

I stood at the rail, holding on with one hand, the other hand resting against the swell of my gown, watching the sunlight on arcs of white sand beaches, cloud shadows moving across the dark bush of the coves and bays of Sydney Harbour – not the angled brightness of coconut palms over Tongan reef, but the comfort of gumtrees and boronia, banksia and bottlebrush, bush orchids and wattle. Soon, very soon, the solid shapes of buildings and the streets of Sydney Town would be visible around the next point. Soon the open arms of my mother, my sisters and brothers would enclose me. Nearly home. . . Thank you, oh, thank you, Lord!

'Mary?' It was only when Walter's voice reached me that I realised that my face was wet with tears.

This afternoon we disembarked and our dear family welcomed us. When my mother put her arms around me, I had no words to greet her, only tears of relief and a hug of such emotion that I knocked her bonnet over one ear! Such a flurry of hugging and greetings. There was Thomas with his wife Anne *and* baby son James, no less, all my precious brothers and sisters, and sister Eliza coming to us with the Rev. William Walker on her arm and saying, 'I'd like to introduce my husband.' They were kissing a rather astonished Henry till he hid his face in my shoulder, and were noticing the generous curve of my waist – I'd quite forgotten that they didn't even know I was pregnant. Everyone was talking at once, laughing, shouting instructions, whispering news.

After seventeen months of separation, it was suddenly too much and I longed to be safely home with the door shut.

Parramatta, New South Wales: Tuesday, November 11, 1823

The child is born.

In all the months of her growth in my body, I pictured how it would be. In the hot restless midnights at Mu'a I saw another miscarriage, or sometimes had nightmares about angry Tongans around our house seeking revenge for some real or imagined offence while my pains gripped me. I imagined childbirth in a gale at sea or exposed to the gaze of interested Tongans, leaning on our elbow-high walls. I even imagined a broken Walter beside a grave and a rough cross inscribed: 'Here lies Mary...'! Walter says that my imagination is too vivid. Over the months the pictures in my mind have haunted me and I prayed and prayed that God would be merciful.

Now we praise God for his mercy to us. On Saturday, the day after the *St Michael* arrived in port, we came to Parramatta. As we travelled along the road, every bend in the way, every roadside shanty, every vista of the Blue Mountains in the distance was infinitely precious and beautiful. The twin towers of St John's Church pointed into the sky, guiding us home. At last we were going through the front door into the wonderful safety of Mother's home, the home of my childhood and growing up.

We sat in the front parlour, feeling in a strange way like visitors. Everything was as I remembered: the same ornaments in their familiar places, the red cedar furniture glowing with polish, the fire-irons on the sandstone hearth, swept clean for summer, Mother's treasured English oaks and lemon trees gilded with ripe fruit through the window, even the remembered aroma of Mother's homemade soap and the rattle of china teacups on a tray. Home.

Mother and my sisters served us tea, insisting that I sit and rest with my feet up while they looked after me and carried Henry off into the garden. They had invited my married brothers and sisters to come, dear Benjamin and Deborah Carvosso and the Mansfields, and the newest and youngest Methodist missionaries, the Rev. William and Mrs Horton. We were crowded into the parlour, with our Tongan friends as well, and they asked us question after question about Tonga. In the same way that we feel that we know little about what has been going on in New South Wales, we need to remember that our family and friends have suffered a long silence with no news at all of us since the *St Michael* sailed in October over a year ago.

There was so much to tell and, even in the telling, we found it hard to express the truth of what we had seen and heard in words that would really communicate – it was almost as if we were speaking a foreign language. I saw young Mrs Horton staring at me with wide eyes and realised that to her, newly arrived in the colony only three weeks ago after two years in Van Dieman's Land, I was an experienced missionary lady. The look in her eyes was of deep respect which struck me as rather amusing. That is how I am sure I must have gazed at Mary Williams, only two years ago. I must be getting old!

That was on Saturday. By last night, four days after the *St Michael* sailed into the harbour, I felt the first pangs of preparation for childbirth and, in the early hours of this morning, our daughter was born. Mother and my sisters were with me, and the doctor and midwife. In the beautiful safety of my own old bedroom, lying on Mother's fresh bedlinen and a deep mattress of featherdown from her geese, there was no terror in the pain, but energy, power and joy. And our daughter is perfect. We have called the child Elizabeth Anna for our mothers, Walter's and mine.

Tonight, with Elizabeth Anna in my arms and Henry leaning heavily on my shoulder, snuggling as close as possible, I asked Walter, 'What have you written about today in your diary?'

He read it aloud for me: 'Nov. 11th. My dear Mary brought to bed early this morning with a fine baby girl. She was remarkably favoured with a quick and easy delivery. She is now in her mother's house among her dear and numerous friends. How very different from being among savages or on board a ship! This is one of the most singularly gracious providences we remember in our lives.'

Amen!

Parramatta, New South Wales: December, 1823

What has happened to our dreams and plans? We thought that God was calling us to take the gospel of Jesus Christ to the poor heathen of the Pacific. We thought that Samuel Leigh would spend years in New Zealand and be the means of bringing many people to faith. We thought that Walter would go to Tonga to bring light to the darkness there. We had thought that we were doing the right thing.

What has gone wrong? Have we made a terrible mistake and misunderstood God's guidance? Because here is Walter, back in New South Wales in disgrace with the Committee, even though he was just beginning to see signs of hope in Tonga. The work that we tried to start is in the hands of two young and inexperienced laymen with no expectation of support soon. Our dear young friend Macanoe

who travelled with us is dead – he died here with us in
Parramatta on November 19, only weeks after our return.
And on the last day of November, the ship *Dragon*
anchored in Sydney Harbour. On board with the Rev.
Samuel Marsden were... Samuel and Catherine Leigh.
Samuel is a broken, sick man, brought away from New
Zealand by Mr Marsden because he was not able to cope
with the strains of the task. So the two new Wesleyan mis-
sions to New Zealand and Tonga have both ended for their
pioneers in ignominy and failure, both men returning to
Sydney in the same month.

In the case of Samuel Leigh, he seems to have been
defeated by health problems and the unexpected pressures
of living in a strange environment. When Mr Marsden went
to New Zealand in August, he took with him the other new
missionaries for the Methodist work there, Nathaniel and
Mrs Turner and Mr Hobbs. The two men set off to walk
across country from the Bay of Islands north to 'Wesleydale' at Whangaroa, while Marsden visited his Church
Mission people. Two weeks later, Marsden sailed to visit
his friend Leigh at Wesleydale, intending to help him with
a land transaction with the Maoris. He was shocked to find
Samuel Leigh a shadow of himself. Leigh was still a big
man, as heavy as ever, but his former competence and
energy were gone and he was suffering from constant
headaches and other mysterious aches and pains. He
seemed to be unable to make decisions or handle even
simple planning. The house building was almost entirely in
the hands of the Rev. William White and the laymen until
Turner and Hobbs arrived, and Catherine Leigh had taken
on all letter-writing and record-keeping for her husband.
Mr Marsden saw that Leigh was quite unfit to stay and,
within a few days, had the Leighs on board the *Brampton*,
sailing for the Bay of Islands.

Mr Marsden intended to bring the Leighs and the still unhappy and rebellious Kendalls away to Sydney. After considerable difficulty he managed to get them all on board the
Brampton on September 7 and set sail out of the Bay of

Islands. The journey was haunted by troubles. The ship struck a rock while still in the Bay. Marsden and the Leighs were hastily rowed off and landed on a small and barren island, to spend two miserable days with little shelter and very little food until they were collected by the mission whale boat.

If Samuel had been feeling unwell before the shipwreck, he felt much worse after it! The *Brampton* was badly holed, but all the passengers and cargo were safely rescued and taken to shore before she sank. The Kendalls announced that they were definitely not going to be talked into leaving a second time and took all their things away to settle permanently in New Zealand. William White, after only six months in the colony, announced that he now wanted to go back to Sydney to look for a bride. Mr Marsden was now without a ship and had to wait till a passing vessel, the *Dragon* on the way from Tahiti to Sydney, called at the Bay of Islands and took Marsden, the Leighs and William White to Sydney. They left New Zealand in the middle of November, leaving the unfortunate New Zealand Methodist work in the hands of Turner and Hobbs who had only been in the country since August and knew almost no Maori language. It seems that the New Zealand mission is having to start at the beginning again and the Tongan mission is only clinging to life.

How can God possibly bring good out of that sort of muddle?

Parramatta, New South Wales: January, 1824

Did we dream that we went to Tonga? Sometimes it seems that Walter and I have been sleeping, unconscious, for a year-and-a-half while everything around us has been changing. Some things are changing for the better, but some things are very troubling.

Some of the chapels, which used to be full, are full no longer. There is still a frightening debt hanging over the new building in Macquarie Street, Sydney, though it is a fine and handsome chapel. A young Scot, a Presbyterian minister of my own age called John Dunmore Lang, has recently arrived and established a Presbyterian congregation out at the Ebenezer Chapel which my father helped to build some years ago. He is a young man of enormous energy and I expect he will be good for the colony.

Another new minister, the Rev. George Erskine, has been sent here from Ceylon to take over the leadership of our Methodist group. He is a good and gentle man, but he is not well and all our Methodist affairs are in such a mess at the moment that we need a leader of considerable strength to help us through. The Anglicans have plans next month to consecrate the building in Macquarie Street that was near our Sydney home and intended for a courthouse. It will be called St James' Church and is almost next door to our Macquarie Street Chapel. The Roman Catholics are building a chapel too, only a stone's throw away and they are calling it St Mary's Chapel. At least Mr Marsden doesn't change and goes on as I remember him.

Our family, too, is not as we left them. It seems very strange to see Thomas a married man, with baby James. Thomas and Anne are living in a small weatherboard cottage not far from Mother's house, near the Parramatta River. Sister Eliza seems very happy with her William Walker. He is a very enthusiastic young man who has begun trying to learn the language of the Aboriginal tribes and is working with young Aboriginal people, including a number of halfcastes. He is trying to establish a training institute for them, though not finding it at all easy. Eliza tells me that she and William got to know each other when he was sick from exposure and overwork last year and, as usual, Mother took him in and gave him a home until he was well again.

Samuel and Lucy on the farm at 'Macquarie Grove' and Jonathan and Mary not far from them at 'Matavai' are thriving and their families are growing. Samuel called their third baby, born while we were away, little Mary. Jonathan's Mary will be having their third child in a few months, so all three of us who were brides together have changed from young girls into mature, married ladies with all the responsibilities of home and family.

Even little sister Susannah is growing up and is special friends with William, the oldest of the Shelley family. My brothers have all become mature adults. Not only is Thomas a respected clergyman with the church, but Samuel, Jonathan and James are becoming more and more like Father, with their generosity to good causes and their willingness to serve on useful committees. All three are serving with other more senior men on the Committee of the Native Institution. (Perhaps they will be able to curb some of the more unwisely impulsive actions of William Walker.)

Mother keeps fussing around me, and I find that my role in the family has changed a little. 'You are so thin, Mary,' she says. 'You must eat more, drink more milk, have more rest.' It is rather strange being back in my mother's house, being treated as a daughter again, after several years as a married woman, particularly as we have lived so far away. I have been 'wife' and 'mother', 'supporter' and 'friend', but not 'daughter'. In some ways it is rather a nice luxury for me to be so pampered and planned for by Mother, but I think Walter will be very glad to move away into our own cottage very soon.

Certainly no-one can suggest that our children are too thin. Walter was writing to his parents the other day and said: 'Elizabeth Anna is doing very well... Henry grows to a fine boy and is one of the fattest children I have ever seen. Mrs L. is quite the reverse. People say that I shall grow fat, though this I think might be questioned.'

Even fashions have changed! After Elizabeth was born and I decided to sew some fresh gowns to replace the tattered remains of my Tongan wardrobe, my sisters wouldn't let me use the familiar pattern. 'No, Mary!' they insisted, quite shocked at my suggestion. 'You'd look so *old-fashioned*! Waists are much lower and more fitted and skirts are a lot fuller than the old styles.' They make me feel as if I have been away a hundred years.

It is not just our families and community that have changed while we were away. No, Walter and I are different people from the pair who went away. We have seen and experienced so many things which our families cannot even imagine. They don't even know the right questions to ask about the life we knew in Tonga and, once they have enquired about the climate and food and how we managed with practical housekeeping, they tend to change the subject and talk about baby James, his first tooth or the latest gossip from Sydney. We still love each other dearly, but we have not shared a large chunk of their lives and they can't even picture the most significant and moving part of ours.

I think I realised how much we had changed on the day of the feast just after Christmas which the Governor gives each year for the Aboriginal tribes. In past years, I have been at the gathering in the Parramatta marketplace and looked with great interest and curiosity at the large circle of Aborigines, with their strange languages and way of life. This time, standing tall and impressive among the onlookers, naval and military officers, clergy and all, were our good Tongan friends, Tama Nau and Malungahu.

They looked magnificent in their native dress, their muscular bodies gleaming in the sun from anointing with coconut oil, heavy war clubs in their hands and their faces expressing intelligence, dignity and... disdain! Our friends were actually looking down their noses at the crowd around them and seemed to be singling out a heavily tattooed New Zealand Maori for their greatest scorn, suggesting that, like ourselves, they found their own people and their own way of doing things superior to that of foreigners. Perhaps to my own surprise, I found that I was very anxious that the crowd gathered should notice how fine our friends were – just as I want people to realise how extremely healthy and handsome are my children, Henry and Elizabeth. Not only that, I was anxious that Tama Nau and Malungahu should be impressed by *us* and that the white population wouldn't disgrace me!

Parramatta, New South Wales: January 9, 1824

We are home and yet we are not home. We are back among our brethren, with my dear family and friends – back to all the familiar activity of church and society in New South Wales, back to safety and plenty – but we are certainly not settled. The whole question of what we should do now looms over our heads, still unresolved.

For the first few weeks after our arrival back in New South Wales, Walter tried to put the matter aside for the time being, allowing time for me to have the baby and recover, giving himself the pleasure of spending time with the Carvossos, the Mansfields and others. They were very eager to hear about Tonga and he was very willing to tell them. But now some definite decisions must be made about our future. The whole thing is so confusing and, somehow, wasteful of time and energy.

Walter came home from one of his meetings with the other Methodist missionaries, troubled and disturbed.

'If I were not so firmly attached to Methodism,' he declared, 'I'd resign! The whole affair is a disaster. I find that we had only sailed for New Zealand and Tonga a few months before the other New South Wales missionaries received the first letters of criticism from London. They sat straight down and wrote answers in detail to each criticism – they have shown me the copy of their replies and it runs to thirty-six foolscap pages! This was happening at the same time as the *St Michael* was sailing and leaving us in Tonga in October 1822.'

'What did they write?'

'They had perfectly reasonable explanations for everything. They had the backing of the Methodist laymen on the question of church hours and the sacraments, and pointed out that it was a bit late to appoint me to Van Dieman's Land as I had sailed five months earlier to my appointment in Tonga. All the things about me that the Committee censured, the local missionaries have praised.

'One part of their letter of reply, referring to the possible origins of the charges, read: ''We believe that their origin may be traced to the influence of that unhappy disagreement which has long existed between Messrs Leigh and Lawry..." and mentioned that very unhappy affair in 1820 when I felt I had to tear out two pages from the published report about New South Wales which Leigh had written before I would distribute it. The whole letter was very painful, specially as they felt that they were being treated very unjustly.

'They wrote: "Our little lion, from a healthy infancy, was growing up toward a vigorous maturity, free from the intrusions of bigotry and persecution and enjoying the friendly smiles of the clergy and the sheltering arm of the civil authorities: the first disquietude she has to deprecate flows from misrepresentation and is threatened by her very parents and guardians! It is this that wounds our feelings — and draws forth our sighs and our tears."

'Anyway, they posted off that long letter and a few months later got more letters of complaint. No wonder they are all depressed and discouraged! They say they have spent hours of wasted time trying to solve their problems with the Committee. I've written asking for permission to return to England to put my case and give my views on wiser planning for mission in the South Seas, but they probably won't let me come. I wrote to my parents: "I would like to live at peace and union with all men. I have actually spent more on the Tonga and New South Wales missions than it has cost the Committee to maintain me all the time I have been a missionary... Had I been a little more servile and wasted my time and the Society's money by sticking to the letter of their instructions, all would have been well between me and them, but how could I have answered it to God and my conscience?"' (I'm glad he still writes to his parents — he has stopped keeping his journal because he says there is nothing good to record.)

'At least the other missionaries have had time to deal with most of the letters,' I commented. 'They are all ready to go on with their work and they are clear about their appointments. But what are we supposed to do?'

'One thing is certain. Whatever else we choose to do, we must make our peace with Samuel Leigh, much as he has hurt us all. He is a very sick man and may well die.'

That was how things stood when we went to Sydney for the Quarterly Meeting, travelling by coach on December 28 after the Aboriginal gathering with William Walker, William Horton and Mr Hutchinson, a young Englishman who was to be received on probation as a missionary. The next day the men met for the Quarterly Meeting in the morning and the District Meeting in the afternoon. The meetings went on for some days and on New Year's Eve we met for a Watchnight Service.

As I reflected on the strange and difficult year of 1823, with all its pain and joy, I found myself trembling as I placed myself in God's hands for 1824. Walter was one of the preachers. As I looked at him there in the Macquarie Street pulpit, I prayed for him with all my heart, that he will find the place where God truly wants him to be.

On New Year's Day, Walter came home from the meeting with a letter in his hand.

'You'd better pray for me tomorrow, my Polly,' he said. 'I am to take this letter to Samuel Leigh on behalf of us all. Young William Horton is to come with me, but none of the original complaints applied to him as he has only just come to New South Wales. So much of the pain has always been between Samuel and me. Our District Meeting wants us to be reconciled with our brother because, however much he has hurt us by his misrepresentations, it is all so long ago, so stale. We are dealing with things that hurt him four years ago, things he said against us three years ago, and censures written by the London Committee two years ago! It is a New Year now; surely it is time for a new beginning.

'I know I have called Samuel Leigh an "ignorant and rotten man" (and have meant it), but tomorrow I am going to take him this letter of reconciliation. There is beautiful peace and harmony between the rest of the brethren – I'll need the Lord to help me make my peace with Samuel Leigh.'

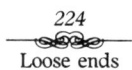
So Walter and Mr Horton visited Mr Leigh. The poor man is so sick. He has been too ill to attend services since his arrival back in New South Wales from New Zealand and has Dr Bland calling every day. Mr Erskine and Mr Marsden both have said that they expect him to die soon. Our Eliza's William Walker has said: 'I think that Mr Leigh has something on his mind which is worrying him and upsetting his body. He has taken such quantities of medicine and submitted to so many bloodings that, combined with his worry over the letters going to and fro about him to London, he probably would get sick again even if Dr Bland could cure him.'

Walter's visit was not easy for either of them. Both men have been too close and too distant, too alike and too different for it to be easy. But at least Samuel Leigh knows that the District Meeting and Walter don't want to remain in a state of disharmony. Forgiving and being forgiven, for both men, will probably be a slow process.

I'm glad that Walter went to see Samuel because the next morning, the last day of the District Meeting, we all met in the Princes Street Chapel for the sacrament of Holy Communion. Catherine Leigh was there, with the other wives of missionaries who were in Sydney at the time, dark, weary rings under her eyes and the strain of the constant care of a very sick husband showing on her face. As we received the body and blood of our Lord, I was glad she was with us and I said a special prayer for her.

Although the 1822 stationing shows Walter appointed to Van Dieman's Land, the District Meeting advised him not to go immediately, but to wait for replies to our letters. Benjamin Carvosso pointed out that an item published in the 1823 *Methodist Magazine* suggested that perhaps Walter is not quite so much out of favour as he feels. Who knows what might happen next?

The missionary notices in the *Methodist Magazine* read: '. . . an extract from a letter from Mr Carvosso states the sailing of Mr Lawry to Tongataboo with the intention of attempting the commencement of the mission there: a measure which the Committee had not in contemplation at quite so early a period, but which we trust may prove the opening of a "great and effectual door" for the preaching of Christ to those interesting islanders, among whom there are no other missionaries of any denomination.'

Walter said that all *that* meant was a polite way of saying that Lawry had gone off to do things his own way again and they just hoped that some good might come out of the mess!

And now, confusion on confusion. The new list of stations has arrived from the Conference of July 1823: Ben has been posted to Van Dieman's Land and the final name was 'Friendly Islands — Walter Lawry, one to be sent.' We'd laugh, if it wasn't so ridiculous.

Parramatta, New South Wales: July 20, 1824

Walter came home tonight after the meeting in Parramatta, stamping his cold feet and rubbing his chilled fingers after his frosty ride home. I threw more wood on the fire and he stood on the sandstone hearth with his back to the blaze while he told me the news.

'Everyone agrees,' he said. 'I'm going to England on the *Midas* as we had planned and everyone thinks you should come with me.'

I took a deep breath. For months while all kinds of ideas have been discussed about Walter and his future, I have been fighting a fear that it might mean separation for us. I couldn't bear that. Some people thought he should go back to Tonga: we hear that a man has been sent direct to Tonga from England, but don't know if it is true. Some thought he should take up an appointment around Sydney or Parramatta. Early in the year, there was serious talk about him moving west of Sydney and beginning a new work at Bringelly. None of these ideas really dealt with the problem that still remained: the Committee in London were still clearly not happy with him and further letters had shown that he was still not reconciled with them.

Ought he to go to England and sort things out with them,

leaving me here in Parramatta? Arrangements have. been made with the *Midas*, a very fast sailing ship, for a passage for Walter, but I was afraid I would be left behind. In fact, he was all ready to sail with the *Midas* in May, but it was delayed. And he has still not received permission to return to England.

Now, staring into the fire, a new part of my life opens up. Again I will face the open ocean with all its dangers. I will be again leaving my mother, brothers and sisters and I know how much I missed them before. There will be the excitement of seeing England, with all its wonders which I have only dreamt about, and the joy of meeting my Walter's family and seeing his beloved Cornwall. Maybe my feelings are understandably mixed.

Yet I'm thankful that a decision has been made. The past months have been very difficult for Walter. He had plenty of work to do in helping the other ministers with services and sharing the pastoral work, but it was made difficult because he didn't have a specific circuit of his own. He longed to have a special place where the people and the work were his responsibility. My brother Thomas has been sharing his feelings about this, because over recent months the Anglican clergy have been dithering over making a decision about *his* appointment – Port Macquarie, Bathurst or the Cowpastures to start a new congregation at Cobbittee – and sister-in-law Anne has been very agitated about the delay.

Walter has been invited to speak at a number of the missionary meetings around the colony about his experiences in Tonga. He likes to talk about it, but finds that people expect to hear only exciting or dramatic things and are not really interested in the ordinary, mundane parts of our life. Perhaps they think that high drama was part of our everyday life, or maybe they just like an exciting tale, whether or not it really expresses what was true.

The average settler, gaping on his backless form in a tiny Methodist chapel at stories of Tonga, is not really any worse than the editors of the *Methodist Magazine*, far away in London. A copy of the 1823 issue with its missionary notices has come, with large parts of Walter's 1822 journal and part of the 1823 journal published in it, describing the work in Tonga and our time there.

'They just choose the parts that suit them,' Walter complained. 'I didn't expect them to print every word, but they have chosen to print all the parts that show us in a good light and the Tongans as curious and rather peculiar pagans, and have left out all the bits where I wrote of failure or discouragement, mistakes on our part or anger. On some occasions they have used articles which were published in the *Sydney Gazette* from my notes, but somehow they have managed to use the material in such a way that an experience which was lively and full of zest sounds merely ponderous and dull. Perhaps they thought they had to alter things to make them sound a bit more "spiritual" because our instructions particularly said that we should record conversions and, of course, we had none to record.'

A small but personal hurt for me was that, in several instances where Walter had originally written my name and mentioned my presence at events, my name was omitted from the published account. I suppose a missionary's wife doesn't count.

So, we are going to England. Walter wants to take one or two of our Tongan friends with us. (Brother Jonathan has agreed to manage my flocks and herds in our absence.) What will that mean to us all? I wonder.

On board the ship *Midas*: August 18, 1824
We have set sail and the coast of New South Wales is only a line on the horizon. Walter has tried to make me go below to our cabin, but I have stayed here, staring back towards my home with a sense of great desolation and loss. Do convicts feel like this, I wonder, when they see England disappearing in the distance? Yet I am not facing a 'life sentence', surely? All I know is that I felt an anguish of spirit which I can't explain when I said goodbye to my mother and my family, and I can't talk about it.

Tama Nau is travelling with us to England and is very excited about it, indeed. I don't think another Tongan has ever been to England before, unless Captain Cook took some – I have heard no stories of it. Tama Nau will be a good man to go back to his people to describe the wonders of civilisation. (The wonders of English civilisation will be just as new to me!)

The Carvossos have gone as directed to Van Dieman's Land and we feel sure they will do a fine work there – they are very greatly loved in New South Wales. To our great relief, Samuel Leigh is well again. He was extremely ill till the end of January, but then began to recover and is now able to take up his appointment at Parramatta. We were able to part from him in peace, thank God. Ralph Mansfield has been asking for permission to take Lydia home to England because she has had one miscarriage after another and is a sick girl, but he has been refused permission – to his great disappointment and distress. William Walker is facing all kinds of difficulties with the Aboriginal work and I have a feeling that he may give up quite soon. I don't know how the Methodist work will go over the next few years – probably not easily.

Saying goodbye to the Marsdens was almost like saying farewell to my own family. Dear Mrs Marsden, after all her long years of being an invalid, is a lovely motherly lady. Mr Marsden, despite his rather gruff exterior, has been the man who has been like a father to me since Father died. I love them both.

As I stand here gazing back for the last glimpse of Australia, I feel as if I am being physically torn away, a tearing that is leaving me damaged and in pain. I am being torn away from a landscape, a place and a people that are home.

Pain and healing

On board the ship *Midas*, South Atlantic Ocean: November 22, 1824

Five years ago today Walter and I were married. On that lovely day, as a nineteen-year-old in Parramatta, I had no idea what it would mean to marry the Rev. Walter Lawry, Methodist missionary. I knew I loved him and wanted to be with him always, but I didn't imagine that being with him would take me to New Zealand, Tonga and now to the middle of the South Atlantic Ocean on our way to England.

Would I have been too frightened to marry him if I had known? I doubt it! For one thing I was sure I loved him enough to go with him to the ends of the earth, and for another I didn't realise, in my innocence, what the ends of the earth might mean. So today we cuddled up together in our cabin, holding each other and our children in one big bundle of love, and we thanked God for letting us live our life together. Holding Henry and Elizabeth tightly, we thought again of our first beautiful Elizabeth – she is still very real to me and an important part of our marriage.

As well as being our wedding anniversary, today has also been important in that we have crossed the equator and for the first time in my life I am in the Northern Hemisphere. Walter was excited because for him it means he is closer to his home. But I am further from mine. He wrote in his diary: 'Shall I ever pass under the sun again? I hope if at all it will only be once more. I have dear friends in each

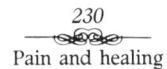
place (New Holland and Great Britain) and must necessarily endure the pain of being absent from one party.'

Our journey in the *Midas* has been reasonably fast so far, but not always easy. The *Midas* is a ship of 430 tons which sailed far south of Australia earlier in the year to collect her cargo of sea-elephant oil and seal skins from Macquarie Island, almost as far south as the Antarctic. Before we sailed, Walter thought that Captain Thompson seemed a reasonable man who promised a comfortable passage, but for the second time we discover that at sea a captain can become very tyrannical and disagreeable. The mate is even worse and the crew tend to be dirty and bad-mannered.

We have been at sea for three months already without calling in at any port. Captain Thompson says that he doesn't intend to stop anywhere until we reach England. And I thought that a month between New Zealand and Tonga was bad enough! We have tossed across the Pacific Ocean through a number of storms and our passage around Cape Horn was terribly rough. (I remembered my parents and the *Duff*, turning away from Cape Horn nearly thirty years ago.) The children and Walter and I have been seasick, weary of being cooped up and bruised from being thrown about in the ship.

Walter, with his usual planner's eye to the future and ideas for efficiency, has been making notes in his journal under the heading 'Preparations for a Voyage', in case we should ever make a similar journey again. We have both been very dissatisfied with the arrangements for food. He thinks that we'd do better to bring all our own food or have a written agreement with the captain about the availability of bread, milk, potatoes, fresh water and so on, and perhaps pay only half our passage money till we know that things are satisfactory.

'Next time,' he says firmly, 'we'll bring our own preserved meats and wine — and insist on sailing on a vessel with a poop deck where we can take some fresh air in peace.' To save on freight costs, we have all our possessions crowded into our cabin with us which is probably

very bad for our things because the cabin is so damp –
Walter calls it 'a well' because it is so often wet.

To make up for some of our discomforts, we have had the
pleasure of the company of a number of Christian friends
on the voyage, including the Butler family on their way
back to England from the Church Mission in New Zealand.
We have been having regular Sunday services and Bible
studies in our cabin, with various preachers. During the
week that the captain said we would need to change the
date because of crossing the dateline, the crew had two
Saturdays but we decided to keep two Sundays instead.

It has been a great help to have Tama Nau with us. He
loves our children and is special friends with Henry, who
is nearly three years old now.

How much longer will this voyage take? I wonder. If we
travel really fast, we just might be in England for Christmas. That would be lovely, I think. I have always heard
stories about the beauties of a wintry Christmas. Last year,
we were just home from Tonga and were being surrounded
with all the love and care of my Australian family. The
Christmas before that was our very strange Christmas Day
in Tonga, where the people had no idea that that day had
a special meaning for us. How are our Tongan friends
now? I wonder. How are Charles and George getting along
alone – will they be able to manage until more staff arrive
to help them? We pray for them all often. With Tama Nau
in our company every day, we can't forget Tonga.

Portsmouth, England: New Year's Day, 1825

Thank God we are safely arrived. After four-and-a-half
months and 18,000 miles of sea across two vast oceans, today we put our feet at last on dry land again. We are all
well and so thankful to be here. A kind Captain Hawtry of
Portsmouth has welcomed us warmly and we will stay
with him here until Tuesday when we will take a coach to
London. Our luggage will be taken to London on the
Midas, but we couldn't wait to leave the ship.

We have missed Christmas in England this year. A week

ago we were still well out to sea and only yesterday did we first see the coast of France and sail up the British Channel. Next year I will have my dream of snow on Christmas Day, and roaring fires and carol singers wrapped in cloaks against the cold.

3 Winkworth Place, City Road, London: January 8, 1825

It wasn't until we had finally arrived at the house of Walter's old friends, the Flemings, here in the heart of this vast city that I realised how tired I was. For months we have been travelling, buffetted about by the ocean, living in miserable conditions, trying to care for two little children, missing my family and excited but a little scared of the future in a strange land. Now that we are here, I have wanted to hide away in my room and sleep and sleep.

Tama Nau and I were just like two little children, jumpy with excitement, on the coach ride over the fifty miles from Portsmouth. Walter laughed at our eagerness (and probably made a note about us in his journal!). We left Portsmouth very early while it was still dark and, as the sky lightened, Nau and I were constantly rubbing clear patches on the frosted windows so that we could see. It was so beautiful. As we jolted along, swaying from side to side with the motion of the coach as it rattled behind the horses, we looked out on a winter landscape unlike anything either of us had ever seen: leafless trees, elegant black-and-white sketches against snowy fields, thick green lines of hedgerows and thickets of pine, villages of tidy cottages, thatched roofs laden with a crusting of snow, signs of industry and prosperity in the towns we passed. When we stopped at a coaching inn for a rest and hot soup, Nau and I picked up handfuls of snow — we hadn't realised that it would be not only very cold, but very wet!

As we entered the outskirts of the city of London, I felt myself not so much impressed as overwhelmed by it all. Buildings were heaped on buildings, crowding closer and closer together, higher and higher, some marvellous and huge in their appearance and some poor and disreputable, almost blotting out the sky and making me feel that they would all fall on me. More and more people were crowded together with traffic on foot, in coaches, chaises, wagons and hackney cabs, wheels upon wheels splattering mud and refuse on passers-by. Noise was pressing against my ears: shouting, the bleat and lowing of flocks of sheep and herds of cattle on their way to market, the crying of wares for sale. Walter heard a woman calling 'Mackerel, fresh mackerel!' and he nearly jumped out of the coach with excitement, knowing it was probably Cornish fish.

My eyes began to sting with the smoky atmosphere. As we had approached London, we had seen great smoke stacks pouring dark clouds of smoke into the sky over the city and my first impression was of a weary greyness lying over everything. Without wanting to give offence to our fellow travellers, I found myself pressing a handkerchief to my nose, which was being assaulted with odours of a range of nastiness. I trembled to think what might be causing so many horrible smells, but even a glance out into the road with the open drains and droppings of a thousand beasts gave me some clues.

'So this is civilisation, the pride of the British Empire,' I thought, with a memory of the fragrance of uncivilised Tonga. When we were finally set down at the coaching inn in the heart of London, I stumbled wearily across the great yard seething with horses and coaches, passengers, luggage, servants and ostlers, and was willing to be guided, almost as if blindfolded, by the good Mr Fleming who had come to collect us and take us home to his house just off City Road. As soon as the children were cared for, I almost fell into bed with a splitting headache and told Walter that I should probably stay there for a week.

3 Winkworth Place, City Road, London: January 15, 1825

For years I have heard of the Committee – always the Committee – this all-powerful Thing: faceless, perhaps with

many heads and tentacles reaching around the globe, prob-
ing blindly at people and places beyond their vision and
beyond their grasp. The Committee has hurt my other self,
my Walter, so I had decided long ago that I didn't like It.

'Don't be silly, Mary; they are only people,' Walter had
assured me. 'Just ordinary men. Well, maybe not really so
ordinary, because most of them are men with exceptional
gifts and unusually deep Christian experience. But the
Wesleyan Methodist Church has asked them to do a very
big task in supervising all their missions around the world.
First, let me try to sort out all my problems with them and
then I'll take you to meet them.'

The day after we arrived in London, therefore, while I
stayed snugly in bed and Mrs Fleming looked after the
children, Walter set off for the offices of the Mission Committee several city blocks away in Hatton Garden. I have
seen the address '77 Hatton Garden' on so many letters,
yet find it hard to imagine *going* to it. Walter tells me there
is no garden there now, but long ago in the days of Queen
Elizabeth, one Christopher Hatton bought a great garden
there from the church on the understanding that the bish-
ops could collect twenty bushels of roses every year.

He came back very deflated indeed.

'So much for a welcome home to the pioneer missionary,'
he said. 'When I arrived at their offices, I was told that the
Committee was busy in a meeting and couldn't see me today. Then Mr Morley, one of the four executive secretaries
of the Committee, came out to see me briefly, then Mr
Taylor and Mr Mason, but the atmosphere in the room was
as chilly as the London weather! They wanted to know
what I was doing in London when they had not given permission for me to come home. Then they suggested that we
missionaries in New South Wales had taken it upon ourselves to make up our own rules and deliberately flout
their directions. I started to give our point of view, and surprised them with a few things I said, but they have told me
to wait until they call me to a formal meeting when they
will hear my case. We parted with bad feelings.'

Poor Walter. I wish I could help, but there is little I can do but love him and pray for him.

'There'll be a storm when we meet, I'm sure. Yet I really believe that I have done what was right, both in New South Wales and in going to Tonga, so I'll just have to bear any rough treatment I get.'

Nine days went by before the Committee called Walter to see them again. He was beginning to think that they had forgotten his existence. We had spent the time busily, with Walter collecting our luggage from the *Midas*, now at anchor on the Thames River, and having a great argument over freight costs with the captain. We were advised to have vaccinations against smallpox (in Australia it is not a problem) and so took the children with us to the infirmary at the huge St Bartholomew's Hospital not far from here to be given the cowpox. Unfortunately it didn't take the first time and will have to be done again. I was feeling much more rested by then and Tama Nau and I had made a few tentative excursions into nearby streets. One delightful surprise had been a visit from our old friends, Mr and Mrs Hosking, who used to be teachers of orphan girls in Sydney and Parramatta. It was so exciting to see their familiar faces.

At last, on January 14 Walter was called to the Mission House again and set off, very tense and nervous, for the meeting he had been imagining for months. When he came home again, he looked much relieved.

'I have to go back again tomorrow,' he said, 'and speak with the full Committee, but today was very important as I spoke with all the four executive secretaries — a few other missionaries were onlookers.'

'Tell me,' I said. My heart had been with him all day.

'We made a very bad start. The chief secretary, the Rev. Richard Watson, came in and, without so much as shaking my hand or greeting me, started straight in with an accusation. "Mr Lawry, you have come home without permission and so virtually exclude yourself from us", he said. Coming home without permission was only the last thing

on a long, long list of things which had annoyed them
about me. When I started to try to justify myself on that
one, he interrupted me to say, ''Are you going to try to
justify every letter you have written and everything you
have done since you left? You Cornishmen are never wrong
– look at that long letter about nothing from Mr Carvosso
we have just received!''

'That made me really angry. I told them that they should
be careful about sending out any more Cornishmen in that
case, because in my opinion Benjamin Carvosso was one of
the very best missionaries they had. They saw how upset
I was and quickly tried to soothe me by saying that they
knew and loved the many excellences of their Cornish
brethren.

'So I calmed down and explained that *of course* I didn't
mean that I had never written an unwise letter (did you
ever see a letter I wrote before we were married, demanding instant permission to marry? It was a masterpiece of an
unsuitable choice of words to write to the church fathers)
or that I had never made a mistake. I just wanted to say
that they didn't understand the background to all the
things of which I was accused and that I was innocent of
those particular accusations. After that, we were able to
talk together much more reasonably and went, point by
point, over the problems – the Parramatta Sunday School
and everything. I had minutes of meetings to show them
and, before long, they were apologising to me for their misunderstanding. They said that their letters had seemed
justifiable and proper according to their understanding
of the case, but now they had changed their minds.

'In the end we agreed not to bring all our disagreements
out into the open before the whole Committee as it would
only mean that poor Samuel Leigh would be in trouble for
long-past problems instead of me and I didn't want to do
that to the man. I was even able to ask them why I had
been accused of so many supposed wrongs, but had never
been thanked for paying for the Parramatta chapel out of
our own pocket. They were quite embarrassed to hear that

as they had not realised what had happened and have promised to reimburse us. That will help our tottering financial position.'

'What about Tonga? What did they think about that? Have you talked to them yet about your ideas for work in the South Seas?' I asked.

'They want me to talk to the whole group about it tomorrow and then we will know.'

Today, Walter returned to Hatton Garden and the Mission House. He went off armed with his careful notes on his suggestions for the whole approach to the South Seas, ideas that he has tossed around in past years with the Rev. John Williams, Rev. Samuel Marsden and Rev. Samuel Leigh, things he has thought through during our visit to New Zealand and our time in Tonga, dreams he has had while poring over his atlas and while soaking himself in scripture. He has an orderly mind and went to the meeting with some clear principles to offer.

When he came back to the house this evening, he came stamping in with the grimy slush of the streets on his boots and his hat and coat wet and cold, but as he came to the fireside his face was alight.

'I've had a wonderful day!' he said, throwing his arms around me. 'Such a change. Mr Watson introduced me to the whole Committee as if I were his long-lost brother (as indeed I think I am) and explained that I had come back to England specially to advise them on their missions in the South Seas, with barely a word about all our other misunderstandings. He asked me to speak to them all about Tonga and New Zealand and, of course, it was the first opportunity anyone in England has had to hear about it first-hand.

'I talked and talked, I don't know how long, and they didn't take their eyes off me. I talked about the Tongan people and hopes for their conversion, of our encouragements and fears, of the problems of isolation with no regular ship, of dangers, of the need for medical help, of the need for a larger and stronger team of workers to support each other. When at last I finished, one of the men, a Mr Butterworth, jumped up and moved that they have a special meeting of the Committee at a future time to hear my detailed suggestions for the better management of their missions to the South Seas. Everyone agreed, and then Mr Watson moved that they formally approve my return to England. And they all agreed to that, except one gentleman who thought it might become "a dangerous precedent".

'At the end of the meeting, they all crowded round me so warmly, welcoming me home, thanking me for coming, assuring me that they had quite changed their minds since they had had the chance to meet me and hear my story. For the first time in well over a year I feel that a terrible load has been lifted and that I'm... free!'

City Road, London: January 28, 1825

What an amazing mixture is this city of London. Parts of it are so wonderful and exciting, and parts are thoroughly miserable.

Walter keeps saying, 'I wish we could winter in Cornwall... at least the sea-mist and the rain is clean.' He has written many letters to his parents saying that we will come as soon as we can, but we have been asked to wait until it is convenient for the Committee to have a special meeting to hear and discuss all Walter's ideas for the South Seas missions – and goodness knows when that will be. All the Committee members are such busy men, rushing here and there to speak to missionary meetings, attending various committees and seeing to the work all around the world. Our great interest in the work in Australia, New Zealand and Tonga must take its turn for their attention with equally demanding needs in the West Indies, in Ceylon and India, in Africa. Walter put a rather acid little note in a recent letter to his parents, saying, 'I am very sorry that our London preachers who form the Committee have so much to do that they do nothing with promptitude or circumstantial accuracy...' So we wait through a London winter.

January to me has always meant heat and flies, dust
and fruit, violent thunderstorms cooling the oppressive
clamminess of hot days, sleeping under a thin sheet or
nothing at all. Not in London! I have hardly felt warm since
we arrived. The sky is grey and dark, and night seems to
fall while it is still mid-afternoon. The snow that was so
beautiful out in the country mixes with the rubbish in the
streets to become slippery and treacherous and the air is
filled with the smoke of thousands of coal fires, all trying
to warm shivering Londoners. I have heard that some
mothers stitch their children into their warm woollen
underwear in autumn and unpick them in spring. Judging
by the aroma around some people, I can believe it.

I think Tama Nau is quite shocked by the difficulties of
being clean in London – despite their pride in their modern
water closets and their acceptance of occasionally sending
a servant up several flights of stairs with a bucket of hot
water for a wash – and he and I are remembering the
delights of bathing at least daily in Tongan waters and the
anointing of coconut oil scented with fresh flowers, on
clean bodies. There is even a tax on soap here in London!

The clothing that we brought with us from New South
Wales has proved to be much too light (and quite un-
fashionable in any case) and so we have tried to stay in the
house as much as possible until I have been able to buy
and sew new things, suitable for the icy chills of winter.
The children and I have terrible colds, Walter and Tama
Nau have had small ones, so the whole house seems to be
full of people sniffing and sneezing, coughing and wheez-
ing. Although the children were outraged at being taken
back for a second dose of cowpox, I'm thankful that the
second vaccination was successful and we don't have to
worry about smallpox.

But, of course, London is an exciting place as well as a
cold and grimy one. Here in City Road we are very close
to London Bridge and the Thames River, crowded with
shipping from all around the world. There are even
astonishing ships on the river which are propelled by

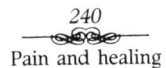
steam! I haven't travelled on it, but Walter says that last year the new invention of a railway, with a steam train travelling along it, has been taking passengers between London and Greenwich. Nau and I keep finding things to amaze us: gas lights in some city streets, the immensity of some of the churches, the bustling Smithfield markets not far away with all their animals, the complexity of the business life of the city, the elegant new suburbs to the west with great squares and parks where all the grand people of society can be seen, the wonderful variety of the shops.

Shopping has been good fun: going into a draper's and having bolts of cloth spread before me of such quality that I am dazzled (and have to remember our financial limitations), searching for a particular cooking book to send to Thomas and Anne in Sydney, working through lists of things that our New South Wales friends asked us to buy for them – a prayerbook and new Bible for Thomas, with commentaries, and all sorts of other things. Both Walter and I have spent hours shopping with the two families who are preparing to go to Tonga, Mr Ray and John Thomas and his bride Sarah, trying to be sure that they take with them the things that will be most useful. John Thomas, a blacksmith by trade, is to be ordained in March before they leave. Tama Nau has been going to school here in London, much to his interest, and will probably return to Tonga when the new missionaries go. Nau has found London so very interesting and the gentlemen of the Committee so kind to him, that he is changing his name to Watson Nau – after his new friend, Secretary Richard Watson. He understands a great deal about the gospel now, but I'm not sure just what he thinks about it.

The best thing about London has been the chance to meet the leaders of the church and to worship with them. Wesley's Chapel, the central heart of Methodism, is here in City Road and last Sunday we went there to chapel. What an experience! The chapel is very fine, I thought, set well back from the road with trees lining the entry beyond the iron gates. We joined the crowd of worshippers streaming in through the pillared entrance and found ourselves sitting up in the gallery which rings the building. Above us rose a high ceiling, beautifully ornamented, and below us were pews filled with people. When the precentor began a hymn, a glorious sound of praise welled up around us, making my skin positively tingle with goosepimples as I joined in. Walter beside me was singing at the top of his voice and I wouldn't be surprised if there were tears in his eyes. I remembered the pathetic attempts of our little group to sing those same songs in Tonga and have decided that there can be great power when a crowd of Christians worships the Lord together.

The central pulpit was immensely tall with three landings one below the other; the preachers stood at different levels to preach, to pray and to read the scripture. When the great Dr Adam Clarke came to preach his sermon, his eyes seemed to be on a level with ours in the gallery and, after the service was over, Walter told me that he felt as if every word of the preacher's message was being spoken directly to him. I could feel Walter beside me absorbing every word as we heard the great man preach an amazing sermon on Colossians 2:27-28: 'Christ in you, the hope of glory: whom we preach, warning every man, and teaching every man in all wisdom; that we may present every man perfect in Christ Jesus'.

After the service, to Walter's delight, he was introduced to Dr Clarke — 'the Rev. Walter Lawry, our pioneer missionary in the Friendly Islands... you may have seen his excellent reports of the work in the missionary notices' — and he had a conversation with that fine father of the Methodist Church.

After the service, Walter took me around behind the chapel to a quiet garden where he showed me the tomb of his hero, the Rev. John Wesley. 'They say he chose this spot himself,' Walter said. 'Wouldn't it have been wonderful to have seen Wesley himself preaching from that high pulpit? You can still feel the spiritual energy in that chapel today. Wesley's bones may lie here, but his God is still just

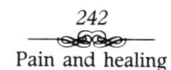
as alive and powerful as ever. We... no, I have been the powerless one.'

Somehow I feel that Walter is at the point of a new beginning in his ministry. Since we left Tonga, he has been unsure about his direction, unsure about his relationship to the Methodist work, without an appointment, a wounded man. But he has been given medicine for his wounds and they are healing so that now he can start again.

As I wrote in a letter to brother Thomas: 'It affords me pleasure to inform you that after some explanations and old writings brought foreward which had not been made public, the Committee quite changed their tone of voice and approved of all that had transpired. They are now well pleased that we came home. They, of course, wish us to return, but at the same time think it reasonable that we should remain a while here.'

For the time being Walter is speaking at a great many missionary meetings on behalf of the Committee and is to be given an appointment in a circuit in Cornwall for long enough for him to spend some time with his family. Since his reconciliation with the Committee, he seems to have been able to take a fresh grasp of his own call to ministry. Since Dr Clarke's sermon from Colossians, he keeps reflecting on 'Christ in you... whom we preach...' He is a good man and I love him. I feel sure that his ministry is going to be more powerful than ever since his recent heavy trials.

Tregarton, near Mevagissey, Cornwall: June 24, 1825

The man that Father Lawry sent down to the post office in the village of Mevagissey has come back empty-handed again.

'Sorry, Mrs Lawry,' he said. 'No mail from Australia again' – and he marched off to return to his farm work.

I wonder if my family at home realise just how eagerly I look for a letter. I begin to realise why our Methodist Committee don't seem to see much urgency in things happening on the far side of the world. Australia and Tonga seem so far away as to be quite unbelievable. But I *know* they are real, and I know that my beloved family is there and I long to have word from them.

My half-written letter to my dear brother Thomas lies before me. A lot of things have changed since last I wrote from London. One very sad day was in April when we said goodbye to dear Watson Nau and the new missionaries, John and Sarah Thomas, on their way to Tonga. Nau has been part of our family since we first met him in Tonga at the end of 1822. He often came to stay with us and help me with the cooking. Since then we have lived in his home area, he has lived in ours and we have travelled all around the world together. Somehow I fear that Mr and Mrs Thomas didn't quite know what to make of Nau, with his lively, mischievous confidence and rather boisterous humour, but we have come to love him.

Our children were heartbroken and I found myself mopping my eyes as we left their ship saying in a wobbly voice, 'I'll never see him again. . .'

Walter was quite brisk about it. 'Why not? We could go back to Tonga one day, you know.' But I don't think we'll ever meet again till we meet in heaven.

After Watson Nau and the others had gone, Walter had his long-awaited meeting again with the Committee and preached at numberless missionary meetings. We were both kept 'on the trot', as Walter described it in a letter, with all sorts of errands for ourselves and our friends at home in New South Wales. At last we were ready to set out for his beloved Cornwall. With two young and very wriggly children on my lap, the coach trip was very exhausting from London, but as we travelled through county after county to the west we saw all sorts of beautiful countryside. It is wonderful to see, specially in all the glory of an English spring, but I still miss the bush of my childhood with the lovely untidiness of a eucalypt draped with ringlets of shed bark or the mysterious messages inscribed on the smooth bark of the scribbly gum.

We are being cared for so lovingly here with Walter's family and I find it easy to call them Father and Mother Lawry. Sister Emma is having to get used to having us and our lively family around, but she is a lovely, kind aunt to Henry and Elizabeth. Sister Anna is a married lady now, Mrs Henry Vercoe, but Walter writes to her regularly and we sometimes see her. The people here in the nearby villages of Gorran and the fishing village of Mevagissey have been delighted to see Walter home again and he has been so very happy to be here. All through winter in London he kept on wishing for the joys of Cornwall. Now that he is home and it is a lovely warm, dry summer, he is prone to say: 'I told you so − I *said* it would be good!'

After the constant problems with colds in bleak London, it is wonderful to have all of us well again. Sometimes we go for walks together, down to Mevagissey village to see the fishing fleet with their haul of pilchards and mackerel, crabs and lobsters, or along windy headlands looking down on a wild rockiness of coastline where smugglers have been said to lurk and probably still do. Walter says it is fine swimming in some of the coves, but the water looks very cold to me, after Australian summer waters or the coral reefs of Tonga. Sometimes we walk along narrow country roads between high, thick hedges, passing little cottages and the refuse heaps of old mine workings and mine shafts, now all grown over with brambles. Everywhere we walk we see vivid colour, green slopes draped with yellow furze, lichens of all colours from deep orange to the darkest mossy green and always the sea in the distance.

It is all very lovely, but I miss my family. I have just written to brother Thomas: 'Do you know, my dear brother, that I have not had one line from any of you or my friends and you must think I am all most brokenhearted. Several ships have come since we arrived and I keep on sending to the post office three miles off in hopes of hearing, but all in vain. What then is England and all its beauties to me if I hear not of my friends? I am now expecting that the end will be their negligence and unkindness will wean me entirely so that I shall never care to return.'

As soon as I had written that, I suddenly wondered whether my dear family might not recognise that I was only teasing and hastily wrote on: 'Do, dear brother, let us hear from you often for you know the rest are not fond of writing. I wish very much to hear if you are at your new station and whether you have another little one and how dear little James and his mother is, and whether your prospects are fair to do good in that place. Nothin will give us more pleasure than to hear of your well fair. If crosses be your lott, do pray let us share them by sympathy.'

The other very important thing I wanted to say to Thomas was about our own future ministry. I wrote: 'My dear W. is absent as he frequently is, for he has been very busyly imployed ever since our arrival, in assisting in missionary meetings. Poor man, he begins to fag thro' travling so much and telling the same story so many times; still it is new in every place...'

Poor Walter complains that he hopes his listeners are getting some good out of his meetings. I'm sure they are — though they just leave him worn out and cranky! I continued: '...next month he proceeds to Bristol to Conference, after which we shall leave our Father's house (where we are at present very comfortable) for a new station, a circuit which shall not be above seven miles from hence. We expect to remain there (in St Austle) one year, after which we do not know which way to stear. We wish to be guided entirely by the providence of God in all things.'

For some reason which I can't explain, except that I felt shy about writing it to my brother, I didn't tell him about the baby I am expecting in December. I am very well at the moment and Henry and Elizabeth are excitedly looking forward to a little brother or sister. I'll tell him about it next time.

I dipped my pen in the ink to complete my letter: 'Mrs H., yourself and babe have our prayers. I can say we most cordially unite in affectionate love to you all. Bear us, my dear brother and sister, on the wings of faith and love in your daily petitions at a mercy seat. From your loving and affectionate sister, Mary C. Lawry.'

St Austell, Cornwall: December 14, 1825

This is our birthday week, with Henry's fourth birthday today and my twenty-sixth birthday two days ago. I woke this morning with a strong feeling that today will be the birthday of our new baby, too. When Henry and Elizabeth came to clamber over us in bed this morning, Henry bouncing with energy and intelligence and Elizabeth such a lovely two-year-old, I whispered to Walter: 'Thank you for giving me such beautiful children. What do you think they will be like when they grow up? Rich? Famous? Will they have happy marriages? Will they travel to Australia? What about their children and their children's children...? More than anything, I want them all to love the Lord and be his children, but it would be rather nice if Henry grew up like you and became a minister of the gospel.'

Walter laughed at me and said, 'You are thinking a long way into the future,' but I was very serious about it. Ever since Sunday I have had the strangest feeling that I wanted to see, to enjoy, to appreciate, to be thankful for all my blessings – almost as if today is the last day I can do it.

Walter is so happy now that we have our home in St Austell, a circuit of his own and he no longer has to make endless journeys to strange congregations. The people of St Austell and all the villages around here – Mevagissey, Charlestown, St Blazey, Tywardreath, Treuarren, Gorran, Fowey, Lanjeth, Coombe, Porthpean, Trethergy, Polgooth and Truan – where Walter travels to preach at Methodist meetings, are all pleased to have him because he grew up in this area. He understands all their needs and preaches in a way that both challenges them and makes them love him.

Many of the people are miners and, during the week,

they are working deep in the earth in the tin mines and the new china clayworks at St Austell. Many of them are faced with unemployment as the tin mines are closing down and, while some farmers are flourishing, many farm labourers are struggling. Even the fishing villages have faced difficult times lately.

Walter has been preaching with real power and there has been what Walter describes as 'a spirit of hearing' on the people. Many have said that they feel that they have been slipping away from the Lord and feel a great need to be right with him again. People are starting to meet in greater numbers for prayer and are beginning to talk about a sense of need in their lives. Something very wonderful is beginning to happen. Walter has just written a happy letter to his dear friend Benjamin Carvosso, far away in Van Dieman's Land, to tell him how very happily and usefully he is settling into his new ministry after all the pain of the past few years.

I'm glad I have come to visit Cornwall and to meet Walter's family. As I get to know his parents and uncles and aunts, I can understand better what makes my other self as he is. They are a clan of people who have been devout Methodists since the days when John Wesley used to preach at the pit-tops in Cornish mining communities, a family of chapel builders and lay leaders of Class Meetings in their own welcoming kitchens. His great-aunt Thomasina's family even founded a new group of believers called the Bible Christians.

I have met Benjamin Carvosso's dear old father, Mr William Carvosso, a wonderful old man who learned to read at the age of sixty-five in a Methodist society so that he could read his Bible. He still walks from end to end of Cornwall, making friends with strangers and leading them to the Lord. Recently a new convert called Billy Bray came preaching in our area and he was so excited about the way God has changed his life from wild drunken behaviour to a whole new person that he sang, skipped and positively danced around the pulpit with the joy of the Lord. The

Cornish are a lively people: fiercely independent and very real and heartfelt in their faith. It is no wonder that my Cornish Walter found the attitudes and rejection of the New South Wales population so hard to accept.

Last Sunday I went as usual with Walter to chapel. Each tiny village chapel has its own character, very simple and bare yet full of atmosphere. As the children and I walked through the door, we moved to the women's side of the room, with all the men sitting solemnly on the other. The only ornament in the room was the row of hatpegs around the walls with the hats, caps and cloaks of the congregation suspended from them. I kept my cloak wrapped around me because it was raining again and I felt cold. They say that 'Cornwall will take a shower every day of the week and two on Sundays'. The constant soft drizzling mistiness is so different from the sunshine of Sydney or the violent tropical downpours of Tonga.

Walter stood high above us in the narrow pulpit, looking down on us over the Bible laid on its fat velvet cushion. The girls around me had put aside their work clothes and the big, floppy sunbonnets which they wear in the mines, and blossomed out in vivid colours. The men were stiff and well-scrubbed in their Sunday-best, the red-stained garments of the tin mines and the mine hats with candles stuck on the front left behind on this day of rest. They sat looking up at Walter expectantly, waiting for a word of hope in their discouragement, a promise of forgiveness in their failures, a call of challenge in their apathy.

As he preached the word of God, the fervent congregation responded to him with whispers of 'Amen!' and cries of 'Praise the Lord!' Walter caught my eye and we smiled at each other, enjoying the eagerness and openness of the people. There was, I think, the merest hint of a wink in his eye, just for me. My body shifted restlessly on the hard, high-backed pew, awkward with the weight of our child soon to be born, but my memory slipped off freely to other scenes where we have been able to worship together: the schoolroom in Parramatta; my parents' front parlour; on the empty block of land at Windsor; in our beloved New Chapel in Parramatta; the elegant new church in Macquarie Street, Sydney, with its uncomfortable pews and even more uncomfortable debt; in the open air and in our communal room with its high thatched roof at Mu'a on Tongatapu, with our tiny alien group of worshippers watched curiously and suspiciously by Tongans; cramped in our cabin on the *Midas* in mid-ocean; the wonderful services in Wesley's Chapel, London; and now here, in Cornish chapels scattered in fishing villages and mining communities.

The scene has changed and the response of the people has changed, but I have realised that the word of the gospel has been just as true in every place and our Lord has been just as present in every place. I watched Walter preaching and I feel sure that he will go on leading people to Christ wherever he is. That is my prayer for him.

*　　*　　*

The lamps have been lit, the curtains are drawn against the windy dark and the midwife has gone home. I feel very weak and tired, but I suppose that is only normal. Walter has been with me and we have held our lovely new daughter in our arms.

'I want her to be called Mary,' he said, 'but what shall we call her for a second name?'

As I had been struggling through the hours of labour, I had been thinking a lot of home, wishing that it was the sure and loving hands of my mother who was delivering my child, not an unknown Cornish midwife with perhaps rather old-fashioned ways. And so I said sleepily, 'Can we call her Mary Australia?'

Now Mary Australia is asleep beside me and I need to sleep too.

*　　*　　*

St Austell, Cornwall: Christmas Day, 1825

Today they brought my son to see me. I think it was to say goodbye.

Little Henry and Elizabeth have been cared for by their grandparents since baby Mary Australia was born. Walter brought Henry on horseback through the snow and they came creeping into my room together. It is a very strange Christmas Day for them and for me. I always looked forward to one day spending Christmas Day in England. I thought it would be lovely if there were snow – but I didn't think it would be like this. Since Mary Australia was born, I have not been well. Since the bleeding started again, I have felt my life flowing away from me. For Walter's sake, I'm glad he is with his family.

I'm not frightened of going to be with God – I feel that he has been my Friend for so long that I will be safe and at home with him – but I am clinging to Walter's hand because it is so hard to be separated. He is my other self and I am his.

Some people seem to think that my dying will be a waste. I hope not. . .

Epilogue

Parramatta, New South Wales: March, 1859

I, Walter Lawry, have never forgotten that bitter Christmas Day when my beloved wife Mary died. I couldn't believe it. She was such a very alive person, so closely meshed into the fabric of my own life that it seemed impossible to believe that she was no longer with me. Months after her death, letters came addressed to her from her family in Australia, the letters she had so longed to see, and I stumbled with them to her grave and wept. Wept because she couldn't read her letters and wept because I had lost her.

After Mary's death, I wrote to my friend Benjamin Carvosso far away in Van Dieman's Land. Only a few months before I had written to tell him how happy we were in our new work and how well. Now, in deep anguish, I wrote of my loss. I had been searching my heart to see if I could see some reason why this had happened to me and to our children. I could find no reason, only the assurance that we were still in God's hands. I wrote to brother-in-law Thomas Hassall: 'My precious Mary is where you and I hope to be... She was to me of all earthly blessings the dearest...'

At the time, it seemed that all that I had left were my beautiful children, now motherless, and my work. My mother and sister helped me with the little ones and I poured all my strength into my work. Wherever I preached, I would find myself looking in vain for her face among the congregation and could not help mentioning her name. Week after week the people would be moved to tears as they shared my sense of loss and the urgency I felt that I must point people to Christ. As that empty first year of my bereavement went on, 1826, I began to realise that some of the seeds I had been watering with my tears had been taking root. More and more people were becoming interested in finding a real faith of their own, the prayer meetings were growing in numbers and in genuine seeking for God, and I felt that my preaching was being given power by the Lord to reach people.

Only two months after Mary's death, we had the first sign of a great new movement of the Holy Spirit among us. An old man who had been godless all his life was at work breaking stones on the road when he was overcome with a great sense of his sinfulness and need for God. That night he couldn't sleep for fear of the future, because he was sure that God could never forgive one so wicked as he. For days he struggled with a lifetime of guilt. Christian friends came to help him, till at last he was able to pray for forgiveness. To his amazement, and the astonishment of all of our people, not only did he find peace and forgiveness but his back, twisted and crippled into a permanent stoop for many years, was miraculously healed and he was able to stand upright!

Not long after, I was preaching in the village of Sticker at a missionary meeting, referring to the spiritual needs of Tonga. A man was powerfully convicted of sin and found peace with God. This made such an impression on the people of Sticker that, as I wrote later: 'From that time on the word of the Lord mightily grew and prevailed in Sticker so that at the annual revel no-one was found in attendance; and when the fiddler came in his usual way to the public house, it is reported that the landlady said to him: 'The feast is removed to the Methodist chapel. All the people are gone thither and I advise you to follow them.'

I still have the report I wrote of those months, written from St Austell in May, 1827. Out of the pain of my preaching and under the hand of God, something was happening. I wrote: 'At St Austle the Spirit of the Lord has descended on the people... In no instance has there been any irregularity or noisy commotion, but a steady, deep and awful "feeling after God". About one hundred souls have been added to our society at this place... At Mevagissey... the work has been very rapid and wide... one hundred and fifty persons have joined; they will require much pastoral care; and, thank God, there are among our leading friends in this society many individuals who are highly qualified to watch over these souls... in other places almost the whole population is in motion Godward. In such copiousness did the Spirit descend on the people of these villages, that they were seized with deep distress for sin, while they were in the bowels of the earth; and many came from different parts of the mines, at the same hour of the day, in the bitterest anguish of soul, desiring some to pray with them; and these individuals seldom left the place until they found spiritual comfort... The bulk of the population is under spiritual arrest; and the general subject of conversation is this great work of the Lord among the people... A great number of conversions [are] among the children of our religious friends; many weeping parents having seen their prodigals return... Our lovefeasts are indescribably blessed... almost every countenance glows with heavenly love and joy.'

Almost a year after Mary's death, letters came from Australia telling of how her family had received the news and it was as if the wound were reopened as I read the letters. Eliza's husband, William Walker, told how the first news had come through a letter from Benjamin Carvosso in Van Dieman's Land, who had received my letter and written to the family and friends in Sydney before other news arrived. He told how Mrs Hassall bore the sad news, how he and Samuel rode out to the Cowpastures to tell Lucy, Jonathan and Mary, how brother James 'feels very acutely and suffers severely', how they wrote to Thomas Hassall in Bathurst, how Elizabeth Marsden, Mary's bridesmaid, wrote: 'I feel her death deeply for she was my earliest friend.'

They sent me cuttings from the *Sydney Gazette*. Somehow it soothed my heart to feel that my Mary was not forgotten in her own home and among her own people. The *Gazette* obituary read: 'The melancholy news has arrived per the *Henry* of the death of one of Australia's daughters... this young lady leaves three children, with an inconsolable husband to grieve over a loss which will be pronounced irreparable to all acquainted with her many virtues. She was not only almost idolized by her numerous connexions in this land, but loved also by those who knew her only by name. An afflicted parent is left to mourn the loss of her first of several daughters. Mrs Lawry accompanied her husband in his mission to Tonga, and despite every entreaty braved the fury of savages. In Tonga she remained about a year, when her condition became so extremely interesting as to render her return to the colony expedient for the sake of medical aid, and she had scarcely been on shore one day when she was delivered of a fine girl. In some few months after, though advised to the contrary, she risked the danger of the ocean and proceeded to England with her husband – and in England she died.'

In the *Methodist Magazine* in England, her obituary read briefly: 'She enjoyed a clear sense of the divine favour and was distinguished by genuine piety and amiable manners. She died in peace...'

The *Gazette* also reported on a sermon delivered by Ralph Mansfield on Jeremiah 15:9 ('Her sun is gone down while it is yet day') and a long anthem composed for the occasion of Mary's funeral service in Macquarie Street Chapel. Some of the words read:

> Shall we no more in social converse share
> The sweet endearments of her friendly care?
> No more her happy countenance survey
> Which smiled with hope of heaven's perennial day
> A sister in the bond of Christian love

The tie which forms the family above;
A friend of genial soul whose hallowed flame
Could fire our praises of Emmanuel's name...

Samuel Leigh also led a special service in the Parramatta
chapel 'to a larger congregation than has been witnessed
for some years. Many of his auditors were those who had
experienced the effects of her benevolent and sympathizing
disposition. Even the memory of the just is blessed.' That
must have been a difficult service for Samuel to lead, I
think, because his life has been intertwined with Mary's
and mine for ten years.

They sent me a report of a memorial sermon which the
Rev. Samuel Marsden preached which says that, when he
referred to Mary, 'his feelings were so strongly excited that
it was with difficulty that he proceeded to the end of his
subject. He had known Mrs L. from her infancy; and that
when the Parramatta Sunday School was established, she
was indefatigable in attempting to promote the best interests of the children.'

Marsden preached from Job 19:25-27 and I have been
reading it again to myself: 'For I know that my redeemer
liveth, and that he shall stand at the latter day upon the
earth: And though after my skin worms destroy this body,
yet in my flesh shall I see God: whom I shall see for myself,
and mine eyes shall behold, and not another...' With
tears in my eyes, I remembered that that last phrase can
also read, 'and not a stranger'. I thanked God that Mary
was with him, the One she had loved, and that when she
saw him he would truly not have been a stranger to her.

That was all many years ago and I am an old man now,
sixty-six years old and crippled since I had a paralytic
stroke. Perhaps Mary would not even recognise me now —
to me she is always young and beautiful. In those days I
was healthy and athletic, exploring Tonga, riding for miles
around New South Wales, jumping overboard from the
Midas in mid-Atlantic for a swim. Not any more.

The years have brought many changes. I remember writing to my good friend and brother-in-law, Thomas Hassall, explaining how many people had recommended that I should remarry for the sake of the children, but how I had not been able to bear the thought for several years. I wrote of our son Henry who 'can read the New Testament and goes on to the Old Testament', of Elizabeth Anna 'who grows fine, healthy and handsome and Mary Australia who is now one year and nine months, is a fine child, very much like her heavenly mother.' Four years after Mary's death, I married Mrs Eliza White, a Falmouth widow some years older than myself – a good, kind woman who has cared for our family with great love.

Over the years, I worked in a series of circuits around England – Falmouth, Helston, Exeter, Dudley and Burslem in the Potteries. Henry grew up and was apprenticed to a printer, but felt called to Christian work. He came to work with me as a lay preacher. Our steady life was unexpectedly upheaved when I was asked to go to New Zealand as General Superintendent of Wesleyan Missions at a time when the New Zealand work was suffering a number of difficulties.

Eliza and I, with Henry, Elizabeth and Australia, sailed from England in September, 1843 and arrived in Sydney in January, 1844. We arrived in time for me to be asked to preach at the opening of the grand new Methodist Church in York Street, Sydney. It was very moving to see the many changes in Sydney, with all the new buildings, and to meet again some of my dear friends from the past.

So many of them had gone. Of the Hassall family, Mother Hassall had gone – as had brothers Samuel and Jonathan, who both died in their thirties. James Hassall now ran the Cowpastures farms and was a wealthy and much respected man. Mary's dear brother Thomas was well established with his own Cowpastures property called 'Denbigh'. He was also the Rector of St Paul's Church, Cobbittee, which he described as 'All of Australia beyond Liverpool'! He is greatly loved by his people and rides hundreds of miles to spend time with people in lonely places – they call him the 'Galloping Parson'. Mary would be very proud of him. Her sisters were now married ladies – Mrs William Walker, Mrs William Shelley and Mrs Robert Mackay Campbell, all three with large families. Both the Rev. and Mrs Marsden had been gone for some years and Parramatta seemed strange without him.

Samuel Leigh returned to England in 1831, a sick man, soon after the sad death of his dear wife Catherine, who died after catching an epidemic disease because of her loving care of the sick and dying in Parramatta. For years his health was poor, but he persisted in travelling around England to speak of the needs of the young churches in New South Wales and New Zealand. Samuel Leigh always seemed better able to inspire others to respond to the missionary cause than to cope with the difficulties of that life personally, but maybe that was his special gift from God. Samuel died in 1852.

None of the Methodist ministers were the men I knew. After about ten years of deep trial and struggle my friends had all gone, a whole new team of missionaries had arrived and the work began to take on new strength under the leadership of the Rev. Joseph Orton. Sometimes I have wondered: would the Methodist work in New South Wales have been able to avoid some of the miseries of the 1820s if Leigh and I had been better friends? Even our dear visionary colleague, John Williams, was no longer in the Pacific. Our friend had been clubbed to death on the beach of Erromanga in the New Hebrides at the beginning of yet another missionary contact with a pagan people.

Our family went on to New Zealand, a New Zealand very different from my memories of the small and divided communities in the Bay of Islands. We settled in Auckland, the new and growing centre. The place was still beset by many problems which I tried to tackle, with varying degrees of success. Some of my more useful projects were in setting up places for training of Maori Christians and in education for missionaries' children.

My son Henry joined the Mission and became in due course the Rev. Henry Hassall Lawry – which would have pleased Mary very much. He married Miss Hephzibah Forsaith. My daughter Elizabeth married Francis Oakes, the son of one of the *Duff* missionaries and long-time friends of the Hassalls. She came to live in Parramatta and died two years ago, a young mother of five. My daughter Australia married the Rev. John Aldred, a Wesleyan missionary in New Zealand.

After ten often difficult years in New Zealand, my health was deteriorating and my eyesight was weakening so I became a supernumerary in 1854 and moved back to Australia, to live in Parramatta in 1856. I expect I will die here, here where my Mary grew up and where we were married, the town where three of our children were born and where we both grew a great deal in our spiritual lives. My good Mrs Eliza Lawry is here, growing old beside me – a dear, short and stout little lady. Perhaps it is as well that she can't see how often I think of a slim, young girl called Mary who once lived here too.

My dear Mary Lawry has not been forgotten. As I sit here tonight in my cottage here in Parramatta, I have been turning the pages of two small books and remembering how much I had longed to have her with me when they were written. The books are the journals of my visits back to Tonga in 1847 and 1850 in my role as General Secretary of Wesleyan Missions in the Pacific and they were published in London by our Mission. With the passing of the years and the balding of my head, my writing has gained respectability and authority. Once the many letters and writings of this rebel Cornishman were viewed with great caution, but now my writing is published in real books with my name elegantly imprinted on the cover.

If only Mary could have gone back to Tonga with me. She shared all the early loneliness and discouragement; if only she could see Tonga now. As I wrote in my 1847 journal: 'The sight of these most lovely islands has filled my whole soul with associations, emotions and feelings of the most

touching kind. . . Here I landed twenty-four years ago. . .
The people then were pagan. . . and now I find a rich harvest.' And *what* a harvest — and what a story of the years
between.

When, on my first return journey to Tonga, the *John
Wesley* came close to the island, a middle-aged missionary, tanned and with a thick thatch of greying hair, came
out in the canoe to meet us. It was hard to recognise in this
senior man the young and rather nervous young blacksmith, John Thomas, who had been in London with us and
whom we had helped prepare for his great adventure.
Thomas had been in Tonga since 1826. When he first
arrived on Tongatapu, Thomas had a co-worker, the Rev.
John Hutchinson and his wife, but they stayed less than
two years whereas Thomas was to stay for thirty years.
George Lilly had recently left Tonga, but Charles Tindall
was still there, struggling to survive the constant threat and
rejection of Fatu. They advised Thomas to settle at Hihifo
with Chief Ata instead of at Mu'a. But Ata was not willing
to change either and, within a year of arrival, John and
Sarah Thomas were seriously thinking of abandoning the
mission in Tonga.

Only the arrival of new, strong staff saved the work from
yet another set-back. They struggled on together and, in
1829 the first few converts were won, one as a result of
helping a missionary translate Matthew's Gospel. Thomas
moved to the northern islands of Vava'u and Ha'apai and,
during the 1830s, there was a wonderful period of growth
with many conversions, dramatic confrontations between
the old ways and the gospel and a people movement where
whole communities turned to God. They called it the Great
Awakening.

But although many Tongans of the northern islands
turned to God, even sending parties of Tongan missionaries in their deep sea canoes over 500 miles of open sea
to take the gospel to cannibal Fiji, many of the communities on our island of Tongatapu still refused to listen.
Though some were converted, there were many fights and

conflicts through the years and the people at our old home of Mu'a were unmoved. The old chief died, still unconvinced about the truth of the gospel. At that time his son and heir, Tungi, was living a wild life and didn't want to give it all up to become a Christian. However, the old man's wife and daughter had become believers, with our friend Eliza Anne now a fine and powerful chief in rank and a leader of a Christian Class Meeting. She told me that her earliest understanding of the gospel had begun when Mary and I were in Tonga and she had often visited our home.

Turning the pages of my 1847 journal I recall that first visit: the joy of meeting some of our old friends again, including Tama Nau who had gone with us to London and is now a local preacher; Malungahu who went with us to Sydney, one of our domestic lads of long ago who is now a fine Christian magistrate; attending a Communion service at Nuku'alofa where 500 Tongans received communion; observing the children of our missionaries; being thankful that a good school for missionaries' children has begun in New Zealand (the last I heard of poor Sarah Henry, the girl Mary always remembered as the saddest example of a missionary's child, was that she was destitute in the poorest part of London in the 1830s); visiting the northern islands and seeing the great work being done there; travelling on from Tonga to Fiji and seeing the impossible dreams we used to dream of the gospel going from island to island across the Pacific being brought to life.

'Mary,' I find myself saying, as if she could hear, 'it *wasn't* hopeless – slow, and difficult, but not hopeless. Why did we so often feel like giving up?'

The second little book is in my hands, the journal of my visit in 1850, and it has fallen open at those pages I have reread and remembered so often. I was in Tonga again, rejoicing in improvement since my last visit: progress of the translation of scripture; fine new schools, particularly at Nuku'alofa; wonderful services of worship with the whole congregation joining in the prayers and singing; wonderful music in the churches with the people singing 'in beautiful harmony . . . in tones like the sounds of many waters'; and the sight of Tongan preachers leading their own people to God. The preachers have begun to wear a shirt like the white missionaries, but often forget that they have it under their arm. They only don their shirt at the beginning of the service, almost as part of the liturgy!

My eyes are not as good as they once were and I find it hard to read the words on the pages, but one memory of that visit can never be blurred. They have built a chapel at Mu'a — on the very spot where our first Tongan home stood. On that place where we did our best to enclose the sides of that thatched, open building to provide Mary with a little privacy from the staring eyes of the people, there is now a house of worship. On the place where Mary spent hours trying to keep our clothes clean, sifting weevils from her flour, battling with mosquitoes, teaching girls sewing, weeping over her miscarriage and watching Henry and his little friend, the chief's son Tungi, at play, I saw the people of Mu'a turning to God.

Tungi was now a powerful young man with great influence over his people. Because he was living what I called 'a life of more than ordinary sinfulness', his people were reluctant to become Christians as so many other Tongans had done years earlier. But now, over some months, Tungi has been disturbed by powerful dreams and he felt that perhaps the Christian God was real, true and more powerful than the old sacred spirits who lived in the ancient symbols of whales' teeth and ancestral war club. Many other people of Mu'a were also feeling their way to God at that time.

On that Sunday morning as I sat in the chapel, there was a feeling of great expectancy, of a people who were open and ready for God to deal with them. The room was crowded with many people bowed in prayer, some quietly weeping over their sins. I looked across the room at the many Tongans for whom I had prayed so often, then out over the wall across the bay, the same view which Mary and I had seen so often as we waited for the return of our ship. And I saw Tungi coming – the great chief who never came to chapel – stumbling along, hurrying to join us, coming to bring himself to God.

Later I wrote: 'And when Tungi entered the chapel and fell on his knees with his people, the sobs and cries of the congregation were irrepressible. Some were called upon to pray; but no-one could speak for some time till the gust of overflowing feeling had subsided, and *then* they broke out as the sun when he ariseth. . .'

What a day! When at last the service of worship was over, the people of Mu'a went all around their area and each one brought out the old gods. There was the most powerful ancient whale's tooth, carefully wrapped and not seen by man for generations, to whom many human sacrifices had been made, a necklace of whales' teeth wrapped in *tapa* cloth and stuck full of little red feathers, the club of generations of priests, each item still with the grime of years of dirt and blood. Their discarded gods were placed in a big Tongan basket and handed to me. 'Take them away,' they said. 'Take them to another land. They have lost their power over us.'

Now I sit with the little book in my hand in which the story is told. I don't need to read it now. I remember going back alone into the quiet chapel after the people had all gone, carrying their basket of powerless gods. I was standing on the very ground where Mary and I had lived and struggled, hurt and embraced, hoped and prayed together.

'Can you see, Mary, my beautiful helpmate?' I whispered. 'Can you know, there in heaven, that our work was not wasted, that we were able to show others that it would be possible to bring the gospel to the people of Tonga? Do you know. . .?'

*   *   *

The Rev. Walter Lawry died in Parramatta on April 7, 1859 and was buried there.

Bibliography

Primary sources

(a) Unpublished

Hassall Correspondence, 1813-1828: Mitchell Library:
* letters of Mary Cover Hassall to Rev. Thomas Hassall
* letters of Rowland, Elizabeth, Thomas, Samuel and Jonathan Hassall
* letters of Rev. Walter Lawry

Rev. Walter Lawry, Diary, February 1818 – February 1825: Mitchell Library

Rev. Walter Lawry, letters to parents and friends, 1815-1825: Mitchell Library

Rowland Hassall Papers: Mitchell Library

Missionary Correspondence, Bonwick Transcripts Box 49-51: Mitchell Library

Marsden Papers: Letters of Mrs Anne Hassall, nee Marsden, 1813-1820: Mitchell Library

Rev. William Horton, Journal, 1820-1828: Melbourne Archives

Rev. Ralph Mansfield, Journal, 1820, Bonwick Transcripts Box 50: Mitchell Library

Robert Howe, Government Printer, Diary-letter to Rev. Walter Lawry, 1 August 1822 – 16 January 1823: Mitchell Library

(b) Published

Rev. Walter Lawry, *Friendly and Feejee Islands: A Missionary Visit to Various Stations in the South Seas in the year MDCCCXLVII by the Rev. Walter Lawry*, edited by the Rev. Elijah Hoole. Published by Charles Gilpin, London, 1848

Rev. Walter Lawry, *A Second Missionary Visit to the Friendly and Feejee Islands in the year MDCCCL*, edited by the Rev. Elijah Hoole, London. Published by John Mason, 66 Paternoster Row, 1851

The Letters and Journals of Samuel Marsden 1765-1838, edited by John Rawson Elder, Dunedin. Published by Coulls Somerville, Wilkie Ltd and A.H. Reed for Otago University Council, 1932

Captain W. Wilson, *A Missionary Voyage to the South Pacific Ocean, performed in the years 1796-1798 in the ship Duff*. Published 1798

John Williams, *Missionary Enterprises in the South Sea Islands*. Published by the Presbyterian Board of Publication and Sabbath Schoolwork, 1334 Chestnut Street, Philadelphia, 1888

Captain Edmund Fanning, *Voyages and Discoveries in the South Seas, 1792-1832*, Salem, Mass. Published by the Marine Research Society, 1924

The Wesleyan-Methodist Magazine: Missionary Notices for 1822, 1823, 1824, 1826, 1827 and 1845. Published by J. Kershaw, 14 City Road, London

The Wesleyan-Methodist Magazine: Missionary Notices 1851, Part II: Published by John Mason, London

William Smith, *Journal of a Voyage in the Missionary Ship 'Duff'*. Published 1813

The Sydney Gazette for 1804, 1811, 1812 and 1818-1826: National Library, Canberra

An Account of the Natives of the Tonga Islands in the South Pacific Ocean, compiled from the Extensive Communication of Mr William Mariner by John Martin, Volume 1. Printed for the author and sold by John Murray, Albermarle Street, London, 1817

*　　*　　*

Secondary sources

Rev. Canon Arrowsmith (editor), *The Cradle Church of Australia: The history of St John's, Parramatta, Part 1 to Year 1910*, Pilgrim International Limited, Sydney, 1975

Australian Dictionary of Biography, Volume 1: 1788-1850 A-H: Melbourne University Press, 1966

T. Barrow, *Women of Polynesia*, Seven Seas Publishing, 1967

J.C. Beaglehole, *The Life of Captain James Cook*, Stanford University Press, California, 1974

Biographical Sketches of Eminent Christians: Second Series, The Religious Tract Society, 56 Paternoster Row, London (n.d. pre-1860)

The Book of Offices, being the Orders of Service authorised for use in the Methodist Church, Methodist Publishing House, 25-35 City Road, London, 1936

F.W. Bourne, *Billy Bray, The King's Son*, Epworth Press, City Road, London, 1937

Peter Buck, *Vikings of the Sunrise*, J.B. Lippincott Company, New York, 1938

Eve Buscombe, *Australian Colonial Portraits*, Tasmanian Museum and Art Gallery, 1979

John Campbell, *The Martyr of Erromanga, or the Philosophy of Missions: Illustrated from the Labours, Death and Character of the late John Williams*, John Snow, London, 1842

Captain Cook: His Artists, His Voyages: The Daily Telegraph Portfolio of Original Works by Artists who sailed with Captain Cook. Printed by Conpress Printing Ltd, Sydney, 1970

W. Carvosso, *The Efficacy of Faith in the Atonement of Christ Exemplified in a Memoir of Mr William Carvosso*. Written by himself and edited by his son (n.d. c.1840)

C.M.H. Clark, *A History of Australia Part I: From the Earliest Times to the Age of Macquarie*, Melbourne University Press, 1962

C.M.H. Clark, *A History of Australia Part III: 1824-1851*, Melbourne University Press, 1973

John F. Cleverly, *The First Generation: School and Society in Early Australia*, Sydney University Press, 1971

Frank Clune, *Serenade to Sydney: Some Historical Landmarks*, Angus & Robertson, 1967

James Colwell, *Illustrated History of Methodism, Australia: 1812-1855*, William Brookes and Company Ltd, 1904

James Colwell, (editor), *A Century in the Pacific*, Chas. H. Kelley, London, 1914

Frank Crowley, *Colonial Australia: 1788-1840, Volume 1*, Nelson, 1980

J.S. Cumpston, *Shipping Departures and Arrivals: Sydney, 1788-1825*, Roebuck, 1977

J.W. Davidson and Deryck Scarr (editors), *Pacific Island Portraits*, A.H. and A.W. Reed, Wellington-Auckland, 1976

Daphne du Maurier, *Vanishing Cornwall*, Victor Gollancz Ltd, London, 1967

Early Artists of Australia, Paul Hamlyn, London, Sydney, 1971

M.H. Ellis, *Lachlan Macquarie: His Life Adventure and Times*, Sydney, 1947

Sarah S. Farmer, *Tonga and the Friendly Islands*, Hamilton, Adams, London, 1855

John Alexander Ferguson, *Bibliography of Australia, 1784-1830: Volume 1*, Angus & Robertson, Sydney, London, 1941

Richard Fodor, *Fodor's London*, Hodder & Stoughton, 1979

John Garrett, *To Live Among the Stars*, World Council of Churches in association with the Institute of Pacific Studies, University of the South Pacific, Geneva and Suva, 1982

Philip Geeves, *A Place of Pioneers: Centenary History of the Municipality of Ryde*

Murray B. Gittos, *Mana at Mangungu: Biography of William White 1794-1875, Wesleyan Missionary at Whangaroa and Hokianga 1823-1836*, M.B. Gittos, Mt Roskill, Auckland 4, 1979

Douglas Gorsline, *What People Wore: A Visual History of Dress from Ancient Times to the 20th Century*, Orbis Publishing, London, 1978

Nesta Griffiths, *Point Piper: Past and Present*, Ure Smith, Sydney, 1970

Niel Gunson, *Messengers of Grace: Evangelical Missionaries in the South Seas 1797-1860*, Oxford University Press, 1978

E.W. Hames, *Walter Lawry and the Wesleyan Mission in the South Seas*, Wesley Historical Society (New Zealand Proceedings, Volume 23, Number 4), September 1967

J.S. Hassall, *In Old Australia*, Brisbane, 1902

Babette Hayes, *200 Years of Australian Cooking*, Thomas Nelson Australia Ltd, 1970

Holdsworth and Findlay, *Wesleyan Methodist Missionary Society History, Volume III*

S.M. Johnstone, *Samuel Marsden: A Pioneer of Civilisation in the South Seas*, Angus & Robertson, Sydney, 1932

Anne E. Keeling, *What He did for Convicts and Cannibals: Some Account of the Life and Work of the Rev. Samuel Leigh*, Charles H. Kelley, London, 1896

Joan Kerr and Hugh Falkus, *From Sydney Cove to Duntroon: A Family Album of Early Life in Australia*, Hutchinson of Australia, 1982

Sione Latukefu, *Church and State in Tonga: The Wesleyan Methodist Missionaries and Political Development, 1822-1875*, Canberra, 1974

Lucy Marshall, Script of Lecture on life of Walter Lawry, Auckland, New Zealand, 1967

Lucy Marshall, *Walter Lawry, Cornwall, Australia, Tonga, New Zealand*, Cornish Methodist Historical Association Occasional Publication, Number 12, 1967

G.E. Mingay, *Georgian London*, B.T. Batsford Ltd, 1975

Rev. William Morley, *The History of Methodism in New Zealand*, McKee and Co., Wellington, 1900

Night of Toil, or A Familiar Account of the Labour of the First Missionaries in the South Sea, by the author of *Peep of Day*. Published by American Tract Society, 150 Nassau St, New York (n.d. c.1840).

J.M.R. Owens, *Prophets in the Wilderness*, Auckland University Press, 1974

Mark Guy Pearce, *Daniel Quorm and his Religous Notions*, England (n.d. c.1850)

T.M. Perry, *Australia's First Frontier: The Spread of Settlement in NSW, 1788-1829*, Melbourne University Press in association with Australian National University, 1963

David Piper, *Companion Guide to London*, Collins, 1964

Ebenezer Proutt, *Memoirs of the Life of the Rev. John Williams*, John Snow, Paternoster Row, London, 1843

Marjorie and C.H.B. Quennell, *A History of Everyday Things in England, 1733-1851*, B.T. Batsford Ltd, London, 1961

Ronald Rose, *This Peculiar Colony*, Rigby, 1981

G. Stringer Rowe, *A Pioneer. Memoir of the Reverend John Thomas, Missionary to the Friendly Islands*. First published London, 1885. Reprinted by Kalia Press, Canberra, 1976

A.F. Scott, *Every One a Witness: The Georgian Age*, Martin Publishers Ltd, London, 1970

Geoffrey Scott, *Sydney's Highways of History*, Georgian House, Melbourne, 1958

Dr J.C. Smee and Mrs J. Selkirk Provis (editors), *The 1788-1820 Association's Pioneer Register: Second Edition, Volume 1*

R.V. Spivey, *Wesley's Chapel*, Pitkin Pictorials Ltd, 1970

Alexander Strachan, *Life of Rev. Samuel Leigh*, Hamilton Adams, London, 1865

Alan R. Tippett, *People Movements in Southern Polynesia: A Study in Church Growth*, Moody Press, Chicago, 1971

Alan R. Tippett, *The Deep Sea Canoe: The Story of Third World Missionaries in the South Pacific*, William Carey Library, South Pasadena, California, 1977

Tongan-English Dictionary

Gloster S. Udy, *Spark of Grace*, Epworth Press, 1977

H. Vane, *Some Girls of Early Australia*, 'Lone Hand', July 1920

Bill Wannen, *Very Strange Tales: The Turbulent Times of Samuel Marsden*, Lansdowne Press, Melbourne, 1962

John Wesley, *A Collection of Hymns for the Use of the People called Methodists*, Wesleyan Conference Office, 2 Castle Street, City Road, London (n.d. pre-1860).

A.H. Wood, *Overseas Missions of the Australian Methodist Church, Volume 1: Tonga and Samoa*, Aldersgate Press, 1975

A.H. Wood, *The History and Geography of Tonga*, 1943. Reprinted by Kalia Press, Canberra

Woolmington J., *Religion in Early Australia*, Cassell Australia, 1976

A.T. Yarwood, *Samuel Marsden: The Great Survivor*, Melbourne University Press, 1977

Doreen Yarwood, *The Encyclopaedia of World Costume*, B.T. Batsford, London, 1978

Cover illustration:
Although the cover illustration of Mary Lawry
is only an artist's impression (no known painting
exists of her), the four men on the cover
are drawn from original portraits. On the front
cover is Walter Lawry and on the back cover
is (left to right) Thomas Hassall, Rowland
Hassall and Samuel Leigh.